Deconstructing
Trauma

Release Chaos, Pain, and Negativity

Renee Frye

DECONSTRUCTING TRAUMA™
Release Chaos, Pain, and Negativity

Copyright © 2023. Renee Frye.

ISBN: 979-8-9885147-2-5

Book Design by
Transcendent Publishing
www.transcendentpublishing.com

Printed in the United States of America.

This Book is Dedicated to Each One
of Us Releasing the Struggle Within.

We are all looking to be loved and accepted.
This information allows us to release the preconceived
notions and stigmas of society.
Through this space we learn we don't have to be afraid
of what we see in the mirror.
Any shortcomings or faults we may experience are
all opportunities to learn and grow.

Our mistakes and lessons don't have to define us,
they are not who we are...

So, who are we?

We are Love, Light, and Grace;
at the very center of our creation, we are pure.

Here we learn how to peel back the layers of trauma
and pain to reveal our true self.

Who are we???
We Are Love, Light, and Grace!
Yes, each one of you!

Embodying Grace

Grace is what emerges from the struggle... Grace is the courage to face the uncomfortable

Grace is our true raw self exposed. Not only in spite of but because of our flaws, this is how we learn. Grace allows us to take our struggles, our trials, our lessons and turn them into wisdom.

Through this Grace, we know we are not our trauma, we are not our suffering, we learn our lessons and move on. Grace allows us to separate negative feelings, triggers, and experiences from our identity.

Grace knows the struggle is real but allows us to release the struggle. We are not the struggle, we are not the pain, we are not the suffering. We are not alone.

Grace is humility in action; humility is not shame.

Being humble takes courage, strength, balance, and Grace.

Grace allows us to support and love others without controlling, manipulating, or running their lives.

Grace allows us to evolve from our trauma.

Grace allows us to let others walk their own journey, without rushing in fixing, saving, and taking away their opportunity for lessons and growth.

Grace allows us to trust others to handle their own journey, not in the way we see fit but in the way that is best served for them. They will learn their lesson... or they won't; this is not up to us. It is our responsibility to be mindful and care for ourselves by removing ourselves from unhealthy situations. It is not our responsibility to change anyone else or make them see the light.

Grace allows us to release this to a higher space, a higher presence. In this way, we learn not to take situations personally.

Grace tells us it's not always about us...What a relief!

Grace allows us to fully and completely love and accept ourselves at the most basic fundamental level.

Grace is our true self realized. Our true self is Love, Light, and Grace.

Grace Embodied...Is You.

Renee Spiritflyer Frye 2022

TABLE OF CONTENTS

PREFACE

Thank you for purchasing Deconstructing Trauma™. We can Deconstruct Trauma by shifting unhealthy, rigid perspectives and negative behavior patterns. Unbiased behavior exploration allows us to identify and modify negative behaviors and damaging core beliefs. Awareness of our thoughts and actions, along with simple positive mindful behavior modification techniques, can assist us in reprogramming negative patterns. Through this process, we Deconstruct Trauma.

Our curriculum is based on positive, personal social development; through this process, behaviors, perspectives, and attitudes are learned, offering long-term positive changes in relationships and interactions involving oneself, peers, and family. As we learn to release negative and unhealthy behaviors that have manifested from our trauma, we are able to reprogram to positive mindsets and healthy behaviors. Our program includes insightful daily awareness tools, mindful behavior modification strategies, a revolutionary positive behavior resilience method, and energy healing therapy. The combination of these specific approaches has a significant impact on the release of trauma, chaos, pain, and negativity.

The Deconstructing Trauma program is a personal and social development tool. Personal social development enhances the quality of life for all members of a community so that they can realize their maximum potential. Through personal and social development, we are able to explore our behaviors and grow in understanding, compassion, and balance.

We can learn more about our speech, gestures, facial expressions, body language, self-regulation, acceptance, resilience, adaptability, tolerance, self-efficacy, consequences of actions and interactions with ourselves, and others.

Our personal social development approach allows each person to check in safely and equitably with where they are at. Through this personal social development process, we begin to identify our negative learned behaviors and understand how to deconstruct the past trauma that is affecting us.

As part of the Deconstructing Trauma program, we acquire the knowledge and skills necessary to retrain ourselves to engage in behaviors and surroundings that are healthy, safe, and appropriate. Our physical, mental, emotional, and spiritual health and well-being, as well as our personal and societal relationships, are all improved as a result of this.

One of the most effective tools you can use in your daily life in any situation is to ask yourself: Is this healthy, appropriate, and safe? This will help us reestablish healthy, safe, and appropriate relationships with ourselves and others around us. This can apply to the way we think, the way we talk, and the way we interact with others and ourselves.

Awareness. Tool: Is this healthy or unhealthy? Is this appropriate or inappropriate? Is this safe or unsafe?

Our programs offer new solutions as well as practical, life-changing resilience tools. Our exclusive Deconstructing Trauma™ Program has created superior results and positive, lasting change for thousands of people. This approach can shift negative thought processes and behaviors by releasing trauma and blockages deep within the mind-body connection.

This information is essential to living a happy and healthy life. It can assist all members of society, including offenders of all ages, trauma survivors, individuals battling addiction, depression, anxiety, anger, fear, suicide, and more. This information is vital for professionals as well as military personnel, medical and mental health professionals, trauma workers, and first responders, among others. We have extensive experience providing deconstructing trauma support in mental wellness, substance abuse, offender treatment, and incarceration programs. Our Deconstructing Trauma program is significantly effective for all and complements MRT—Moral Reconation Therapy®.

We have all been affected by trauma in some way. By creating health, wellness, resilience, and balance in all areas of our lives, we have the opportunity to reduce trauma, toxic stress, sadness, depressive states, low energy, anxiousness, panic, ACEs, substance abuse, addiction, mental health challenges, compassion fatigue, burnout, absenteeism, and more. We believe in a healing-centered approach and holistic care, focusing on the whole person; in this way, we become our own best resource. We all need healthy life-support skills. There is hope; we are not alone.

Note: The author, Renee Frye is a Trauma-Healing Holistic Specialist and the owner and founder of Sacred Sol Healing Institute®. She provides mental wellness and substance abuse recovery support resources through her deconstructing trauma program and indigenous clearing and trauma healing. She is, first and foremost, an indigenous traditional healer; her modalities are all holistic and deeply rooted in Native American teachings.

Note: Each person's experience will be different because we are all unique. We are in no way diminishing or condoning past trauma. This is simply a different perspective, with unique opportunities to deconstruct trauma. If you are working on healing trauma, please be sure to establish a professional medical and mental health support team to guide you through that process.

<u>Notice:</u> All content, information, resources, and services offered through Sacred Sol Healing Institute is for informational and holistic healing purposes only and does not replace medical advice. Our resources reflect our opinions and experiences and are not intended to diagnose, treat, cure, or prevent any disease. Please consult licensed medical and mental health professionals for your medical and mental health needs. If you are experiencing an emergency, please call 911.

The Deconstructing Trauma Program at Sacred Sol Healing Institute includes the resources and knowledge gained during at least forty Deconstructing Trauma Healing sessions, valued at over $5800. We have compiled the contents of those sessions into our guidebook, Deconstructing Trauma, in an effort to solve barriers to access and complete our mission. Our mission is to solve barriers to access by providing trauma-responsive healing resources worldwide.

This book's format is unique: it is a guidebook that offers simple, information in quick and easy-to-understand sections. There is so much amazing healing information available. This book draws some of the basics together, much like the pieces of a puzzle. Integrating these pieces of information, allows us to begin seeing why we are uncomfortable in our daily lives and how we tend to automatically think in a negative way.

This book includes articles and studies that are in alignment with our positive approach. The way we present our concepts and format is unique. I write in the same way I speak, with statements. It is direct and with purpose. It may read differently from what you are used to. It is not a lacking appropriate grammar; it is designed intentionally in this way.

We have chosen a Q & A (question and answer) format for easy reference. Each chapter lists the questions and answers that guide us through the concepts of our innovative Deconstructing Trauma Program (DTP). This program requires awareness and action to achieve the desired results. Our concepts are repeated intentionally throughout the book because the more familiar we are with something, the easier it is to get back to. We have gathered and compiled this information through thousands of hours of research, training, education, and practical lived experience. We have been extremely diligent in the creation of this book and its material. However, there is always the possibility of a mistake in grammar or punctuation. To that end, I pass along a teaching.

When we bead, we are taught to always add an off-color bead to our work for the following two reasons: One, we add the off-color bead to note that we are human, and mistakes will be made because they are part of life; this is how we learn. This keeps us humble and open to learning. Second, the off-color bead is a signature. We use the same color bead in all our work, and people will recognize our work and our medicine in that way.

Pay special attention to the awareness tool and mindful behavior modification techniques throughout the book. They are also gathered together at the end of this book into a simple reference resource, called the Deconstructing Trauma Toolkit, also available to download in full-size color pdf; see the next page for information. You can easily access these tools as you need them. When you are having a tough time, check out the toolkit to see what awareness tools and mindful behavior modification tools will be the best fit for your current challenge.

The awareness tools are powerful, simple statements. They are positive affirmations and wisdom that help teach us positive behavior resilience. Reminding us how to keep a positive, balanced, and unbiased perspective in life, therefore improving our daily experiences as well as our relationships with ourselves and others. Our mindful behavior modification tools are techniques and exercises that help us reprogram negative thinking and habits.

Through the Deconstructing Trauma Program, you can learn to shift the familiarity of chaos, pain, and negativity. Learn to reprogram to positivity, peace, and joy.

You can start using this information immediately by applying these techniques and tools in your daily life. Combine the Deconstructing Trauma guidebook with our interactive curriculum workbooks at https://sacredsolhealing.com/wellness-store/. The Deconstructing Trauma interactive workbook is available in two versions: the Substance Abuse Recovery Edition and the Personal Social Development Edition.

As we heal ourselves, the world around us begins to heal. Begin reading to unlock this life-changing information.

BONUS!

Welcome! In the back of this book you will find the Deconstructing Trauma Toolkit. As a thank you for purchasing the Deconstructing Trauma guidebook, we would like to gift you a color pdf version of the toolkit.

Our Deconstructing Trauma Toolkit combines all the tools that have been offered throughout the Deconstructing Trauma Guidebook in one convenient reference space, plus bonus material. Many additional tools that are not offered in the book have also been included in the toolkit.

Please visit deconstructing-trauma.com to access your complimentary bonus gift.

Walk in Beauty

One of our biggest teachings is learning to "Walk in Beauty" daily, in the world around us as well as in the world inside of us. It requires moral, spiritual, physical, mental, and emotional endurance, integrity, commitment, and patience. "Walking in Beauty" is an intentional life journey; it is a way of life that takes work and dedication. It is not easy, but it is simple.

Many times, life complications will unwind on their own when we are not feeding them with an exhausted, frantic negative mindset. We do not have to become stressed or exhausted to fix what is not working.

The Deconstructing Trauma program teaches us how to "Walk in Beauty," utilizing social development life skills and tools that allow us to step back from the challenges and not take them personally. We do not ignore the challenges, but rather choose a mindset of peace and openness, appreciating the lessons and moving through them, rather than feeding the negativity around them.

These lessons are how we grow in mind, body, and spirit. We have been given the gift of knowledge; if we are able to process, learn, and use this knowledge, it will manifest as wisdom that we can use in our lives. This is how we learn to "Walk in Beauty".

"Walking in Beauty" is challenging, but it is how we live our best life. "Walking in Beauty" doesn't mean that everything is perfect. It means we get to choose how we show up in the world. How we live our best lives, reflecting beauty, grace, strength, light, compassion, resilience, peace, respect, kindness, balance, joy, and love, daily for ourselves and others.

"Walking in Beauty" is the human challenge; it reminds us and teaches us how to respect the sacred hoop of life and all that resides within it. The earth, the elements, the people, and the animals. How can you apply "Walking in Beauty" to your daily life? It is a continual dance filled with highs and lows. You are the medicine; you are the beauty; allow your heart to guide you on this journey to self. You are the miracle you've been looking for, "Walk in Beauty."

2023 - Renee Frye

INTRODUCTION

We all have negative tendencies. We are here to learn. This information is only here to raise awareness. It is not an attack on anyone's character or actions.

I used to be the most angry and hateful person I knew. I didn't even realize it; it was a way of life because I felt bad inside. Through years of intensive study and research, I learned that it was okay to look at the challenging toxic behavior patterns I had acquired over time.

The day I realized that my behaviors, thoughts, and emotions don't define me was the day that changed my life. Whhewww! What a relief!

I am, of course, responsible for my own actions and behaviors, but knowing that they are not my identity has allowed me to dig deeper into self. What I found was okay; I could change what wasn't appropriate and keep what was!

Knowledge gives us the opportunity to evolve and grow. Even if parts of this book bring up a bit of uncomfortable information, it can be worth your time and effort.

Deconstructing Trauma by releasing chaos, pain, and negativity allows healing. It is life-changing!

··•◆◆•··

We live in a very negative, toxic world. Our thoughts are negative, our surroundings are negative; we are led by chaos, pain, and negativity. This is what we know.

We are told to suck it up, move on, don't cry, don't show emotions or feelings. We are told that everything is fine... until one day, it's not. No wonder we have extreme behaviors, dependencies, unhappiness, anxiousness, stress, tension, depressive states, anger, addiction, and more.

We haven't been taught to create balance between the body, mind, and spirit.

We run blindly from one thing to the next, trying to fulfill our need for support and love by overextending ourselves, which creates continual mental, physical, and spiritual health crises.

We unknowingly reach out to find our value and worth in acts of service to others, without realizing that this can be inappropriate and unhealthy if we are using these acts as a catalyst to feel better about ourselves. Once we realize this, we are able to see that when we are balanced and healthy our value and worth is found within.

That of course doesn't mean we need to stop the acts of service and kindness, but maybe we are able to evaluate first why we are doing them. If we are the one who needs to save the world and everyone in it, we will be out of balance. It is dangerous for us, as well as for the people we are "saving." We each have a responsibility to work through our own experiences so we can resolve trauma, chaos, pain, and suffering. When we rush in to fix it for others, that doesn't allow them to learn or solve their own challenges. They become dependent on us solving their challenges, and we become dependent on solving them so we can feel good about ourselves. This perpetuates the cycle of trauma for both parties.

If we don't tend to our past trauma, we don't know that we can process it and heal. We have been caught up in an extremely dysfunctional generational "follow-the-leader," not knowing that we can heal, not understanding that we do not have to continue to be a perpetual product of our trauma and suffering. We check-out with drugs, alcohol, food, social media, gambling, shopping, anger, passive-aggressive behavior, controlling others, withdrawing, and more.

Negativity affects us in every way. It is poisonous to the body, mind, and spirit. It manifests as disease – physically, mentally, emotionally, and spiritually. The more familiar we are with something, the easier it is to get back to it. We have become so familiar with chaos, pain, and negativity that it is our new normal. Our bodies have become used to living in fight-or-flight. And because the body is not meant to continually live in fight-or-flight, it begins to break down. From there, we become frantic. We become sick, and then eventually we *need* to be sick; we are labeled with a diagnosis and we feel validated in our discomfort.

What if we shifted that thought process for a moment? What if we started to consider the option of healing, of not becoming our diagnosis? What if we were open to the possibility that we could process and release trauma, misery, and suffering, and, along with that, reduce the dis-ease of the body, mind, and spirit? Of course, there are times a diagnosis is valid, and medication is necessary. But so much of what's going on in our world can be improved if we are open to the possibility of change and committing to the steps that bring about that change.

Bringing in awareness, knowledge, and action can change our lives. When we are aware of our actions, our thoughts and our emotions, we are able to understand, process, and commit to the action of releasing our negative experiences. In this way, we learn that we are not our experiences; they are not who we are. Instead, the experience manifests as a learning opportunity. We can learn and release the challenges and lessons because they are no longer needed, instead of holding onto them, pushing them down where they grow and become toxic, poisoning us and negatively affecting our daily lives.

Toxic stress and negativity have the power to damage all portions of our lives. Learning to identify our addiction to chaos, pain, and negativity is crucial. Not only is it okay to see and understand this predicament, but it is appropriate to learn how and why we are addicted to negativity. By learning and arming ourselves with knowledge and tools, we can mitigate (lessen) and release toxic stress and negativity. We can live in freedom, peace, love, happiness, safety, and joy!

Through this journey to self, we learn to understand our daily triggers and learned behavior. What we find along the way is okay because we are not our trauma, we are not our pain, we are not our suffering, we are not our feelings, we are not our emotions, we are not our experiences. These things come to us so we can learn and evolve, not suffer and punish ourselves.

When we release negativity, we are able to heal trauma. As we seek change, we are able to reprogram to positive behaviors, thoughts, and actions. Whatever we are most familiar with, we come back to easier. So, as we begin to shift the familiarity of negativity, we begin to release and resolve toxic stress, triggers, and negative learned behavior patterns that have caused pain and suffering in our lives.

Suffering is imminent in general, but especially when there is no hope or change. At times, circumstances or events may feel like they are happening to us for no other reason than to hurt us. We may identify ourselves in that pain and damage, which then increases our suffering.

Suffering is part of how we learn and heal. When we are willing to look at the discomfort that has caused the suffering, we are able to begin healing. Through shadow work—seeing, observing, resolving, and releasing our dark and negative tendencies, impulses, and experiences—we are better able to understand our challenges and move past the pain and suffering.

As we begin to realize that we can shift and release the feelings and experiences that cause suffering, we learn that suffering can be changed. This comes about by allowing a new perspective: "It's not happening to me, it's just happening." *(*Note: We are not referring to victim crimes. If you have been the victim of a crime please reach out to a trusted support, such as a family member or friend, as well as contacting law enforcement and/or seeking out appropriate health care professionals.)*

By understanding and resolving suffering, we are able to differentiate between suffering and struggling. Struggling is much different from suffering. Struggling is uncomfortable, whereas suffering is an unbearable, unchanging state of despair and hopelessness. Both are necessary to learn and evolve, but suffering does not have to be a constant part of our lives. Once we resolve the chaos, pain, negativity, anger, fear, guilt, shame, grief, abandonment, self-loathing, and toxicity that have entered our lives, we are able to release suffering and change our lives in a positive way.

As we learn to understand, let go, and heal suffering, we can see that general life struggles are also inevitable and necessary; we must struggle to grow. Struggling is part of the process; only through the struggle can we gain the strength we need to move forward to the next space. As things fall apart they will rebuild in the intended way. It is part of rebirth and transformation. Through this insight we understand it is okay to not be okay; it is okay to be uncomfortable and struggle; it is temporary and has purpose. The butterfly must struggle to break out of the cocoon because it needs to build the strength in its wings to fly. If we open the cocoon so the butterfly doesn't have to struggle, it will die because it hasn't had the opportunity to create strength in its wings.

We can apply this knowledge to our daily lives, realizing that struggling is part of creating strength and learning balance. Through this wisdom we begin to look forward to coming out on the other side – stronger and wiser, knowing that the lesson will pass, instead of suffering and being doomed and subject to our misery (creating more suffering).

We are able to achieve lasting change in our lives as we reprogram to positivity. Through this process, with the appropriate tools and information, we begin to develop healthy relationships, not only with the world around us but especially with ourselves and the world inside of us. Understanding how to speak in positive, trauma-sensitive language changes our lives and the lives around us. We gain empowerment, resilience, and balance through learning techniques and positive options to incorporate into our daily lives.

We are not meant to be miserable; we are meant to thrive in positivity, love, and joy. No one else can do this for us, only we can be the change we seek. Each one of us has infinite worth and value. Our value and our worth is not defined by our actions; however, our actions may not always reflect our value and worth. The key is to learn from our experiences and move forward, evolving and growing.

No matter where you've been, no matter what you've done, no matter what has happened to you, your worth, your value, is infinite. It always has been and always will be. Here, we peel back the layers to access that space. Everything you need is contained within.

Through this information, and by utilizing these tools, you can release chaos, pain, and negativity. You can discover the missing peace.

We all struggle, we can all heal. You are not alone.

You are the miracle you've been looking for.

Welcome to the Deconstructing Trauma Program.

PART I

Build Empowering Foundations

We Are All Challenged With Past Trauma And Learned Negative Behavior That Affects Our Daily Lives. The Struggle Of Not Being Enough Is REAL.

Our Past Trauma Will Continue Until We Actively Do The Work To Release And Reprogram.

Life Experiences Leave Trauma, Negative Imprints, Triggers, And Blockages That Affect Us Daily; This Trauma And Pain Can Be Resolved.

Our Deconstructing Trauma Program Shifts Negative Thought Processes and Behaviors.

Discover How To Reprogram To Positive, Healthy Thoughts and Behavior Patterns As You Learn How To Identify Negative Triggers and Unhealthy Learned Behavior.

You Are Not Alone!

CHAPTER 1

AWARENESS

In this chapter we address these questions and answers...

What is Awareness? Why is it Important?

What is Self-Awareness? Why is it Important?

What is Trauma? Why it is Important?

What are Adverse Childhood Experiences (ACEs)? Why are they Important?

What is Re-traumatization? Why is it Important?

What is a Trauma-Informed Approach? Why is it Important?

What is Trauma-Responsive Care? Why is it Important?

The Journey of Deconstructing Trauma Starts with Awareness

What is Awareness?

According to the neo-ren blog, "Awareness is the state or ability to perceive, to feel, or to be conscious of events, objects, or sensory patterns. In this level of consciousness, sense data can be confirmed by an observer without necessarily implying understanding. More broadly, it is the state or quality of being aware of something."[1]

Awareness is understanding what our surroundings are and acknowledging our presence within the space.

Why is Awareness Important?

Awareness is important because when we are aware of the environment around us and inside of us we are able to make different choices and decisions. We have the ability to choose what happens when we are aware of what is transpiring around us. Awareness reminds us of our environment and brings attention back to our surroundings.

We can observe the interactions within ourselves and with others impartially because we are not our thoughts, we are not our feelings, we are not our emotions, we are not our trauma, we are not our suffering. We do not have to attach to others' behaviors.

Awareness Tool:

Awareness allows us to understand that we are not our thoughts, we are not our feelings, we are not our emotions, we are not our trauma, we are not our suffering. RF

What is Self-Awareness?

This article defines Self-awareness as "the ability to focus on yourself and how your actions, thoughts, or emotions do or don't align with your internal standards. If you're highly self-aware, you can objectively evaluate yourself, manage your emotions, align your behavior with your values, and understand correctly how others perceive you." [2]

Highly self-aware people are able to interpret their actions, emotions, and thoughts without feeling bad about themselves. It is a unique talent because many of us perceive our circumstances based solely on our emotions, rather than actual facts. Being self-aware is crucial because it enables us to evaluate our progress and effectiveness and alter our course as needed. Through true self-awareness, we are able to choose the way we interact with ourselves and the world around us. As we learn to understand our reactions, we can then begin to understand our emotions. We resolve our negative experiences rather than ignoring our feelings, perpetuating a toxic cycle.

Organizational psychologist and coach Tasha Eurich founded her practice on the importance of self-awareness. *In an article published by Harvard Business Review*, Eurich explores what true self-awareness is – learning to truly understand and communicate what we believe, think, and desire. People who are self-aware also have an accurate realistic picture of their strengths and weaknesses, behaviors, and impact on those around them. As a result, they experience a greater sense of self-reliance and satisfaction, both in their careers and personal relationships. According to Eurich, true self-awareness is rare, ranking between 10% and 15%.[3]

Many of us have been taught at a young age to ignore, minimize, or repress our emotions. We have to push them down; we are not allowed to have a feeling that someone doesn't want to hear. "Quit crying"; "Don't be a sissy"; "Grow up"; "Don't cry;"; "Don't be mad," et cetera.

The only problem with that is we *DO* have feelings, so when we push them down and pretend that they are not there, they begin to poison us inside. This creates a mix of chaos, pain, and negativity. We develop toxic trauma as these suppressed emotions poison us, leading to anger, rage, guilt, shame, depressive states, grief, anxiousness, addiction, drugs, alcohol, despair, disease, eating disorders, identity crises, and more.

Why is Self-Awareness Important?

Betterup.com has a great post on the importance of self-awareness in all aspects of life. *Self-awareness is important* because "this kind of introspection allows us to look at behaviors and beliefs for what they are. With self-awareness, we can examine old patterns and stories that do not serve us, and then we can move on. Asking the right questions empowers us to make different choices that bring different results."[4]

The greatest journey starts with the first step...

The first step is awareness. Through this awareness we can access understanding and knowledge that we can then place into action to facilitate change.

Through this awareness, we can step back and observe. When we observe we don't have to take things personally. We can see each part of the interaction without judgment or ego.

Yes, This Takes a Lot of Practice, But It Is So Worth It!!!

Awareness allows us to see why we might have an issue, how we are acting, and why we are acting that way. It also allows us to see why others might have an issue, how they are acting, and why they are acting that way.

Awareness of Trauma

Awareness Tool:

Becoming aware of trauma can lead to healing. RF

What is Trauma?

Trauma is a deeply distressing or disturbing experience.[5]

Trauma comes in many forms and can include psychological, physical, emotional, sexual abuse, or domestic violence. *The Substance Abuse and Mental Health Services Administration (SAMHSA) describes* individual trauma as resulting from "an event, series of events, or set of circumstances that is experienced by an individual as physically or emotionally harmful or life-threatening and that has lasting adverse effects on the individual's functioning and mental, physical, social, emotional, or spiritual well-being."[6]

Awareness Tool:

We have been passing on EXTREMELY dangerous information for decades. When we don't allow others or ourselves to process feelings and emotions, we are denying an inborn human response. RF

Awareness Tool:

*Our emotions and trauma **will** come to the surface. We can't stop it; it will happen eventually, and most likely in a very damaging way, if it has been stuffed down and ignored. RF*

Why Do We All Have Trauma?

We all have trauma because we have all had negative experiences occur in our lives. These negative experiences create trauma because they negativity impact our interactions with the world around us, as well as the world inside of us.

Our past trauma will affect us all in our daily lives until we understand our trauma responses. These trauma responses are meant to keep us alive. We can begin to understand that we have become programmed to protect ourselves, either by submission and backing away or by anger and fighting back. Different situations, as well as different personalities and past experiences, will dictate how we respond in certain situations.

Many times, our past trauma can serve as a learned lesson that can keep us safe, moving forward. For example: We learn the stove is hot by touching it and burning our hand, however, that experience keeps us from continuing to touch it and burn ourselves.

Understanding our learned triggers and impulses is so important; they can teach us how to identify the difference between a real threat or a perceived threat and can change the course of events.

An impulse is a powerful, sudden urge to take action. These impulses can save our lives. Impulses are bound to happen from our environment; we do not have to act like it's okay and everything is fine if we have learned experience that shows us something is dangerous or not healthy. A trigger will lead to the impulse; when that happens we can stop and make a choice. We don't have to make choices based on reactions and impulses.

Awareness Tool:

There are times when we can become bitter about life
and worn out by our personal experiences. When this happens
joy and enthusiasm for life seem to disappear. RF

Why is Trauma Important?

Trauma is important because it has and will continue to impact our lives in negative ways until it is resolved. *Research on trauma has produced* two certain conclusions. First, trauma is prevalent. More than half of Americans report having at least one adverse childhood experience (ACE), and many adults also endure potentially life-altering traumatic events. Second, exposure to trauma at any point in the life course can limit human potential and compromise quality of life. In fact, trauma is one of the leading causes of disorder, disability, disease, and death.[7]

Our past trauma does and will continue to affect our lives until we take an active role in healing that trauma. This information does not label us or condemn us. What has happened to us, where we have been, and what we have done does not define us. Rather, it gives us insight and an opportunity to learn and evolve from where we've been. Also, it's important to note that none of this work condones anyone's bad behavior or harmful actions, including our own. Through this space we learn to observe, discovering awareness of the situation and the challenge, without *becoming* the situation or the challenge.

Awareness Tool:

We are not our trauma. We are not our pain. We are not our suffering. RF

What is the ACEs Study and Why is it Important?

Potentially traumatic events that may occur during childhood (0-17 years) are known as adverse childhood experiences (ACEs).

Description of Adverse childhood experiences (ACEs).. Adverse childhood experiences (ACEs) can have a significant impact on the outcome of an individual's life. Potentially stressful events that may occur during childhood (0-17 years) are known as adverse childhood experiences (ACEs).

ACEs can have long-term detrimental repercussions on health, well-being, and life chances such as education and employment. These factors may increase the risk of injury, sexually transmitted infections, personal physical and mental health challenges, teen pregnancy, pregnancy issues, fetal death, sex trafficking, cancer, diabetes, heart disease, or suicide.

For example, being hurt by violence, abuse, or neglect, seeing violence at home or in the community, or having a family member try or die by suicide are all examples of traumatic events. There are also things in the child's environment that can make them feel less safe, stable, and connected; for example, if you grew up in a home where there were problems with drugs or mental health, where there was a lot of chaos because your parents split up, or where someone in the home went to jail/prison. These are not the only negative outcomes that can occur. There are a lot of other traumatic events that could potentially harm physical, mental, emotional, and spiritual health and happiness.

ACEs are linked to long-term health problems, mental illness, and problems with using drugs or alcohol as a teen or adult. ACEs can also damage a person's ability to learn, get a job, and make money; however, preventing ACEs is possible.

Awareness Tool:

ACEs are relevant because they may have long-lasting, negative impacts on health, happiness, and may reduce options for education and employment. RF

ACEs and other social factors that affect health, like living in poor or racially segregated neighborhoods, moving a lot, or not having enough food, can cause toxic stress (extended or prolonged stress). Toxic stress from ACEs can hurt a child's brain development, immune system, and ability to deal with stress. Changes like these can affect a child's ability to pay attention, make decisions, and learn.

When children are young, toxic stress can make it hard for them to make healthy, stable relationships. They may also have unstable jobs as adults and have problems with money, jobs, and depressive states throughout their lives. Consequently, these issues may be passed on to future generations. Some children may be exposed to more toxic stress because of past and ongoing traumas caused by racism, or the effects of poverty caused by a lack of educational and job opportunities. [8]

Awareness Tool:

The ACEs Study: Adverse Childhood Experiences.
It is important because this study can help us identify
trauma that has occurred in our lives. RF

Our future doesn't have to be determined by our past. We can use this knowledge to seek change and resolve our past and present trauma. Trauma therapists, medical practitioners, holistic practitioners, and mental health professionals are all good resources! Your healing journey can begin here!

Adverse Childhood Experience (ACE) Questionnaire[9]

This asks questions about events that happened during your childhood; specifically, the first 18 years of your life. The information you provide by answering these yes or no questions will allow us to better understand problems that may have occurred early in life and how those problems may be impacting the challenges you are experiencing today. Write YES or NO for each question. Each "yes" response will equal one point.

While you were growing up, during your first 18 years of life:

1. Did a parent or other adult in the household often:

Swear at you, insult you, put you down, or humiliate you? OR

Act in a way that made you afraid that you might be physically hurt?

Yes or No... If Yes, enter 1 _____

2. Did a parent or other adult in the household often:

Push, grab, slap, or throw something at you? OR

Ever hit you so hard that you had marks or were injured?

Yes or No... If Yes, enter 1 _____

3. Did an adult or person at least 5 years older than you ever:

Touch or fondle you or have you touch their body in a sexual way? OR

Attempt or actually have oral, anal, or vaginal intercourse with you?

Yes or No... If Yes, enter 1 _____

4. Did you often feel that:

No one in your family loved you or thought you were important or special? OR

Your family didn't look out for each other, feel close to each other, or support each other?

Yes or No... If Yes, enter 1 _____

5. Did you often feel that:

You didn't have enough to eat, had to wear dirty clothes, and had no one to protect you? OR

Your parents were too drunk or high to take care of you or take you to the doctor if you needed it?

Yes or No... If Yes, enter 1 _____

6. Were your parents ever separated or divorced?

Yes or No... If Yes, enter 1 _____

7. Were any of your parents or other adult caregivers:

Often pushed, grabbed, slapped, or had something thrown at them? OR

Sometimes or often kicked, bitten, hit with a fist, or hit with something hard? OR

Ever repeatedly hit over at least a few minutes or threatened with a gun or knife?

Yes or No... If Yes, enter 1 _____

8. **Did you live with anyone who was a problem drinker or alcoholic, or who used street drugs?**

   YES or NO

9. **Was a household member depressed or mentally ill, or did a household member attempt suicide?**

   Yes or No... If Yes, enter 1 _____

10. **Did a household member go to prison?**

   Yes or No... If Yes, enter 1 _____

ACE SCORE (Total "Yes" Answers): _____

Awareness Tool:

*The ACEs we have experienced growing up will continue
to have negative impacts on the rest of our lives,
until we resolve that trauma. RF*

The ACE Study revealed five main discoveries:

1. ACEs are common...nearly two-thirds (64%) of adults have at least one.

2. They cause adult onset of chronic disease, such as cancer and heart disease, as well as mental illness, violence and being a victim of violence.

3. ACEs don't occur alone...if you have one, there's an 87% chance that you have two or more.

4. The more ACEs you have, the greater the risk for chronic disease, mental illness, violence and being a victim of violence. People have an ACE score of 0 to 10. Each type of trauma counts as one, no matter how many times it occurs. You can think of an ACE score as a cholesterol score for childhood trauma. For example, people with an ACE score of 4 are twice as likely to be smokers and seven times more likely to be alcoholic. Having an ACE score of 4 increases the risk of emphysema or chronic bronchitis by nearly 400 percent, and suicide by 1200 percent. People with high ACE scores are more likely to be violent, to have more marriages, more broken bones, more drug prescriptions, more depression, and more autoimmune diseases. People with an ACE score of 6 or higher are at risk of their lifespan being shortened by 20 years.

5. ACEs are responsible for a big chunk of workplace absenteeism, and for costs in health care, emergency response, mental health, and criminal justice. So, the fifth finding from the ACE Study is that childhood adversity contributes to most of our major chronic health, mental health, economic health and social health issues.[10]

As mentioned earlier, while the findings of this study are comprehensive they do not cover all types of adverse childhood experiences. You may have a score of 0 on the quiz and still have experienced one or more ACEs that are affecting your life.

Awareness Tool:

We are not placing blame or passing off our current actions because we are identifying our past trauma. Through this experience we are learning more about our challenges so we can identify, resolve, and evolve! RF

So, how do we mitigate and resolve our past trauma?
Where do we start?

<u>**Awareness Tool:**</u>

Congratulations! We have already started to resolve our trauma, by learning and raising our awareness! Continuing to learn will manifest knowledge and awareness; it will set us free. RF

Awareness of Re-traumatization

Digging a little deeper into understanding trauma, we refer to Re-traumatization.

What is a Re-traumatization?

A re-traumatization is a conscious or unconscious reminder of past trauma that results in a re-experiencing of the initial traumatic event. It can be triggered by a situation, an attitude or expression, or by certain environments that replicate the dynamics (loss of power/control/safety) of the original trauma.[11]

What can Trigger a Re-traumatization?

Triggering Re-traumatization
Some of the main causes of re-traumatization are:

Feeling like you don't have control, going through changes you didn't expect, feeling threatened or attacked, feeling weak, discouraged, low, scared, or feeling shame.

Why is a Triggering Re-traumatization Important?

Triggering re-traumatization is important because when we are unaware we can inadvertently re-traumatize and continue this dangerous cycle in our lives, causing chaos, harm, unhappiness, negativity, anger, addiction, and more.

Awareness Tool:

We live in a re-traumatized state to some extent until we are able to release our trauma and start reprogramming negative learned behavior. RF

So where does this leave us???
Are we doomed to live in our trauma forever???
Absolutely Not!!!!

We do have free will and can exercise that free will! We can choose to address and release our past trauma and learn how to reprogram ourselves to a positive mindset, thus changing the course of our unhealthy patterns.

We can begin this healing journey by seeking trauma-informed and trauma-responsive services and resources.

Awareness of Trauma-Informed

We continue with a brief understanding of what trauma-informed and trauma-responsive means. We must first understand and learn to apply this for ourselves before we can begin to apply it in relationships around us.

What does a Trauma-Informed Approach Mean?

A Trauma-Informed approach means speaking to the person about the trauma that happened without calling them "bad" or "broken." A trauma-informed approach means that you understand, plan for, and respond to each person's experience, hopes, and special needs.

Why is it Important to Take a Trauma-Informed Approach?

A Trauma-Informed approach is important because it keeps us from re-traumatizing people or blaming them for attempting to deal with their reactions to a traumatic event.

A Trauma-Informed approach starts with knowing how trauma affects a person on a physical, social, mental, and emotional level.

There are three parts to a Trauma-Informed approach

1. Being aware of how prevalent trauma is.
2. Being aware of how trauma affects everyone.
3. Acting on this knowledge by putting it to use.

Each person's experience of trauma can be different, which can test their coping skills and cause them to start utilizing survival strategies.

Trauma may be the result of a single event (for instance, a natural disaster or seeing or being a victim of violence) or a series of events (long-term abuse).

Trauma changes how we see ourselves ("I'm helpless"; "I'm worthless"); how we see the world ("The world is dangerous, no one can protect me"); and how we see our relationships with other people ("I cannot trust anyone.")

These ideas affect how we act toward ourselves and the rest of the world.

Awareness Tool:

The knowledge that We Are Not Our Trauma is a life-saving tool. RF

Why is Trauma-Informed Care Important?

Trauma-Informed Care is important because through Trauma-Informed Care we are able to begin the healing process because the key concepts of Trauma-Informed Care support our recovery to a whole and healthy self.

The Key Concepts: Trauma-informed Care are:

Safety, Trustworthiness, Choice, Collaboration, Empowerment

What are the Benefits of Trauma-Informed Care?

The benefits of Trauma-Informed care are we are able to realize our past trauma, identify how the trauma has affected us, and respond with positive decisive action to release and reprogram this trauma.

This process changes negative learned behavior, reprograms unhealthy thought patterns, and redirects our lives in a good way. Putting our newfound knowledge into practice allows us to receive the desired outcome of positive change in our lives.

And finally, we reach Trauma-Responsive Care. Trauma-Informed is where it starts, and Trauma-Responsive takes it to the next level and puts the Trauma-Informed theory into action, allowing healing!

Awareness of Trauma-Responsive

What is Trauma-Responsive Care?

Trauma-Responsive care is attempting to resolve problems in a helpful and understanding way. Trauma-Sensitive approaches ask, "What's happening?" or "How can I help?" rather than, "What's the matter with you?"

Why is Trauma-Responsive Care Important?

Trauma-Responsive care is important because it has a significant favorable effect on future levels of addiction, criminality, violence, and other societal disorders. Trauma-Responsive care is crucial. It provides compassion, hope, and encouragement. It offers sympathy, support, and hope. How can we assist and heal? It provides strategies, solutions, life-changing information, plans of action, and resources for minimizing and resolving past trauma.

What are the Benefits of Trauma-Responsive Care?

The benefits of Trauma-Responsive care are lasting change and improved whole health and wellness. By applying and implementing our Deconstructing Trauma principles and tools, we are able to reprogram and release trauma triggers and negative learned behavior.

In this way we heal, we are enough...

Now that we have awareness of what trauma is and a basic understanding of trauma-informed and trauma-responsive approaches and care, we can begin to seek modalities that allow us to heal and assist us in positive, productive ways.

We begin to understand that we are not alone. Utilizing the knowledge and wisdom that each of us is acting through a lens of trauma, we realize that we have the power to address and heal our trauma. This empowers us to move forward in a good way.

We can all participate in Trauma-Responsive care toward ourselves and others. This brings us hope and improves relationships with ourselves and others.

This next statement will blow your mind!

Awareness Tool:

"Each person is acting appropriately for their level of trauma."
~ Andrea Kremko[12]

This information is shocking but true! Think back and remember the last person who really seemed to hurt your feelings... What might change when you consider that they were acting appropriately for their level of trauma?

We might be open to seeing that they could have been hurting, struggling with feelings of fear, or battling an inadequacy they felt deep inside. Most times when people are reactive, they are not aware that something deeper is going on, that they are fighting to keep themselves safe because they are living their past trauma.

Now, maybe thinking back to the last time you might have hurt someone's feelings... What changes when you consider that you were acting appropriately for your level of trauma?

We might be open to seeing that you could have been hurting, struggling with feelings of fear, or battling an inadequacy you felt deep inside. Most times, when we are reactive, we are not aware that something deeper is going on, that we are fighting to keep ourselves safe because we are living our past trauma.

While this information is astounding and none too easy to wrap your head around, it can change your life! This, however, does not excuse anyone's behavior by any means. We are ultimately responsible for our actions; because we are acting appropriately for our level of trauma does not give us excuses or greenlights to continue inappropriate and hurtful behavior. We are still responsible for changing our actions and healing.

Awareness Tool:

We are not responsible for other people's actions, but we are responsible for changing our actions, releasing trauma, and healing from the past. RF

Trauma is part of all of our stories, but it's not who we are. Life is full of learning experiences that are meant to challenge us to grow and evolve. We can choose to reduce our suffering, but it will take effort and action to manifest. By choosing to do nothing we are also making a choice.

Our interactions with others will not manifest the same experience for all involved, because what they need to learn will be different from what we need to learn. We all are in our own unique experience; through this space we are able to learn to respond with awareness and knowledge in difficult situations, not only for others but also for ourselves.

We are not broken; we don't need to be fixed. We just need options and information to move past the trauma, pain, and suffering that we all experience one way or another on this human journey.

As we change our perception, this allows our perspective to shift. Everything we need is contained within, here we peel back the layers to access that space.

A great Trauma-Responsive tool for interaction can be to behave toward everyone as if we are receiving a great guest. Not all guests will need the same thing, nor will the conversation be the same with all guests; however, we treat each guest with honor and respect.

Awareness Tool:

We are infinite beings; we are not meant to suffer;
we are meant to learn evolve and pass healing information
on from one cell to the next. RF

Our hardest lessons are designed to push us to choose a deeper understanding. This deeper understanding allows us to realize that others in our lives are complementary to our lives. They are like an accessory, in a good way! We love to put on hats, jewelry, and extras because they make us feel special, but they are not the main outfit. We are our own main outfit; our self-worth and value comes from within. It is inappropriate and dangerous to expect others to fulfill that space for us.

As we face challenging situations, stress, anxiousness, or depressive states are quite normal. Not to minimize it, of course, but normalizing sometimes is helpful, knowing that what we are going through is valid and will pass. It is temporary. Anything that comes up is okay, even if it's uncomfortable; it's just passing through so it can release. We don't have to attach to it, we can just see it moving through, like clouds in the sky, observing and releasing.

Be patient with yourself and others. We want to hurry up and be done already, but this process takes time and dedication to work through; there are things that need to shift and change along the way. Understanding our past trauma and present challenges that have manifested is a journey, and if we hurry up to get to the end we miss everything in the middle. It would be like only baking a cake for thirteen minutes instead of thirty-five because we don't want to wait. We will not end up getting the result we want because it not done yet. If we rush it, or don't see it all, it will skew the outcome in a negative way.

You are exactly where you should be; just allow the time you need to heal and re-program. It is all part of the process! You are not alone.

AN AUTOBIOGRAPHY IN FIVE CHAPTERS

Chapter 1

I walk down the street.
There is a deep hole in the sidewalk.
I fall in.
I am lost...I am helpless.
It isn't my fault.
It takes forever to find a way out.

Chapter 2

I walk down the same street.
There is a deep hole in the sidewalk.
I pretend I don't see it.
I fall in, again.
I can't believe I am in this same place.
But it isn't my fault.
It still takes a long time to get out.

Chapter 3

I walk down the same street.
There is a deep hole in the sidewalk.
I see it is there.
I fall in...it's a habit...
But, my eyes are open.
I know where I am.
It is my fault.
I get out immediately.

Chapter 4

I walk down the same street.
There is a deep hole in the sidewalk.
I walk around it.

Chapter 5

I walk down a different street.

-Anonymous
Author: Portia Nelson, Design: Andrea Kremko

Chapter 1: Awareness.
Summary/Key Takeaways

What is Awareness? Why is it Important?

- *Awareness is* understanding what our surroundings are and acknowledging our presence within the space. *Awareness is important* because when we are aware of the environment around us and inside of us we are able to make different choices and decisions. We have the ability to choose what happens in our lives when we are aware of what is transpiring around us.

What is Self-Awareness? Why is it Important?

- *Self-awareness is* the ability to pay attention to yourself and how your actions, thoughts, and feelings match or don't match your own standards. *Self-awareness is important* because it allows us to see why we might have an issue, how we are acting, and why we are acting that way. It also allows us to see why others might have an issue, how they are acting, and why they are acting that way.

What is Trauma? Why it is Important?

- *Trauma is* a profoundly stressful or upsetting event. Trauma can take various forms, including psychological, physical, emotional, sexual, and domestic abuse. We all have trauma because we have all had negative experiences in our lives. These negative experiences are referred to as trauma, and they affect our interactions with the world around us as well as the world inside of us. Trauma is prevalent in our lives and can comprise human potential and diminish life quality. One of the primary causes of disorder, disability, illness, and mortality is trauma. *Trauma is important* because it has and will continue to impact our lives in negative ways until it is resolved. Our past trauma does and will continue to affect our lives until we take an active role in healing that trauma.

What are Adverse Childhood Experiences (ACEs)? Why are they Important?

- *Adverse childhood experiences, or ACEs, are* potentially stressful events that may occur during childhood (0-17 years). ACEs are linked to long-term health problems, mental illness, and problems with using drugs or alcohol as a teen or adult. *ACEs are important* because they can damage a person's ability to learn, get a job, and make money; however, preventing ACEs is possible. The ACEs Study can help us identify trauma that has occurred in our lives. Once we are aware of our trauma we can take steps to release and heal this trauma.

What is Re-traumatization? Why is it Important?

- *A re-traumatization is* an intentional or unintentional reminder of past trauma that triggers a re-occurrence of the original traumatic event. A circumstance, an attitude or expression, or specific situations that mimic the dynamics (loss of power, control, or safety) of the initial trauma might trigger it. *Triggering re-traumatization is important* because when we are unaware we can inadvertently re-traumatize and continue this dangerous cycle in our lives, causing chaos, harm, and addiction.

What is Trauma-Informed Approach? Why is it Important?

- *A Trauma-Informed approach means* speaking to the person about the trauma that happened without calling them "bad" or "broken." A Trauma-Informed approach means that you understand, plan for, and respond to each person's experience, hopes, and special needs. *A Trauma-Informed approach is important* because with this approach we avoid re-traumatizing or blaming individuals for trying to manage their traumatic reactions. Understanding the physical, social, and emotional consequences of trauma is the first step in a Trauma-Informed approach, this allows the individual to be met where they are at and to heal and overcome their trauma.

What is Trauma-Responsive Care? Why is it Important?

- ***Trauma-Responsive care is*** attempting to resolve problems in a helpful and understanding way. Trauma-sensitive approaches ask, "What's happening?" or "How can I help?" rather than "What's the matter with you?" ***Trauma-Responsive care is important*** because it has a significant favorable effect on future levels of addiction, criminality, violence, and other societal disorders. Trauma-Responsive care is crucial. It provides compassion, hope, and encouragement. It offers sympathy, support, and hope. How can we assist and heal? It provides strategies, solutions, life-changing information, plans of action, and resources for minimizing and resolving past trauma.

- We can all participate in Trauma-Responsive care toward ourselves and others.

A great method for releasing trauma and tension is TRE®. TRE is an innovative series of exercises that assist the body in releasing deep muscular patterns of stress, tension and trauma. TRE is designed to be a self-help tool. https://traumaprevention.com/. Renee Frye of Sacred Sol Healing Institute is a TRE trained provider.

Awareness is so powerful!
Are you ready to continue?
In the next chapter we will learn to...
Identify the Addiction to Negativity.

What Causes Conflict in Your Life

Anger · Neglect · Mental Abuse · Physical Abuse · Alcohol

Drugs · Criticism · Sex · Relationships · Arguing · Anxiety

Victim · Hate · Co-Dependence · Annoyances · Irritable

Addiction · Damaging Core Beliefs · Gambling · Death · Food · DHS

Lack of Self-Respect · Lies · Sexual Assault · Lack of Self-Worth

Spiritual Abuse · Abandonment · Child Abuse · Environment

Bullying · Dissociation · Belittling · Shame · Not Being Forgiven

Pride · Poor Decision-Making · Downgrading · Comparing

Resentment · Self-Blame · Ego · Lack Of Confidence · Suicide

Righteous Religion · People Pleasing · Recklessness · Labeling

No Self-Love · Depression · Lack of Approval · Boredom

Isolation · Self-Medicating · Lack of Respect · Loneliness · Spite

Lack of Responsibility · Wrath · Vengeance · Jealousy · Greed

Perfectionist · Excuses · Envy · Rage · Selfishness · Judging

Adopting Others' Opinions · Cheating · Assumptions · Bills

Self-Sabotage · Meddling · Guilt Frustration · Family · Finances

Negligence · Disappointment · Lack of Work · False Identity

Bad Choices · Assumptions · Disease · Suffering · Trauma

Negativity weighs heavy on us. If each one of these words weighed
5 pounds it would be over 400 pounds...way too much to carry.
That weight transfers to our body, mind, and sprit.
Release the negative, find positivity and hope. You are not alone!

CHAPTER 2

IDENTIFY THE ADDICTION TO NEGATIVITY

In this chapter we address...

What are Negative Thought Patterns? Why are they Important?

What does Negative Thinking do to Your Body?

Why are We so Hyper-focused on the Negative Aspects of Existence?

Why do We Glorify Struggle and Conflict?

What are Examples of Negative Patterns?

What is Cognitive Distortion? Why is it Important?

What Habits Lead to Cognitive Distortion?

What is Mindfulness? Why is it Important?

Identifying the Addiction to Negativity

Now that we know the benefits of awareness we can continue to apply that awareness to specific subjects. This will increase our desired results, allowing focused information and knowledge to be obtained.

*<u>**Awareness Tool:**</u>*

*Repeated unhealthy, negative patterns can occur from
of our past trauma, and can jeopardize our ability
to live a healthy happy life. RF*

What are Negative Thought Patterns?

Negative thought patterns are repeated unhealthy negative thoughts, that damage our lives, and alter the body's chemistry in a harmful way. Negativity affects us at a cellular level.

On a daily basis, changes in gene activity are possible. *If the perception in your mind* is reflected in the chemistry of your body, and if your nervous system reads and interprets the environment and then controls the blood's chemistry, then you can literally change the fate of your cells by altering your thoughts.[13]

Have you ever found yourself unable to stop thinking negative thoughts? Do you punish yourself for having negative thoughts, which leads to you having more negative thoughts? Negative thinking causes us to focus on the negative aspects of a situation rather than the positives.

According to Sage Neuroscience Center in New Mexico, "Negative thought patterns, or cognitive distortions, can manifest as incorrect assumptions, unrealistic self-criticisms, and even the denial of reality itself. The effects of this thinking can be all too real for someone struggling with their mental health."[14]

Negative thinking patterns can manifest as fears, unwanted thoughts, repetitive thoughts, chaos, anger, resentment, insecurity, chronic fatigue, burnout, low energy, depressive states, anxiousness, chronic continual illness, self-loathing, and even total rejection of reality.

Awareness Tool:

We all struggle with our mental health at one time or another in our lives. This is not because we are weak or should be ashamed, but because we are human, and this is how we learn. RF

As mentioned in Chapter 1, many of us grew up with the message that we should not show our emotions, so we attempt to ignore or suppress them. These negative emotions poison and harm us. We either internalize them (resulting in anger, resentment, depressive states, despair, and resignation), or we externalize them and blame, discount, or bully others. Negative thought patterns have a damaging impact on our physical, mental, emotional, and spiritual health.

Awareness Tool:

Reaching out for assistance and support of our mental health takes courage and strength. We ALL need mental support. You are not alone! RF

Why is Recognizing Negative Thought Patterns Important?

Recognizing negative thought patterns is important because your thoughts and values can determine the way you see yourself and the world around you. Thoughts and beliefs that are grounded in pessimism can negatively impact your feelings, emotions, and mental health. These harmful perceptions are common issues that can contribute to the symptoms of mood and chronic disorders. Negative thinking makes you feel bad about the world, about yourself, about the future. It contributes to low self-worth. It makes you feel you're not effective in the world. Psychologists link negative thinking to depression, anxiety, chronic worry and obsessive-compulsive disorder (OCD).

What does Negative Thinking do to Your Body?

Negative thinking can cause chronic stress and feelings of help-lessness and hopelessness, which disrupts the body's hormone balance, depletes the brain chemicals required for happiness, and damages the immune system. Chronic stress can actually shorten our lives. Negativity, like many other things in life, can become a habit. Criticism, cynicism, and denial can all create neural pathways in the brain that promote sadness and depressive states.

According to mental health professionals, depression begins as a state of health – nothing is right, everything is critical, everything is negative.

The longer we stay in this state of negativity, the more it becomes habitual. When it becomes habitual, our cells begin to adapt to this negativity and accept it. This is extremely dangerous because at a cellular level our body adapts to the depressive state as its main state of being. The mind and spirit follow.

Why are We so Hyper-focused on the Negative Aspects of Existence?

We are so hyper-focused on negativity because it is all we know; it is what we are most familiar with.

Brain chemicals like dopamine cause exhilaration. Negative ideas become habits because they "reward" us. Uncontrolled negative thinking is a common problem. Addiction occurs when our brain thinks that something destructive is good.

Awareness Tool:

People engage in physically or emotionally self-destructive behaviors to get an unconscious hormone response.
This is why we are addicted to negativity. RF

We are all addicted to chaos, pain, and negativity. We are constantly looking to other people, places, and things in an effort to validate our own sense of value and worth. We have become accustomed to getting our own way and thinking that we should have perfect conditions – not too hot, not too cold; rain, but not too much rain; no destruction from weather, et cetera.

Awareness Tool:

We have become so out of balance that we expect the world around us to provide an environment that we find favorable. RF

Example: We may be down because of the cloudy weather. We are blue and sad because there is no sunshine. This ruins our day, putting us in a bad mood, affecting all around us because we do not have the desirable conditions we want.

Why is the weather responsible for continually providing that light that makes us feel good? These expectations are not reasonable, nor will anybody thrive or learn in this way. It is our responsibility to take action and to create the light and happiness that we need inside of ourselves, when we notice that it is needed, rather than complaining about it and suffering.

We have been conditioned, however, to expect our environment to create perfect conditions and when it doesn't we are disappointed. You are not alone, I totally understand! We used to have a thing called the "Frye (my last name) Luck." My husband and I have been together for eighteen-plus years and from the moment we met if anything could go wrong, it would and did!

We had some of the strangest things happen, for real!

So, we would have these negative discussions about how awful our luck was and even decided to name it the "Frye Luck." We just knew nothing was ever going to turn out good and so it didn't. We drew this vibration of negativity into our lives, named it, and gave it such a great home it wasn't ever going to leave! Why would it?

The vibration that you perceive yourself to be in is what will manifest! Even on the rare occasion something good happened we still couldn't enjoy it because we knew that something really bad was around the corner to wipe out the good – and it never disappointed!

Since then, I have learned that this life is about challenges and what we do with them. We now draw in positivity, and we receive that positivity right back! Ninety percent of our life is positive, and even when it's uncomfortable we can learn and adjust to get through the tougher times without thinking the world has a master plan against us!

Of course, things will happen – it's the natural order of the Universe. A wave must go up *and* come down; there has to be balance. So, when we are going through tough times I know that someone else out there is going through moments of ease. It is all for a purpose.

We are each responsible for our own level of happiness, and we are each responsible for our own level of unhappiness. Stress and challenges will happen. The reason they happen is so we can learn, grow, and become stronger from the experience, not so we can adopt them as our identity and concede to suffering. We can learn to be grateful instead of hateful.

Awareness Tool:

The experience of chaos, pain, and negativity stimulates the brain's reward centers, which in turn leads to an unconscious addiction to chaos, pain, and negativity. RF

Why do We Glorify Struggle and Conflict?

We glorify struggle and conflict because we are addicted to the chemicals the body releases when in a state of stress. We call the brain's reward centers "pleasure centers," so it makes sense that when someone is addicted to drugs or alcohol the brain lights up and makes them want more. We know about that kind of addiction.

But you don't need drugs or alcohol to make a self-reinforcing addiction circuit in your brain. Anything that turns on the dopamine or beta-endorphin pathways will work. The beta-endorphin and dopamine pathways are also turned on by pain and negative emotions like self-pity, anger, and guilt. These pathways are lit up by chronic jaw pain or painful thoughts in the same way they are by drugs. Because of this, we can get hooked on those feelings.

In this case, the biological process is simple: pain and bad feelings turn on the brain's reward centers, which makes the person unconsciously addicted to those bad feelings.

Awareness Tool:

*Good news!!! You are not your thoughts, your emotions,
or your feelings! You can learn to identify and
reprogram negative patterns. RF*

According to The Sage Neuroscience Center[15],

> Breaking free from negative thought patterns requires learning how to cope effectively with the feelings and triggers that lead to negative thinking. Someone experiencing mental health struggles can be led into a depressive spiral of negative thoughts by any number of possible triggers—from unhelpful advice to minor relationship issues—and those negative thoughts can take on a variety of different forms.

What are Examples of Negative Patterns?

Mental health experts have identified many types of negative thinking patterns, including:

1. Polarization or Dichotomous Thinking:
When complex issues are oversimplified so that they become black or white, yes or no, good versus bad, me versus them, that's dichotomous thinking. This all-or-nothing mindset makes it hard to approach issues with any sort of room for compromise. The idea that "there is no second place" (i.e., you must be the absolute best to be considered a success) is a common example of harmful dichotomous thinking.

2. Emotional Reasoning:
When a person insists that something is factually true even though their only evidence is their own feelings, they are engaging in emotional reasoning. Someone in the throes of emotional reasoning is difficult to engage with productively because they center their reasoning around negative emotions rather than any sort of logic. The emotional reasoner starts with the premise that their negative feelings must be true and justified simply because they exist and then builds a narrative to support that. "I'm anxious about going to school, therefore going to school must be dangerous," would be an example of emotional reasoning.

3. Overgeneralization:
Overgeneralization means fixating on one negative detail or experience and assigning it an overblown significance in your life. For example, a waiter breaks a glass clearing a table which leads them to exclaim, "I'm the most useless waiter to ever live!" This despairing notion is not proportionate to the event that triggered it. Only by overgeneralizing their entire career in the context of this mundane mistake could someone come to such a conclusion.

4. Labeling:
Putting negative labels on yourself and the people and things around you is another very common type of harmful thought pattern that many people engage in every day without really thinking about it. If someone consistently sees themselves as "a loser" or "stupid" or "a bad father," they can eventually grow into that mold because their negative perception leaves them no room to live outside those labels or grow beyond them.

5. Jumping to Conclusions:
Most of us have been guilty of a mistaken assumption at some point. However, when someone experiencing mental health struggles jumps to a negative conclusion about something – usually themselves – it can become extremely difficult to correct or change that belief.

6. Mental Filtering:
When someone chooses (consciously or otherwise) to remember only the bad parts of a situation, they're engaged in mental filtering. A depressed athlete who forgets their many excellent plays and instead rants about one blown assignment and how it cost their team the game would be an example of mental filtering.

7. Fortune-Telling:
Another type of negative thought pattern involves repeatedly predicting that situations will turn out poorly. Projecting pessimism onto the future can create a self-fulfilling prophecy where your negative vision of the future is so strong it impacts your ability to behave in a way that would lead to positive outcomes. For example, a student with an upcoming test believes they're going to fail, so they don't bother to study, which does indeed lead to a failed test.

8. Mind-Reading:
Fortune-telling and mind-reading may sound like amazing psychic abilities, but when we're talking about cognitive distortion, neither

of them are particularly helpful. Mind-reading in this context means assuming you know exactly what someone else thinks and feels, especially what they think and feel about you. Assuming someone hates you because they gave a short, hurried response to a question (when perhaps they were just flustered by something unrelated) would be an example of negative mind reading behavior. We create a false story.

9. Magnification or Catastrophizing:
Most of us have been guilty of this in a heated moment. Magnification, sometimes called catastrophizing, simply means blowing an issue out of proportion. Allowing a bad taxi ride to ruin an entire vacation is an example of catastrophizing.

10. Inability to Be Wrong:
Everyone likes to feel correct, but this desire becomes a cognitive distortion when the need to be right outweighs evidence, logic, and material reality. Growth – including the growth needed for mental health recovery – requires allowing yourself the room to be forgiven and to grow. If you can never be incorrect in the first place, there's no space for that growth to occur.

11. Control Fallacies:
A control fallacy can manifest in two possible forms. One is that you despair because you have no control over anything in your life and are therefore powerless to change it. The other is that you despair because you have absolute control over everything in your life and are therefore entirely to blame for any negative or difficult circumstances.

12. Fairness Fallacies:
The age-old adage "the world's not fair" is usually spoken in response to someone struggling with a fairness fallacy. Analyzing situations in

terms of how just or unjust they are often not helpful in the context of personal mental health.

13. Change Fallacies:
Believing or assuming that someone or something will eventually change to suit your needs is a fallacy of change. This is essentially a matter of projecting your own needs and desires onto the world around you.

14. Minimizing or Discounting:
Not all negative thought patterns are actually centered on negative thoughts. Another form of cognitive distortion occurs when someone fails to appreciate positive things in their life and instead ignores or marginalizes them. This refusal to acknowledge the good allows negative feelings to flourish unchecked. Writing off all of your accomplishments as "luck" is an example of minimizing.

15. Personalization and Self-Blame:
When you take issues or details that have nothing to do with you and make them all about yourself, your feelings, or your role in matters, you are experiencing the cognitive distortion called personalization. An example of personalization is a child blaming themselves for their parents getting divorced.

16. Imperatives:
Framing things in terms like "should" or "must" can be a big part of negative thinking. For example, someone who gets nervous talking on the telephone might berate themselves because they believe they "should" be able to make a simple phone call without feeling anxious. This minimizes their ability to accept that it's okay to feel anxious, and in turn, prevents them from doing the work of actually coping with anxiety. Instead, they remain distraught that the anxiety exists at all.

Not every pattern of negative thought will fit neatly into one of the above definitions, and oftentimes two or more forms of cognitive distortion will manifest together. In other cases, one type of negative thinking will lead directly to another, creating larger and more complex patterns that can require a lot of hard work and support to break.

What is Cognitive Distortion?

More from Sage Neuroscience...

Cognitive Distortion is when repeated harmful thought patterns occur, this meets the definition of a cognitive distortion. The term "distortion" is used because these negative thoughts lead to untrue and unrealistic conclusions or even distortions of reality itself.

In the simplest terms, cognitive distortions are errors in thinking. More specifically, the term refers to insecure, self-destructive, or nihilistic thinking that leads people to hold harmful false beliefs about themselves and their place in the world. This, in turn, can cause or exacerbate mental health issues such as depression and anxiety.

Common cognitive distortions include thinking yourself unworthy of love or success, believing everyone hates you, blaming yourself for your parents' divorce, and other self-destructive beliefs. Cognitive distortions are not always self-deprecating, however. They can also be projected onto other people and the world around you, such as believing everyone is lying, blaming a person or institution for your personal problems, or obsessing over a partner's feelings towards you.

Awareness Tool:

A thought distortion occurs when harmful, negative thought patterns occur on a regular basis. RF

Why is Cognitive Distortion Important?

Cognitive distortions are important because they are dangerous and can create a lifetime of trauma, chaos, and negativity. Learning to identify cognitive distortions can help someone break free of them. By recognizing and coping with the issue when the negative thought pattern is first beginning, you have a better chance of disrupting this pattern before it spirals into a larger mental health crisis.

Please consult licensed mental health professionals to fully understand how to resolve cognitive distortions and for any other mental health needs.

Awareness Tool:

Learning to spot and stop negative thoughts and attitudes can help you prevent negative outcomes. RF

What Habits Lead to Cognitive Distortion?

Habits that lead to Cognitive Distortion. In order to improve your mental health, you must recognize patterns within patterns. You might be bringing certain attitudes and mental practices into daily life that cause negative thought cycles. You can help yourself by becoming adept at spotting them as they happen and putting a stop to them before they take you somewhere bad.

1. *Overthinking:* It's important to consider all options before making a decision, but if your indecision about where to eat lunch is caused by feelings of insecurity and uncertainty, you may be engaging in a negative thought pattern. When you overthink something, you consider every decision you make from every angle imaginable and attempt to mentally simulate every possible result. At best, this can be draining, and at worst, it can be disastrous if your carefully thought-out predictions are proven to be false. Limit your thinking to avoid overthinking. Set and adhere to deadlines for yourself when making decisions. For a healthy way to clear your mind of some of those extra thoughts, consider yoga, a good workout, or doing breathing exercises.

2. *Self-criticism:* Self-reflection and self-awareness can be lovely things, but they can also be devastating if your thought process is clouded by negativity and despair. Do you frequently focus on shortcomings and errors rather than opportunities for improvement? A cyclical pattern known as negative ruminating causes you to project your flaws onto your imagined future and convinces you that things will only get worse. When you initially become aware of yourself becoming fixated on negative thoughts, break the cycle by doing something else. Avoid spending too much time alone with your thoughts. Read a book, watch a movie, engage in a hobby, or speak with a friend (but don't just use these activities as a convenient way to get rid of your bad thoughts). Don't use food or alcohol as distractions. Intoxication and overeating can make things worse.

3. *Hostile Mindset:* Cynical hostility is a mental attitude in which one harbors resentment, mistrust, condemnation, or contempt for others. These emotions might be the result of insecurity, projection, or unfinished business. Maintaining a network of support is challenging when you view other people as inherently harmful, evil, or unreliable. Such a hostile attitude has been linked in studies to high blood pressure and heart disease. Empathy can counter cynical hostility. Try to look at a situation from all angles rather than automatically assuming distrust. Look for ways to frame events in a cooperative rather than a competitive way.

Why do the following behaviors manifest?

Example 1: *Bully Behavior.* He is a bully because he was bullied and beat up at a time when he couldn't defend himself. So, he has adopted a way of coping; his protection and defense mechanism is diminishing people to make himself feel bigger and safer. This is not actually helping him be safe but it has become his altered sense of security. It is the only way he knows how to operate; it is based on fear. He is looking to find his value and self-worth through harming others because that's all he knows.

Example 2: *Over-giver Behavior.* He had such a big heart and wants to help everyone but does not know his limits or when he should balance so he continues to give until it comprises him. People in his life will continue to take, because he doesn't know how to stop offering. He cannot stop this runaway cycle because he is looking to find his self-worth and value through others rather than himself because that's all he knows.

> ***Both examples are using external situations***
> ***to attempt to solve an internal disfunction.***

Solution Example 1: We can definitely work through the fear and anger to release all that pain and suffering so his value and self-worth will not come from hurting others. It would be so much healthier for him and everyone around him.

Solution Example 2: We can definitely work through the fear and self-doubt to release all that pain and suffering so his value and self-worth will not come from giving to others until he hurt himself. It would be so much healthier for him and everyone around him.

Examples 1 and 2 both display inappropriate, unhealthy interactions because of their trauma from past experiences. Even though their behavior is inappropriate and dangerous for all involved, they are acting appropriately for their level of trauma. The solution is to unwind, and release the trauma that has caused the misguided behavior that attempts to keep them safe. As we begin to resolve and release the trauma that has caused this behavior, the behavior will shift as the threat that caused the original unstable behavior is no longer significant. In this way they can both move forward with happiness, peace, and joy, sure of self and safe within.[16]

Awareness Tool:

Negativity weighs heavy... If you feel like something's too much it's because it is! RF

This information is an awareness tool. We are not supposed to handle all the things that come to us. No one would expect you to pack four cars around on your back, so why do we think we are supposed to keep handling all the things that happen without unloading some of them first?

We are all drawn to see the negative; it is learned behavior. Unless we put in constant conscious effort to see the positive, we will live in a negative state, invoking our fight-or-flight distress response. Living in this state has grave effects on our physical, mental, and spiritual health and well-being. By hanging onto negative emotions, we are punishing ourselves.

Learning to reframe our beliefs to reinforce the actions we want to keep *is* possible. When we prioritize the belief that allows us to act in accordance with our values we are less likely to experience inner turmoil.

Try this exercise: Visualize 10 balloons. The balloons represent our beliefs. Begin to inflate your balloons with the positive beliefs that you would like to incorporate into your life.

Examples: Inflate: Love, Safety, Peace, Joy, Happiness, Independence, Financial Safety, et cetera.

The negative damaging thoughts will slowly deflate as you focus on your positive top priorities. This awareness and action allows you to reprogram negative belief systems.

Examples: Deflate: Anxiousness, Stress, Anger, Sadness, Hopelessness, Depressed feelings, Financial Struggle, et cetera.

We can continue to dispute our beliefs and thoughts, replacing them with more positive and realistic ones. When we start confronting our negative views, we begin to notice how many of them are not true in our lives. Instead of assuming the worst, we may realize that we feel disappointed if we did not reach a certain goal, but also accept that we are learning and growing from our mistakes and setbacks.

It's okay to feel out of balance. It happens to all of us, especially in tumultuous situations. We have been taught to put a piece of tape over the "check engine" light. We have been taught to stuff down our emotions or we will be seen as weak, that nothing's wrong even when it is. There is no greater strength than to see the uncomfortable and sit with it. Not drown or wallow, but just observe. It's okay to not be okay! What is the lesson? What can we learn?

We can sit with it, be aware of it, observe it, allow it ... no judgment, no ego. By allowing the imbalance, we find balance.

By recognizing our own weaknesses, flaws, and wounds, we can start to heal. As we take responsibility for our actions, we are able to reprogram negativity and reduce chaos, leading us to happiness and joy.

Awareness Tool:

The greatest show of strength is honesty with oneself.
Rather than searching to fix or heal those around us,
we start with what's inside – no illusions, no judgment,
no ego, only facts. RF

When we are in pain, our suffering can be magnified by the fear that the pain will never end. When we are enjoying ourselves, the unfortunate reality is that nothing lasts forever. How do we strike a balance between these shifts? We can learn to nurture the space between by not pulling toward or pushing away, allowing us to be fully present to every change in our lives.

We spend so much energy on what we already know has a negative outcome. Redirecting that energy, releasing what has happened in the past and moving to a new future, will change our lives. In this way, we learn to choose wisely where we put our energy and intentions. They are truly powerful tools.

How do we unload in a good way? How do we achieve this? Through awareness and mindfulness.

Identifying Mindfulness

What is Mindfulness?

Mindfulness is our natural ability to focus our attention on something specific in the present moment. When properly trained and practiced, mindfulness is the practice of being in the present moment without judgment, and it has been shown to help people in important ways, both mentally and physically. Mindfulness is the practice of remaining nonjudgmental, with heightened awareness of one's thoughts, emotions, and experiences from moment to moment.

Mindful practice starts with awareness of the breath. If you can breathe, you can find equanimity, you can heal yourself, you can change your life. Mindfulness is a mental state achieved by focusing one's awareness on the present moment, to be fully present, without distraction judgment or ego.

"Mindfulness protects us, our families, and our society. When we are mindful, we can see that by refraining from doing one thing, we can prevent another thing from happening. We arrive at our own unique insight. It is not something imposed on us by an outside authority, it is our choice." ~ Thich Nhat Hanh[17]

Why is Mindfulness Important?

Mindfulness is important because mindfulness protects us, our families, and our society. Mindfulness creates a safe space of support to heal and balance our past experiences and to build resilience. With the help of mindfulness, we can access our own awareness in a calm manner and avoid getting drawn into a never-ending stream of frantic thoughts.

Self-Awareness and Mindfulness

You are the observer. You can watch your own thoughts and how one thought leads to another without reacting to any of them. When you separate yourself from the situation or even your own thoughts, you can see things clearly. People who know themselves well can look at their actions, feelings, and thoughts without ego or judgment. It's a rare skill because most of us interpret our situations based on how we feel. Self-awareness is important for us all because it allows us to evaluate our growth and effectiveness and change course if we need to.

Through mindfulness, we develop the ability to observe and accept what is happening in the mind in each moment, while letting it go without criticism or malice. We use awareness to be aware of the thoughts, feelings, and sensations that come to mind. RF

How does one practice mindfulness, as opposed to just being aware of their surroundings? Being mindful means giving one's full attention to the activities and events unfolding right now. Awareness is knowledge or perception of a situation or fact. Combining mindfulness and awareness can change our perception, therefore changing our lives.

Awareness Tool:

Ask yourself daily: "What am I thinking, what am I speaking, what am I doing, what do I mean, how do I feel?" RF

At Sacred Sol Healing Institute (SSHI), we have created the Deconstructing Trauma Program. This process connects positive behavior resilience and mindful behavior modification to mindfulness by applying the actions it takes to reprogram negative learned behavior and false identities. Below are a few examples for you to try.

Simple Mindfulness Practices

- When you are upset, pause, take a moment, ask yourself, "Why am I upset?" Whatever answer you come up with is okay – sit with it. You don't have to act immediately. It will still be available at a later date and time! If it still matters at a later date and time it can be dealt with then.

- If you are unhappy, ask yourself why. "Why am I unhappy? Am I unhappy because of my expectations?" When we expect something we can be let down. Our expectations put limits not only on us, but the world around us. We can move forward with an idea rather than an expectation, because an idea is flexible and expectations are not.

- Clearing Breath: Inhale through the nose, let the belly and chest expand. Big exhale out the mouth, releasing pressure.

- Positive Breath: Inhale through the nose, drawing in positivity at the top of the head; exhale negativity out the mouth.

- We can use positive affirmations to reprogram negative behavior and emotional complications. For example, "I am capable, I am loved." When we add breath work and imagery with the affirmation, we will have a much deeper result.

SSHI Balancing Exercise:

Visualize positive light at the top of the head,
Inhale through the nose, drawing that light into your body,
Gently exhale that light out the mouth, letting it flow over your body toward the earth. Say, "I am capable, I am loved."
Repeat five times and see how you feel! Try it out!

To see all our MBM Awareness Tools all in one convenient spot, download our Deconstructing Trauma Toolkit. DT Toolkit: deconstructing-trauma.com

As we learn to release our trauma, negative learned behavior, sadness, depressive states, stress, anxiousness, anger, addictions, and self-doubt, we are able to begin changing our lives. This is our choice. It is not imposed upon us; we cannot be forced into a change that we don't want, or it will not manifest in a good way.

Choosing daily to practice balance, mindfulness, and gratitude allows us to begin living from a space of peace and love. Life has many challenges, and we will have times when we are unhappy, upset, and feel bad – that is natural, but we don't have to live in that way. Whatever we are familiar with we will come back to easier, so if we ***choose*** happiness and peace as our primary, or default, state we will be able to return to it easier.

SSHI Heart Breath

This exercise recalibrates the heart space and balances the central nervous system. This is a meditation that brings in happiness and love for ourselves. We spend a lot of time trying to find happiness and love in the world around us instead of the world inside of us. This heart breath has been created specifically to be simple and effective. The reason for this simplicity is that when you are in panic you don't need more to think about, you need less to think about! This meditation can reduce negativity, panic attacks, stress, anxiousness, sadness, grief, depressive states, fear, anger, doubt, self-loathing, self-doubt, reoccurring mind traps, and more.

Heart Breath Exercise

Find a place to sit for a moment...

1. **3 Clearing Breaths: Inhale through the nose, let the belly and chest expand. Big exhale out the mouth, releasing pressure.**

2. **Place both palms flat on center of chest.**

   We learn at a deeper level when we incorporate one or more of our senses.

   The sense used here is touch.

3. **Gently close or soften the eyes.**

   When our eyes are wide open we are receiving information for the outside world. Here, we turn inward. The sense used here is inner sight.

4. **Gently begin to visualize positive light at the top of the head. Inhale through the nose, drawing that light into your body.**

   The sense used here is sight.

5. **Gently bow the head and exhale that light and positivity out the mouth, letting it flow into the heart. Filling up the heart.**

   The senses used here are sight, touch (feeling) of the breath and sound.

6. **Continue breathing in this same way for 5-10 breaths.**

   The breath doesn't change; it's always inhale through the nose, bring in positive light at the top of the head, and exhale that positive light out of the mouth and into the heart. Our heart will fill with this positive light, then it will begin to flow over from the heart to the inner body. It will continue to flow from the inner body to the outer body, eventually building a positive glowing circle of protection all the way around us, from the inside out.

7. **Pause for a few moments to enjoy this peace and safety you are creating. This is available to you at any time.**

   Eventually, just placing your hand on your heart (or even imagining the hand on the heart) will bring you to that peace. Remember, the more familiar we are with something, the easier it is to get back to. Here, we reprogram to become familiar with positivity, peace, joy, happiness, and safety. RF

Chapter 2 Summary/
Key Takeaways

What are Negative Thought Patterns? Why are they Important?

- *Negative thought patterns are* repeated unhealthy thoughts that damage our lives and alter the body's chemistry in a negative way. Negative thinking patterns can manifest as incorrect assumptions, unrealistic self-criticisms, irrational fears, unwanted and/or repetitive thoughts, anger, resentment, insecurity, chronic fatigue, burnout, low energy, depressive states, anxiousness, chronic continual illness, self-loathing, and sometimes even refusal to acknowledge the existence of external realities. *Recognizing negative thought patterns is important* because your thoughts and values can determine the way you see yourself and the world around you, as well as negatively affect your physical, mental, emotional, and spiritual well-being.

What does Negative Thinking do to Your Body?

- *Negative thinking can* cause extreme harm to the body. Thoughts and beliefs that are grounded in pessimism can negatively impact your feelings, emotions, and mental health. Our lifespan can actually be shortened by persistent stress. Negativity is one of many things in life that can develop into a habit. Denial, cynical thinking, and repeated criticism can build neural pathways in the brain that support depressive states and sadness.

Why are we so Hyper-focused on the Negative Aspects of Existence?

- *We are so hyper-focused on negativity* because it is all we know; it is what we are most familiar with. When your brain releases reward chemicals like dopamine, you experience elation. These negative thoughts are frequently repeated and turn into habits because they "reward" us. The issue is that unchecked negative thinking is a habit as well. An addiction develops when something is perceived as beneficial, even though it is harmful, by our brains. We are all addicted to negativity and chaos. We are trying to fulfill our own value and worth through other people, places, and things.

Why do We Glorify Struggle and Conflict?

- **We glorify struggle and conflict** because we are addicted to the chemicals the body releases when in a state of stress. Chaos, pain, and negative emotions stimulate the brain's reward centers, resulting in an unconscious addiction to these negative emotions. We are addicted to the chemical release in the brain and body that happens from negative thoughts and chaos.

What are Examples of Negative Patterns?

- Polarization or Dichotomous Thinking, Emotional Reasoning, Overgeneralization, Labeling, Jumping to Conclusions, Mental Filtering, Fortune-Telling, Mind-Reading, Magnification or Catastrophizing, Inability to Be Wrong, Control Fallacies, Fairness Fallacies, Change Fallacies, Minimizing or Discounting, Personalization and Self-Blame, and Imperatives.

What is Cognitive Distortion? Why is it Important?

- **Cognitive distortions are** repeated harmful thought patterns and errors in thinking. "Distortion" is used because negative thinking often leads to skewed perceptions of the world and false assumptions. **Cognitive distortions are important** because they are dangerous and can create a lifetime of trauma, chaos, pain, and negativity. Recognizing cognitive distortions is the first step toward eliminating them from our thinking. We have a better chance of preventing the negative thought pattern from becoming an unhealthy life pattern and spiraling into a larger mental health crisis if we recognize and deal with the issue at the earliest stages of its development *Please consult licensed mental health professionals to fully understand how to resolve cognitive distortions and for any other mental health needs.*

What Habits Lead to Cognitive Distortion?

- *Habits that lead to Cognitive Distortions are:*

  <u>Overthinking</u>: obsessively thinking about the same thing over and over.

  <u>Rumination</u>: focusing on shortcomings and errors rather than ways to make things better.

  <u>Cynical Hostility</u>: directing rage, distrust, condemnation, or contempt toward others. These emotions might be the result of insecurity, projection, and unresolved trauma.

What is Mindfulness? Why is it Important?

- *Mindfulness is* the mental attitude of paying close attention to the present moment without evaluating it or letting it affect us negatively. Mindfulness is a mental state achieved by focusing one's awareness on the present moment, to be fully present, without distraction, judgment or ego. *Mindfulness is important* because it protects us, our families, and our society. When we are mindful, we can see that by not doing one thing we can avoid the occurrence of another. In the end, we come to our own conclusion. It wasn't imposed on us by someone else; it's our choice.

*Identifying the Addiction to Negativity is
so powerful! Are you ready to continue?
In the next chapter we will learn to...
Understand Daily Triggers
& Learned Behavior.*

YOU ARE WHOLE YOU ARE FREE

YOU ALWAYS HAVE BEEN

YOU ALWAYS WILL BE

HERE WE PEEL BACK THE LAYERS

TO ACCESS THAT SPACE

EVERYTHING YOU NEED IS

CONTAINED WITHIN

UNDERSTAND DAILY TRIGGERS AND LEARNED BEHAVIOR

In this chapter we address...

What is a Trigger? Why are Triggers Important?

What is Learned Behavior? Why is it Important?

What are Negative and Positive Learned Behaviors? Why are they Important?

What is Negative Talk of Others? Why it is important?

What is Negative Self-Talk? How do We Reduce it? Why is it Important?

Why do We Feel like No One Listens, or that No One Cares?

Why are We Always Giving More Than Receiving, Feeling Unappreciated?

Why do We React Instead of Respond when We are Not in Danger?

What is a Real Threat? What is a Perceived Threat?

Understanding Daily Triggers

What is a Trigger? Why are Triggers Important?

A *trigger,* also known as a stressor, is an event or circumstance that may result in a negative emotional response. A stimulus known as a trigger can bring back an unpleasant memory, emotion, or symptom.

We generally go through a range of emotions every day, including excitement, unease, frustration, joy, and disappointment. These frequently correspond with specific events, like attending a meeting with your supervisor, running into an ex-partner or friend, remembering the anniversary of a loss or traumatic event, hearing terrifying news, having too much on your plate, feeling overwhelmed, experiencing conflict in the family, ending a relationship, spending too much time alone, receiving a large bill, et cetera. Depending on your state of mind and the situational factors, your reaction to these events may differ.

We don't talk enough about triggers in the ongoing conversation about mental health. Most frequently, the topic of conversation centers on what transpires after being triggered, which is the point at which the problem is most difficult to resolve. It can be more empowering and efficient to recognize triggers, understand them, and take steps to resolve, and or avoid, them.

Awareness Tool:

An emotional trigger is anything – a memory, an experience, or an event – that causes a strong emotional reaction, regardless of your current state of mind. Observing the circumstances under which you experience intense emotions is crucial for identifying your triggers. RF

Understanding Triggers

Events that serve as triggers are highly subjective and can look very different depending on the person. Heavy breathing, jaw clenching, upset stomach, trembling, chest pain, dizziness, crying, and sweating are all physiological responses that can be triggered.

An emotional reaction can be set off by a thought, such as, "I am being attacked, blamed, controlled, smothered, disrespected, rejected, betrayed, criticized, ignored, unwanted, judged, and/or having my beliefs challenged."

When you experience a trigger, you might feel angry, hurt, overwhelmed, powerless, afraid, helpless, depressed, anxious, sad, hopeless, unloved, weak, disconnected, alone, heavy, or in pain. Tackling these emotions can be incredibly challenging and can have serious consequences for our mental health.

The consequences of a person's emotional reaction to something can range from mildly disruptive to extremely dangerous, such as acts of violence. An individual's susceptibility to and intensity of an emotional reaction to a trigger may increase significantly, relative to those of an individual in the same situation who is not exposed to the trigger. Some people may also lack insight into their reactions and have impaired judgment after experiencing a trigger.

Awareness Tool:

It is important not to assume that you understand the emotional response of someone who has been triggered, or suggest that someone who has been triggered is overreacting, being "too sensitive," or being irrational, even if the trigger may seem insignificant to you.[18]

Types Of Triggers

Triggers can manifest in many different ways and are strongly influenced by past experiences. Extreme distress, conflict, illness, and other negative outcomes may result from such triggers.

External triggers *are people, places, things, activities, and situations.*

<u>Example</u>: When I quit drinking alcohol, I had to stay away from places that carried alcohol and people who drank. It was a trigger for me to think about it, let alone see or smell it. My physical body would shake like I was going through withdrawals all over again. <u>Resolution</u>: I resolved this by not being around alcohol at all until the severity of the trigger reduced (1-2 years).

Internal triggers *are feelings or thoughts that people have before or during a situation.*

<u>Example</u>: I was triggered and felt abandoned when my spouse avoided me in order to avoid conflict. I would explode in anger because I had severe abandonment issues from childhood trauma. <u>Resolution</u>: I resolved this by telling my spouse how avoiding conversation made me feel because of my past, and he assured me that he would not leave me.

Trauma triggers *are negative emotional/physical responses to a previous threatening situation.*

<u>Example</u>: Being in close proximity to the hospital where I endured a traumatic hospitalization. Every time I passed it, I was "retraumatized" and reminded of my hospitalization. <u>Resolution</u>: After being repeatedly triggered, I decided to avoid the hospital by walking in a different direction.

Symptom triggers *are negative experiences that arise from other symptoms.*

<u>Example</u>: A lack of or reduced amount of sleep triggers my anxiousness. <u>Resolution</u>: In this situation, I quickly address any sleep disruption with meditation and breath work. This brings me back to peace and a resting heart rate, allowing restful sleep.

Why are Triggers Important?

Triggers are important because as we begin to recognize what affects us in our daily lives we are able to mitigate, or lessen, negativity and heal our trauma. As we resolve the triggers and negativity in our lives, we are able to live in balance, happiness, and peace.

Our senses play a big part in our lives. We are affected at a deeper level as our sensory information is stimulated.

Awareness Tool:

Understanding the emotions we encounter on a daily basis is the first step in learning how to deal with triggers. RF

A memory is easier to recall the more sensory information that has been stored. The brain frequently stores sensory stimuli from a traumatic event in memory. We can still link the triggers to the trauma even if we come across the same stimuli in a different setting.

For example: I may be shopping in a mall and smell the same cologne I smelled when I was beaten years before. If I have not resolved this trauma, the very faintest scent of that cologne can bring me back to the same trauma I was experiencing in that moment twenty years ago. My body can elicit a trauma response from my sense of smell. It transports me back there and I begin flinching, sweating, and breathing heavily. *True story.*

According to Good Therapy, "In some cases, a sensory trigger can cause an emotional reaction before a person realizes why they are upset. Habit formation also plays a strong role in triggering. People tend to do the same things in the same way. Following the same patterns saves the brain from having to make decisions."[19]

This is where habits and awareness come in. We all build habits into our daily lives (i.e. driving a certain way to work, eating at particular places, et cetera), because it is comfortable and efficient. Becoming aware of our patterns, and what we are thinking and feeling while engaging in them, allows us to make changes that reduce the severity of triggers.

Awareness Tool:

The five senses are frequently the source of emotional triggers, so pay attention to what you see, hear, smell, taste, and touch as these could cause an emotion or a behavioral reaction. RF

So, how do we resolve these triggers and habits?

Means of Dealing with Triggers and Difficult Circumstances

There is a wide range of responses one can take. Methods have been developed to prevent, delay, or lessen the intensity of an emotional response to a triggering event. We all have the opportunity to learn from our experiences. Different coping strategies may be effective for various stimuli and emotions.

Become aware of unhealthy coping skills such as violence, uncontrolled anger, emotional, psychological, sexual, or financial abuse, making justifications for harmful behavior, self-harm, or the emergence of bad behavioral compulsions.

Learn to recognize: Take into account your responses to previous triggers; who or what was involved; and where, when, and why they occurred. To avoid a repeat of the situation, look for patterns and obvious warning signs of risk. Try tracing the source of these emotions by recalling previous experiences that gave rise to the feelings you are currently experiencing.

Develop a strategy: Develop a strategy to deal with emotional outbursts and triggering events. You may want to talk to loved ones or your treatment team to let them know how they can best help you when you are experiencing triggers. Be sure to carefully address triggers that occur repeatedly, as the emotional reaction may become more intense with each subsequent occurrence of the trigger.

Consider a problem-solving approach: Address the source of your stress or begin taking steps to alleviate it.

Consider emotion-focused positive action: If you can't avoid a trigger, try an emotion-focused positive action to reduce its impact. Meditation reduces stress, anxiousness, and depressive states.

Communicate through the trigger: If someone is triggering you, talk to them about it. Most of the time, someone who triggers another person does not mean to do so. Talk to them about your trigger and how it affects you to clear up confusion. Consider possible solutions together, talking in a calm, open, and understanding way. It may be best to establish clear boundaries if the person who is triggering you isn't able to show compassion or understanding.

Trauma-Specific Therapy: Certain therapies can reduce triggers. Cognitive behavior therapy and emotionally-focused therapy help reduce trauma triggers.

Reasonable Thought Check: It can be helpful to "reality check" one's thoughts to determine how plausible they are in order to prevent an unwarranted escalation of emotions. This can help reduce the intensity of one's thoughts and feelings.

Reasonable Thought Check Options:

1. **Verification of the facts:** Think about the facts and ask yourself if they support your interpretation.
2. **Recognize thought distortions:** Identify inaccurate ways of thinking, perceiving, or believing something.

3. **Reprogram:** Shift your default negative thoughts to positive ones.

4. **Proportionality:** Ask yourself if the response is out of proportion to the triggering event.

Trigger warnings: Trigger warnings can help you avoid content that might upset you, especially content about suicide or violence. At the beginning of an article, TV show or film, sometimes a trigger warning is given.

Personal Health Care: Personal health care or self-care can assist in prioritizing mental health and help you resist triggers. Talk to a loved one, friend, or licensed therapist. Mindfulness, meditation, deep breathing, and journaling may help.

We can learn from our triggers even though controlling them is hard. We can use what we learn to prevent retriggering. Though it's challenging, experience can teach us how to better manage our reactions. We must consider both the trigger and what we can do to resolve it.

Downplaying the significance of the trigger or ignoring the importance of taking preventative measures is detrimental; instead, we can concentrate on what we can do to avoid being triggered in the first place. We have the ability to prevent and solve the problems that cause triggers! One of the most important aspects of emotional health is being aware of the factors that can set off your negative emotions, as well as the strategies you can use to manage them.

Awareness Tool:

Triggers can teach us how to manage our reactions before they become problematic. We can stop triggers. Good emotional health requires knowing and managing your emotional triggers. RF

Understanding Learned Behavior

What is Learned Behavior?

Learned behavior is a pattern of behavior that is acquired through previous experience.

The opposite of learned behaviors are innate behaviors, which are predetermined by one's genes and can be carried out even in the absence of any prior experience or training.

Why is Learned Behavior Important?

Understanding learned behavior is important because by identifying that we have learned a particular behavior we are able to understand that it can also be unlearned. We have the ability to reprogram and modify our behaviors. We are not helpless; we can take action to change what is inappropriate and unhealthy and keep what is appropriate and healthy.

Awareness Tool:

We have the ability to reprogram and modify our behaviors.
We are not helpless and can take action. RF

What is Negative Learned Behavior?

Negative learned behavior develops through our experiences. If we have not been guided or supported through a challenging experience, we may adopt a negative learned behavior trait because of this experience.

Example: If you are told you can't do anything right when trying something new, you will most likely be defeated and begin to believe that you CAN'T do anything right. This can then become part of a negative false belief system that will affect you negatively throughout your life.

Why is Negative Learned Behavior Important?

Understanding negative learned behavior is important because by identifying that we have learned a particular behavior we are able to understand that negative behavior equals negative results. We have a choice; we are not helpless and can take action to change this.

Negative experiences create blockages over time; they become tangled with other experiences and blockages, building layers of pain, trauma, and suffering that lead to extreme discomfort.

So, how do we untangle these blockages? It is a matter of unwinding, releasing, and peeling back the layers one at a time. As we begin to understand the purpose of our experiences, we are able to start the healing process. It is like peeling back the layers of an onion. It is awesome when the top layer is released, but that does not untangle all the layers at once. It takes a bit of work to untangle reactive learned behavior, especially when we are strongly set in negative patterns. We will learn how to release these blockages through awareness and action!

Awareness Tool:

We can change our experience and release the negative patterns that have been a continued cycle in our lives. RF

What is Positive Learned Behavior?

Positive learned behavior develops as a result of experience. If we have been guided and supported through a challenging experience, we adopt a positive learned behavior trait because of this experience.

Example: If you are told you CAN learn to accomplish your goal when trying something new, you will most likely be empowered and begin to believe that you can accomplish anything you set your

mind to. This then becomes part of a positive belief system that car-
ries you through a successful, fulfilling life.

Why is Positive Learned Behavior Important?

Understanding positive learned behavior is important because by
identifying that we have learned a particular behavior we are able to
understand that positive behavior equals positive results. We have a
choice; we are not helpless and can take action to continue positivity
in our lives.

Awareness Tool:

Negative and positive behaviors are a result of our experience.
Whatever we are familiar with will continue to manifest.
We will seek out the same negativity and chaos
that destroys us because it is what we are used to. RF

Caution!!! We all have negative tendencies.

This section is only to raise awareness; it is not an attack
on anyone's character or actions. I used to be the most
angry and hateful person I knew. I didn't even realize it;
it was a way of life because I felt bad inside. I learned that
it was okay to look at challenging behavior patterns I had
acquired over time. Knowledge gives us the opportunity
to evolve and grow. Resolving negative talk patterns
can open us up to a whole new world.

What is Negative Talk of Others?

Negative talk of others is when we put people down instead of
speaking kindly or saying nothing at all.

Are we constantly finding fault in others? Is nothing ever good
enough? It reflects pessimism, anxiousness, and a general sense of
mistrust when others engage in negative conversation.

People's perceptions and opinions are all different. We can view a difference of opinion as a threat to our safety. We are generally comfortable and feel safe when others think in the same way we do.

If we really understood that people's perceptions and opinions don't define us, that they are just opinions, it would change our lives. We literally live in the vibration of the reality we perceive we are in; each person's perception of reality will be different.

Does it seem like there are unhealthy patterns and situations in your life that repeat themselves like a broken record? We can take a close look at these situations and ask what we need to learn so we can move forward. There is something that we need to understand and learn before we can end this cycle and begin a new one. The way to find these lessons is to look for repeated patterns. Once we do the necessary work to learn the lessons, we can then apply those lessons to open new doors, leading us to a healthy, happy, balanced, and productive life.

Why is Negative Talk of Others Important?

Negative talk of others is important because it is a reflection of what is going on inside us. A post on *Psychology Today's Sapient Nature* blog describes negative talk of others as "a thinly disguised cry for help, a need to feel respected, loved, and in control."[20] People talk negatively of others because they are not happy with themselves. This comes from past trauma, and negative learned behavior patterns that then form negative habits.

Example: Imagine being discouraged from pursuing your dreams on a regular basis because so few people achieve success. Or consider being constantly cautioned against learning a new skill because it is too risky. Or hearing daily how awful the neighbors are.

Being routinely exposed to negative evaluations of other individuals creates negative learned behavior patterns in our psyche. We then begin to unknowingly project this negativity to the world around us, which then in turn begins to manifest negativity in the world around us.

Awareness Tool

Constant exposure to negativity can significantly deplete our positivity, causing us to either become negative (doubtful, anxious, and distrustful), indifferent, uncaring, or even cruel. RF

Understanding the reasons for negative talk of others.
The following is taken from the same Psychology Today post:

In brief, almost all negativity has its roots in one of three deep-seated fears: the fear of being disrespected by others, the fear of not being loved by others, and the fear that "bad things" are going to happen. These fears feed off each other to fuel the belief that "the world is a dangerous place and people are generally mean."

It is easy to see how, from the perspective of someone operating from such fears, it makes sense to question the wisdom of pursuing dreams (failure seems all but guaranteed) and to be averse to taking risks even if it is obvious that doing so is necessary to learn and grow. It is also easy to see why people with these fears would find it difficult to trust other people.

The fears that negative people harbor manifest themselves
Thin skin: Quick to take offense or be annoyed at others' comments. "You look good today" is interpreted as, "You mean I didn't look good yesterday?"

Judgmentalism: The tendency to impute negative motivations to others' innocent actions; thus, guests who don't compliment a meal are judged as "uncouth brutes who don't deserve future invitations."

Diffidence: A sense of helplessness about one's ability to deal with life's challenges, leading to anxiety in facing those challenges, and to shame or guilt when the challenges are not met.

Demanding nature: Although negative people are diffident about their own abilities, they nevertheless put pressure on close-others to succeed and "make me proud" and "not let me down."

Pessimism: The tendency to believe that the future is bleak; thus, for example, negative people can more readily think of ways in which an important sales call will go badly than well.

Risk aversion: Especially in social settings. This leads to reluctance to divulge any information that could be "used against me," ultimately leading to boring conversations and superficial relationships.

Controlling Others: The need to control others' (especially close-others) behaviors. For example, negative people have strong preferences on what and how their children should eat, what type of car their spouse should drive, and so on.

Notice a common feature across all of these manifestations of negativity: The tendency to blame external factors (other people, the environment, or luck) rather than oneself, for one's negative attitudes.

Thus, negative people tend to think, "If only people realized my true worth. If only people were nicer, and the world wasn't fraught with danger. If only my friends, relatives, and colleagues behaved like I want them to, then I'd be happy."

It might seem strange that negative people can simultaneously feel helpless about themselves and feel entitled to others' respect and love, as well as feeling negative about their own future and yet goad-ing others to succeed. [21]

Awareness Tool:

Negative people demand the respect and love of others and strive for control because they don't feel sufficiently respected and loved and in control of their own lives. RF

Awareness Tool:

People who are constantly negative and angry are trying to protect themselves or fit in. Recognizing one's negativity is helpful, but for lasting change we must reprogram the subconscious thought patterns, the underlying negative belief system. RF

While this brings us a deeper understanding of why people act in a negative way, it is not a free pass for bad behavior.

Healthy ways to deal with negative people

1. Have compassion *for the negative person.*
Note how much pain and suffering they must be going through. We can practice reflective listening, without rushing in to save them. They are on their path for a reason – they have lessons to learn and if we rush in to save them we are not doing them, or ourselves, any favors.

We can't learn what we need to learn if someone else always rushes in to save the day. When a baby is learning to walk, they must fall down to gain strength and balance. Their body is not ready to hold their weight for long periods of time. This is why they fall. If we decided to rush in and "save" the baby by scooping them up so they don't have to fall, we would be doing them a huge injustice. They would never develop the strength or balance to walk.

Example: "Wow, it sounds like you are going through so much. I will keep you in my thoughts and prayers."

2. Take ownership for our happiness and well-being despite the other person's negativity.
Despite the negativity of the other person, we must take responsibility for our own happiness and well-being. Not blaming others for your unhappiness entails accepting personal responsibility. Finding ways to be content despite the (negative) actions of others and the environment around you is what this means.

An individual who has accepted personal responsibility is aware of an essential truth about happiness: our level of happiness is greatly influenced by our attitude rather than by objective, external circumstances. In this way we adopt a mindset that is more optimistic.

3. Take the higher road when interacting with a negative individual.
Realize that the most effective way to persuade a negative person to adopt a more positive outlook is to demonstrate positivity yourself.

Example: A negative person tells you that you will never accomplish your goals. You can say, "I would rather take the chance than not try at all. Every time I try something new I learn useful skills."

Positivity builds confidence and hope for the future.

Awareness Tool:

People who are truly content rarely engage in negative talk. It is not appealing for them to talk negatively. RF

There is such wisdom in silence and in softly spoken words.

The ones who are meant to hear you will, the ones who don't notice are caught up in themselves; it's not a reflection of you. Your thoughts, your words, are precious medicine; we don't have to convince anyone of anything.

What is Negative Self-Talk?

Negative self-talk is constantly finding fault in yourself, engaging in negative self-talk. Nothing ever lives up to expectations.

We each have a critical voice within us. When it warns us that what we're about to eat is unhealthy or that what we're about to do might not be the best course of action, this little voice can actually be useful and keep us motivated toward goals. Nevertheless, this voice can frequently be more detrimental than beneficial, particularly when it enters the realm of excessive negative thinking. This is what psychologists refer to as negative self-talk, and it has the potential to bring us to our lowest points.

Negative self-talk is something that almost all of us will experience at some point in our lives, and it can show up in a number of different ways. If we are not careful, it also causes a significant amount of stress for the people around us, as well as for ourselves.

Self-criticism takes many forms, such as, "I'm terrible at everything I do"; "I can't ever do anything right"; "I'll never amount to anything," et cetera.

Your inner critic might sound very similar to a judgmental parent or ex-friend from your past. It may proceed in the same way as common cognitive distortions, such as catastrophizing and placing blame.

Awareness Tool:

Negative self-talk is thinking that undermines our ability to make positive shifts in our lives. Negative self-talk is stressful and limits our success, self-confidence, and potential. RF

Why is Negative Self-Talk Important?

Negative self-talk is important because it can affect us in damaging ways, including mental health challenges, depressive states, anxiousness, toxic stress, insomnia, anger, addiction, hopelessness, despair, unhealthy relationships, and more.

> *Our reality becomes altered to create an experience*
> *where we don't have the ability to reach the goals*
> *we've set for ourselves.*

The following, taken from a verywellmind.com article,[22] further illustrates the pervasive, far-reaching effects of negative self-talk.

Negative self-talk can lead to a lowered ability to see opportunities, as well as a decreased tendency to capitalize on these opportunities. This means that the heightened sense of stress comes from both the perception and the changes in behavior that come from it.

Other consequences of negative self-talk can include:

- **Limited thinking**: The more you tell yourself you can't do something, the more you believe it.

- **Perfectionism**: You begin to really believe that "great" isn't as good as "perfect," and that perfection is actually attainable. In contrast, high achievers tend to do better than their perfectionistic counterparts because they are generally less stressed and are happy with a job well done. They don't pick it apart and try to zero in on what could have been better.

- **Feelings of depression**: Some research has shown that negative self-talk can lead to an exacerbation of feelings of depression.[23] If left unchecked, this could be quite damaging.

- **Relationship challenges**: Whether the constant self-criticism makes you seem needy and insecure or you turn your negative self-talk into more general negative habits that bother others, a lack of communication and even a "playful" amount of criticism can take a toll.

One of the most obvious drawbacks of negative self-talk is that it's not positive. This sounds simplistic, but research has shown that positive self-talk is a great predictor of success.

For example, one study on athletes compared four different types of self-talk (instructional, motivational, positive, and negative) and found that positive self-talk was the greatest predictor of success. [24]

Awareness Tool:

It is not as important to remind someone how to do something as it is to let them know that they are doing a good job and that others have noticed. RF

How do We Reduce Negative Self-Talk?

VeryWell.com outlines some excellent methods for shifting the way we speak to ourselves.

Catch Your Critic

Learn to notice when you're being self-critical so you can begin to stop. For example, notice when you say things to yourself that you wouldn't say to a good friend or a child.

Remember That Thoughts and Feelings Aren't Always Reality

Thinking negative things about yourself may feel like astute observations, but your thoughts and feelings about yourself can definitely not be considered accurate information. Your thoughts can be skewed like everyone else's, subject to biases and the influence of your moods.

Give Your Inner Critic a Nickname

There was once a *Saturday Night Live* character known as "Debbie Downer." She would find the negative in any situation. If your inner critic has this dubious skill as well, you can tell yourself, *"Debbie Downer needs a time-out!"*

When you think of your inner critic as a force outside of yourself and even give it a goofy nickname, it's not only easier to realize that you don't have to agree, but it becomes less threatening and easier to see how ridiculous some of your critical thoughts can be.

Contain Your Negativity

If you find yourself engaging in negative self-talk, it helps to contain the damage that a critical inner voice can cause by only allowing it to criticize certain things in your life or be negative for only an hour in your day. This puts a limit on how much negativity can come from the situation.

Change Negativity to Neutrality

When engaging in negative self-talk, you may be able to catch yourself, but it can sometimes be difficult to force yourself to stop a train of thought in its tracks. It's often far easier to change the intensity of your language. "I can't stand this" becomes, "This is challenging." "I hate..." becomes, "I don't like..." and even, "I don't prefer..."

When your self-talk uses more gentle language, much of its negative power is muted as well.

Cross-Examine Your Inner Critic

One of the damaging aspects of negative self-talk is that it often goes unchallenged. After all, if it's going on in your head, others may not be aware of what you're saying and thus can't tell you how wrong you are.

It's far better to catch your negative self-talk and ask yourself how true it is. The vast majority of negative self-talk is an exaggeration and calling yourself on this can help to take away its damaging influence.

Think Like a Friend

When our inner critic is at its worst, it can sound like our worst enemy. Often we'll say things to ourselves in our heads that we'd never say to a friend. Why not reverse this and – when you catch yourself speaking negatively in your head – make it a point to imagine yourself saying this to a treasured friend. If you know you wouldn't say it this way, think of how you'd share your thoughts with a good friend or what you'd like a good friend to say to you.

This is a great way to shift your self-talk in general.

Shift Your Perspective

Sometimes looking at things in the long term can help you to realize that you may be placing too great an emphasis on something. For example, you may ask yourself if something you're upset by will really matter in five years, or even one.

Another way to shift perspective is to imagine that you are panning out and looking at your problems from a great distance. Even thinking of the world as a globe and of yourself as a tiny, tiny person on this globe can remind you that most of your worries aren't as big as they seem.

This can often minimize the negativity, fear, and urgency in negative self-talk.

Say It Aloud

Sometimes when you catch yourself thinking negative thoughts in your mind, simply saying them aloud can help. Telling a trusted friend what you're thinking about can often lead to a good laugh and shine a light on how ridiculous some of our negative self-talk can be. Other times, it can at least bring support. Even saying some negative self-talk phrases around under your breath can remind you how unreasonable and unrealistic they sound.

This will remind you to give yourself a break.

Stop That Thought

For some, simply stopping negative thoughts in their tracks can be helpful. This is known as "thought-stopping" and can take the form of snapping a rubber band on your wrist, visualizing[25] a stop sign, or simply changing to another thought when a negative one enters your mind. This can be helpful with repetitive or extremely critical thoughts like, "I'm no good," or "I'll never be able to do this," for example.

Replace the Bad With Some Good

This is one of the best routes to combating negative self-talk: Replace it with something better. Take a negative thought and change it to something encouraging that's also accurate.

Repeat until you find yourself needing to do it less and less often. This works well with most bad habits: replacing unhealthy food with healthy food, for example.

It's a great way to develop a more positive way of thinking about yourself and about life.[26]

**Now that we understand the devastating effects
of negativity toward ourselves and others, we can dig
a little deeper to begin understanding some common
daily challenges.**

Why do We Feel like No One Listens, or that No One Cares?

We may feel like no one listens or cares because each of us is operating with a different set of expectations. Even though someone might be listening, we feel that they aren't if we don't receive the response we think is correct, in the way we think is correct.

Example: My partner and I both arrive home after a ten-hour workday. His way of decompressing is to be quiet and watch tv. My way of decompressing is to talk and share every detail of my day. I may feel that because he doesn't want to talk that he isn't listening or doesn't care. That is simply not true. He does care, he is just tired.

It is inappropriate for me to base the value of our relationship on a difference of opinion; we each have our own needs.

We can both receive what we need if we understand how to balance our needs. During the week we can keep it quieter after work and on the weekends we can go for walks where I can chat away to my heart's content. We don't have to necessarily be interested in every single thing the other person has to say. We can listen and hold space because we care.

Awareness Tool:

Our expectations are based on our prior experiences. Others will have different experiences, and therefore have different expectations. It is inappropriate to base the value of a relationship on a difference of opinion; we each have our own needs. RF

Why are we Always Giving More Than Receiving, Feeling Unappreciated?

Many times, we feel unappreciated because we are giving too much in order to feel loved and accepted. We may do way more than is needed to show how much we care.

Frantically running from one thing to the next is an inappropriate way of seeking love and acceptance. This behavior puts others in a bad position because no matter how much they appreciate us, it is never enough. This behavior also puts us at risk because we are doing way too much and are completely overextended, causing toxic stress and physical and emotional suffering. When we begin to give ourselves the love and acceptance we are looking for, we do not need constant validation from others. We can reduce the number of things we are doing for others and allow balance and joy in our lives.

Why Do We React Instead of Respond When We Are Not in Danger?

We react instead of responding because we feel threatened, either physically, mentally/emotionally, or spiritually. This threat comes from past experience, and because we have not resolved traumatic past experiences we will still have the same reaction as when the threat was real and imminent. A reaction (quick and aggressive behavior) is part of fight-or-flight. A response (pausing to have compassion for both parties) is a choice we have thought about.

Awareness Tool:

*Critical thoughts of self and others keep us in
a constant state of fight-or-flight. RF*

Awareness Tool:

*We react instead of respond because we feel threatened
and are trying to keep ourselves safe. RF*

What is a Real Threat? What is a Perceived Threat?

So, how do we tell the difference between a real threat and a perceived threat?

A real threat is a bear chasing us. *A perceived threat is* someone cutting us off in traffic.

Example: If a bear is chasing you in the woods... that is a real threat! You had better run immediately or stay and fight to save your life.

Example: If someone cuts you off in traffic (not dangerously), or steals your parking spot, that is a perceived threat. It makes us super angry, and fight-or-flight is activated, but we can reason with ourselves to come back to a calm state. We do not need to stay in fight-or-flight with a perceived threat because our lives are not in danger.

Awareness Tool:

We can begin to examine situations that upset us to determine if the threat is real or perceived. With this perspective we can change our lives drastically by reducing stress and anger. RF

Awareness Tool:

The reality we perceive ourselves to be in is the truth and reality we will live in. We have become used to chaos, but we have the ability to change that. Whatever we are most familiar with is what we automatically go back to. RF

Because of our traumatic experiences, the hypothalamus shuts off – we stay in fight-or-flight and are unable to make cohesive, cognizant choices. We become numb and continue to look for chaos because it is the most familiar place we know how to operate from.

We are unable to shift from this pattern and that creates more chaos. In order to break the cycle, we can reprogram the synapses (firing points) in the brain to release this damage and reset, creating a different storage of memories. Once the brain has reset, so will the body. We will not continue to have a visceral body reaction once the brain resolves the trauma.

There are many tools that allow us to reprogram to a space of safety, but the breath is by far the most effective! The breath can balance the central nervous system. When the central nervous system is balanced, this activates the parasympathetic central nervous system, which allows peace, safety, happiness, and joy to be received.

When we have activated the parasympathetic nervous system we have deactivated fight-or-flight (the sympathetic nervous system). They **cannot** both be activated at the same time. We are either in drive or reverse. We are either safe or unsafe.

Awareness Tool:

Many times, the world around us, accompanied with our past traumatic experiences, will send us into a space of unsafety. Learning the skills and tools to return yourself to a state of safety can change your life. RF

Try working with the Self-Critical Thought Record for at least one week to identify triggers and learned behaviors.

SELF-CRITICAL THOUGHT RECORD

SITUATION-TRIGGER:

EMOTIONS:

PHYSICAL SENSATIONS:

SELF-CRITICAL THOUGHTS:

ALTERNATIVE POSITIVE THOUGHTS:

HOW COULD THIS HAVE CHANGED YOUR OUTCOME:

Chapter 3 Summary/ Key Takeaways

What is a Trigger? Why are they Important?

- ***A trigger,*** also known as a stressor, is an event or circumstance that may result in a negative emotional response. A trigger is a stimulus that can bring back an unpleasant memory, emotion, or symptom. ***Triggers are important*** because as we begin to recognize what affects us in our daily lives, we are able to mitigate, or lessen, negativity and heal our trauma. As we resolve triggers and negativity in our lives we are able to live in balance, happiness, and peace.

What is Learned Behavior? Why is it Important?

- ***Learned behavior is*** a behavior that develops as a result of experience. In contrast to learned behaviors, innate behaviors are genetically hardwired without training. ***Understanding learned behavior is important*** because by identifying that we have learned a particular behavior we are able to understand that it can also be unlearned. We have the ability to reprogram and modify our behaviors. We are not helpless. We can take action to change what is inappropriate and unhealthy and keep what is appropriate and healthy.

What are Negative and Positive Learned Behaviors? Why are they Important?

- ***Negative learned behavior develops*** as a result of experience. If we have not been guided or supported through a challenging experience, we may adopt negative learned behavior traits. ***Positive learned behavior develops*** as a result of experience. If we have been guided and supported through a challenging experience, we adopt positive learned behavior traits. *Understanding negative and positive learned behavior is important* because it allows us to choose the behaviors to keep and behaviors to release in our lives.

What is Negative Talk of Others? Why it is Important?

- *Negative talk of others is* when we put people down, instead of speaking kindly or saying nothing at all. Negative talk of others brings people's mood down; it reflects pessimism, anxiousness, and general sense of distrust. *Negative talk of others is important* because it is "a thinly disguised cry for help, a need to feel respected, loved, and in control." People talk negative of others because they are not happy with themselves. This comes from past trauma, and negative learned behavior patterns that then form negative habits.

What is Negative Self-Talk? How do we Reduce it? Why is it Important?

- *Negative Self-talk is* constantly finding fault in yourself. Nothing is ever good enough. We all have an inner critic. This voice can often be more harmful than helpful, especially when buried in excessive negativity. *Reduce negative self-talk by becoming aware of it, wanting to stop it, and taking action to implement tools and techniques that reprogram negative learned behavior. Negative self-talk is important* because it can affect us in damaging ways, including mental health challenges, depressive states, anxiousness, toxic stress, insomnia, anger, addiction, hopelessness, despair, unhealthy relationships, and more.

Why do We Feel like No One Listens, or that No One Cares?

- *We may feel like no one listens or cares* because each of us is operating with a different set of expectations. Even though someone might be listening, we feel that they aren't if we don't receive the response we think is correct, in the way we think is correct. Our expectations are based on our prior experiences. Others will have different experiences and therefore have different expectations. It is inappropriate to base the value of a relationship on a difference of opinion. We each have our own needs.

Why Are We Always Giving More Than Receiving? Why Do We Feel Unappreciated?

- **Many times, we feel unappreciated** because we are giving too much in order to feel loved and accepted. Frantically running from one thing to the next is an inappropriate way of seeking love and acceptance. This behavior puts others in a bad position because no matter how much they appreciate us, it is never enough. This behavior puts us at risk because we are doing way too much and are completely overextended, causing toxic stress and physical and emotional suffering.

Why Do We React Instead of Respond When We are Not in Danger?

- **We react instead of respond** because we feel threatened physically, mentally, emotionally or spiritually. This threat comes from past experience, and because we have not resolved traumatic past experiences we will still have the same reaction as when the threat was real and imminent. A reaction (quick and aggressive behavior) is part of fight-or-flight. A response (compassion for both parties) is a choice we have thought about.

What is a Real Threat? What is a Perceived Threat?

- **A real threat is** a bear chasing us; a perceived threat is someone cutting us off in traffic. We can begin to examine situations that upset us to determine if the threat is real or perceived. With this perspective we can change our lives drastically by reducing stress and anger. The reality we perceive ourselves to be in is the truth and reality we will live in. We are used to chaos. We have the ability to change that. Whatever we are most familiar with is what we automatically go back to.

Understanding Daily Triggers and Learned Behavior is So Powerful! Are you ready to continue? In the next chapter we will learn how to... Reprogram to Positive Actions.

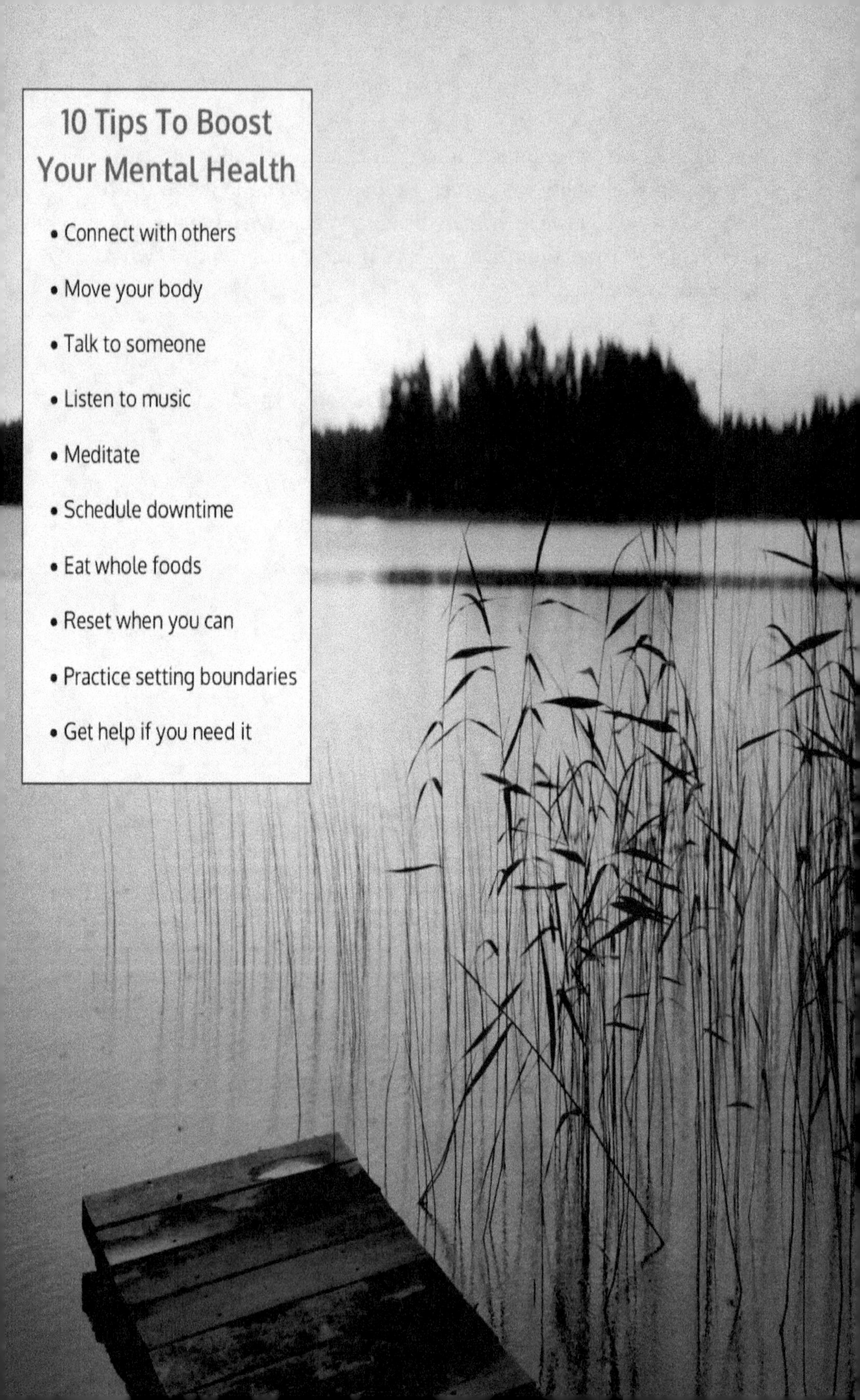

10 Tips To Boost Your Mental Health

- Connect with others

- Move your body

- Talk to someone

- Listen to music

- Meditate

- Schedule downtime

- Eat whole foods

- Reset when you can

- Practice setting boundaries

- Get help if you need it

PART II

Achieve Lasting Change

People Who Have Successfully Made Life Changes,

Have Released Limiting Beliefs, Fears, and Low Self-Esteem.

Our Deconstructing Trauma Program Shifts Negative Thought Processes and Behaviors.

You Can Add Positive Beliefs, Skills, and Tools that Allow Abundance and Heal Your Relationships with Others and with Yourself.

Reclaim Your Life, Find Freedom and Joy, and Reprogram to a Positive Self-Belief System. Step Into a Happier, Healthier Life.

You Are Not Alone!

CHAPTER 4

REPROGRAM TO POSITIVE ACTIONS

In this chapter we address...

What do Our Personal Challenges Look Like? Why is this Important?

Why is Someone Else's Opinion so Important? How Do We Overcome That?

How Do We Label Ourselves and Others? Why is this Important?

What Thoughts, Behaviors, and Ideas Do We Project onto Others? Why is this Important?

How Does Our Past Trauma Play an Integral Role in Our Present Lives?

How Do We Release Expectations and Attachment? Why is this Important?

How Do We Know We are Enough? Why is this Important?

How to Reprogram to Positive Actions

What do our Personal Challenges Look Like?

Our personal challenges will look different for all of us. There are times throughout our lives when we can become bitter and worn

out by our personal experiences. When this happens, joy and enthusiasm for life seem to disappear.

Common personal challenges can be...

- Health Crises
- Workplace Issues
- Emptiness
- Friendship Issues
- Relationships
- Family Issues
- Financial Crises

- Career Pressure
- Unfair Treatment
- No Inner Peace
- Obstacles, Challenges
- Mental Health
- Grief, Loss

- Moral Compass
- Failure
- Impulse Control
- Moving Past Your Story
- Haunting Past
- Safety, Security

Others include:

Abandonment	Exaggeration	Martyrdom
Absentmindedness	Excessive Focus on	Materialism
Abuse	Others	Mediocrity
Accidents	Excessive Sleeping	Minimizing
Accusing	Excuses	Moodiness
Acting the clown	Extremism	Narrowness
Addictions	Failure	Needing to Please
Aggression	Fantasizing	Others
Ambition	Faulty Beliefs	Negativity
Analyzing	Fears	No Fun
Anger	Feeling Needy	Non-Supportive
Anxiety	Fixed Ideas	Habits
Arguing	Focusing on the Past	Numbness
Arrogance	Foolishness	Obsessions
Attachment	Forgetfulness	Opportunism
Avoidance	Frustration	Overeating
Judgmental	Futility	Over-emotional

Opinionated	Future Thinking	Over-exercising
Reactive	Glamours	Over-spending
Scattered	Greed	Overwhelmed
Ungrounded	Guilt	Over-working
Blaming	Hate	Pain
Blind Devotion	Hopelessness	Perfectionism
Boredom	Humorlessness	Phobias
Bossiness	Humor	Poor Health
Busyness	Ignorance	Poor Self-Esteem
Can't Be Alone	Ignoring	Possessiveness
Carelessness	Illness	Poverty Mentality
Co-Dependency	Illusions	Prejudice
Complaining	Impatience	Pride
Compromise	Impractical	Procrastination
Compulsion	Impulsiveness	Rationalization
Conflict	Inaccuracy	Rebellion
Confusion	Indecision	Repression
Control	Indifference	Resentment
Cowardice	Inertia	Resistance
Criticism	Inflexible character	Ridicule
Cruelty	Injury	Rudeness
Cynicism	Insecurity	Running Away
Deceitfulness	Insensitivity	Sadness
Deception	Intellectualization	Sarcasm
Defensiveness	Intolerance	Seeking Approval
Defiance	Isolation	Self-obsession
Denial	Jealousy	Self-Centeredness
Dependency	Judging	Self-Deception
Depression	Justifying Limitations	Selfishness
Deviousness	Lack of Commitment	Self-Pity
Discounting	Lack of Confidence	Self-Sabotage

Dishonesty	Lack of Creativity	Shame
Disorder	Lack of Discipline	Shyness
Disoriented	Lack of Energy	Solitude
Dominance	Lack of Purpose	Status
Doubt	Lack of Trust	Stress
Drama	Laughing It Off	Stubbornness
Dreaming	Laziness	Suffering
Egotism	Living in the Past	Timidity
Emotions	Loneliness	Unexpressed Emotions
Envy	Low Energy	Vacillation
Escape	Lying	Vanity
	Malnutrition	Violence
	Manipulation	Withdrawal
		Worry[27]

Awareness Tool:

We are each playing a role in every situation.
What can you learn? What is your lesson? We don't have
to take experiences personally. RF

Why is Recognizing Personal Challenges Important?

Recognizing our personal challenges is important because as we begin to see our challenges and struggles, we can then begin to address and resolve them. We are not our challenges. These challenges and experiences do not define us. We can regard them as life information to learn and grow from.

Awareness Tool:

We are each responsible for learning our own lessons. It is not
our job to make sure others learn their lessons. RF

Why is Someone Else's Opinion So Important?
How Do We Overcome That?

Other people's opinions are important because we are social beings who are concerned about the thoughts and feelings of others; the viewpoints of others hold a great deal of weight for us. People's opinions do affect us. They can make us feel included and important, and they can even make us feel like we have some control over our surroundings. When we find out that someone thinks in the same way we do, it makes us feel safe without us even realizing it. When someone doesn't agree with us and has different ideas, we may feel threatened and unsafe. We may feel like our belief system or morals are threatened because they don't believe in the same way.

One of the main reasons others' opinions are so important is because we have not been taught that an opinion is just an opinion, that we can all have different opinions, and that they don't define us or the other person. An opinion is just an opinion. Opinions change constantly as a direct result of our ever-changing experiences.

Studies show that the opinions of others alter a very basic mechanism of the human brain that reflects an immediate change in our values. Social influence at such a basic level may contribute to the rapid learning and spread of values throughout a population.[28]

Why is Overcoming Someone Else's Opinion Important?

Overcoming someone else's opinion is important because opinions are formed and shaped by experiences and environment. If a person's experience and environment have not been healthy or positive they will continue to share a cycle of trauma, negativity, and destruction. This is very toxic and gets passed on just like a disease. We then end up with generational trauma that poisons us all.

We live in reactive states until we decide to shed the layers that have kept us trapped there and move past our story, past our pain. When we're able to connect to a higher vibration, our story then becomes a tool, an example to help guide others as well as ourselves. We have learned from our experiences and have chosen to move past that space.

Once we work through releasing attachment to others' opinions, we are truly free to realize unity, freedom, and Grace within all things. We are able to move forward, "Walking in Beauty."

How Do We Label Ourselves and Others?

We label ourselves and others by constantly assigning labels that pass judgment and make assumptions. We categorize certain people as addicts, lazy, weak, narcissistic, needy, etcetera. These labels carry with them the idea that a person's behavior reflects their true nature, even though it may be a fair reflection of how they are acting in the moment. When someone treats us poorly, we interpret that as proof that they are a bad person, not just that they might be a good person who unintentionally did something bad.

Awareness Tool:

Labels are dangerous and defeatist. They can lead to addictions, anger, fear, disorders, despair, health issues, and more. RF

Negative labels can hurt us deeply. Labels are like poison – once you believe them, you'll live up to them. Labels create trauma-related failures and unrealistic assumptions and expectations. They can destroy positive self-image. They can and do live with us for a lifetime, or at least until we learn to resolve and release them. Once we realize we are not the label, we are then able to untangle the false identities and damaging core beliefs we have adopted over time.

A common way in which we label others is by calling them words that describe personality disorders, like

*"bipolar" and "narcissist." Behavior does not define
a person. There is a difference between having certain
behaviors and being diagnosed with a disorder
by a medical or mental health professional.*

Let's Work a Bit With the Common Label of Narcissist...

Narcissist Definition: a personality disorder characterized by a life-long pattern of exaggerated feelings of self-importance, an excessive need for admiration, a diminished ability or unwillingness to empathize with others' feelings, and interpersonally exploitative behavior. These patterns develop by early adulthood and are associated with significant distress or impairment. [29]

The following is taken from the Avalon Malibu blog:

Personality disorders are mental illnesses that involve chronic patterns of unhealthy attitudes and behaviors, inflexible thoughts, and false beliefs. Narcissistic Personality Disorder (NPD) is a personality disorder that's characterized by an inflated sense of self-importance, a deeply-ingrained need for admiration, and a lack of empathy for others. Beneath the excessive show of confidence, people with NPD usually have an extremely fragile self-esteem and are unable to cope with even slight criticism, according to the Cleveland Clinic.[30]

People with Narcissistic Personality Disorder often use drugs or alcohol as a way of dealing with the inevitable relationship problems and other interpersonal issues that result from this disorder, which also commonly co-occurs with other mental illnesses like depression, eating disorders, and bipolar disorder.

Due to the complexity of Narcissistic Personality Disorder, one of the most effective treatments for this condition is cognitive behavioral therapy, which can be modified to treat a wide range of conditions, including depression, anxiety, and substance abuse and addiction, which often co-occur with NPD. [31]

Awareness Tool:

Narcissism is a disorder that hinders healthy, satisfying relationships. Narcissists have lower life satisfaction and quality. Trauma and fear dominate their relationships, causing anger. RF

If we have a strong reaction to the label narcissist, we most likely are on the other side of the label, mirroring codependent tendencies. When we begin to label it starts a downward spiral. How many stones do we want to throw?

Calling someone a narcissist during an argument does not mean they have NPD, and it might be best to refrain from throwing labels out there, as it will not improve communication.

Another common label we place on others is "codependent."

Awareness Tool:

Codependency is a disorder that hinders healthy, satisfying relationships. Codependency, also called "relationship addiction," is marked by one-sided, abusive, or emotionally abusive relationships. RF

Let's Work a Bit with the Common Label of Codependent...

***According to Mental Health* America,**[32] *"Co-dependency is a learned behavior* that can be passed down from one generation to another. It is an emotional and behavioral condition that affects an individual's ability to have a healthy, mutually satisfying relationship. It is also known as "relationship addiction" because people with codependency often form or maintain relationships that are one-sided, emotionally destructive and/or abusive."

The article goes on to say that: Co-dependents have low self-esteem and look for anything outside of themselves to make them feel better. They find it hard to "be themselves." Some try to feel better through alcohol, drugs or nicotine - and become addicted. Others may develop compulsive behaviors like workaholism, gambling, or indiscriminate sexual activity.

They have good intentions. They try to take care of a person who is experiencing difficulty, but the caretaking becomes compulsive and defeating. Co-dependents often take on a martyr's role and become "benefactors" to an individual in need. A wife may cover for her alcoholic husband; a mother may make excuses for a truant child; or a father may "pull some strings" to keep his child from suffering the consequences of delinquent behavior.

The problem is that these repeated rescue attempts allow the needy individual to continue on a destructive course and to become even more dependent on the unhealthy caretaking of the "benefactor." As this reliance increases, the co-dependent develops a sense of reward and satisfaction from "being needed." When the caretaking becomes compulsive, the co-dependent feels choiceless and helpless in the relationship, but is unable to break away from the cycle of behavior that causes it. Co-dependents view themselves as victims and are attracted to that same weakness in their love and friendship relationships.

Characteristics Of Co-Dependent People Are:

- An exaggerated sense of responsibility for the actions of others
- A tendency to confuse love and pity, with the tendency to "love" people they can pity and rescue

- A tendency to do more than their share, all of the time
- A tendency to become hurt when people don't recognize their efforts
- An unhealthy dependence on relationships. The co-dependent will do anything to hold on to a relationship; to avoid the feeling of abandonment
- An extreme need for approval and recognition
- A sense of guilt when asserting themselves
- A compelling need to control others
- Lack of trust in self and/or others
- Fear of being abandoned or alone
- Difficulty identifying feelings
- Rigidity/difficulty adjusting to change
- Problems with intimacy/boundaries
- Chronic anger
- Lying/dishonesty
- Poor communications
- Difficulty making decisions[33]

The following is excerpted from the River Oaks Treatment Center: "What is Co-Dependency Treatment"

While some individuals may be able to break out of patterns of codependent behavior on their own, often it requires professional treatment. Cognitive-behavioral therapy helps individuals focus on understanding behaviors and changing reactions.

Other types of therapy can include couples therapy to help both partners in codependent relationships; or family therapy to help reduce the impact of codependency among parents, children, and extended family.

Steps to break out of codependent behavior patterns include:

- Carving out time alone to explore oneself
- Reconnecting with work or hobbies outside the codependent relationship
- Finding ways to say "no" to requests for help
- Reconnecting with outside friends and family
- If anyone in the codependent relationship struggles with substance abuse, it will be imperative to get treatment for this condition along with treatment for codependency.[34]

Awareness Tool:

We can find compassion for people that are suffering instead of labeling them. If you come across a person with unsafe qualities... remove yourself from the situation, send them positivity, and let them continue on their journey. When we label people it keeps us trapped in that negative energy and vibration. RF

Awareness Tool:

Mental health is a serious issue, and we can ALL make a huge impact by not labeling each other. Whether there is a diagnosis or not, it is not appropriate for us to engage in that diagnosis, unless we are the person with the diagnosis. RF

Here are a few of the struggles people are facing:
Attention-Deficit/Hyperactivity Disorder (ADHD), Anxiety Disorders, Autism Spectrum Disorder, Behavioral and emotional disorders, Bipolar affective disorder, Conduct Disorder, Depression, Disruptive

Mood Dysregulation Disorder, Dissociation and dissociative disorders, Eating Disorders, Gender Dysphoria, Intellectual Disability, Internet Gaming Disorder, Major Depressive Disorder and the Bereavement Exclusion, Mild Neurocognitive Disorder, Obsessive-Compulsive and Related Disorders, Paranoia, Paraphilic Disorders, Personality Disorders, Post-traumatic Stress Disorder, Psychosis, Schizophrenia Sleep-Wake Disorders, Specific Learning Disorder, Social Communication Disorder, Somatic Symptom Disorder, Substance and Addictive Disorders.

Awareness Tool:

The world is suffering with so much trauma and pain.
You are not your diagnosis. You are not your pain;
you are not your suffering. There is hope.
You are not alone. RF

According to the National Alliance on Mental Illness (NAMI), "A mental illness is a condition that affects a person's thinking, feeling or mood. Such conditions may affect someone's ability to relate to others and function each day. Each person will have different experiences, even people with the same diagnosis."

Here are some "Fast Facts" from NAMI to help us understand the prevalence of mental illness in the U.S.

1 in 5 U.S. adults experience mental illness each year.

1 in 20 U.S. adults experience serious mental illness each year.

1 in 6 U.S. youth aged 6-17 experience a mental health disorder each year.

50% of all lifetime mental illness begins by age 14, and 75% by age 24.

Suicide is the 2nd leading cause of death among people aged 10-34.[35]

__Awareness Tool:__

*When we label or are labeled, we view ourselves
as separate. This affects us at a fundamental level.
If we are separate there is no harmony.
We feel like we don't belong. RF*

Why is it Important to Stop Labeling?

It is important to stop labeling because labeling is destructive and unhealthy. Let the professionals diagnose and treat because that can produce productive, positive results. The general public hurling labels and accusations at each other is not productive or positive.

What we feed will grow. If we feed negativity and hate, it will grow. If we feed positivity and understanding it will grow. If we were trained to understand that negative personality characteristics are not necessarily a diagnosis and that people can change if they have the opportunity to Deconstruct Trauma, we might realize that it is not appropriate to define or label ourselves or others by current behavior. We are all learning and growing through our experiences.

We have been shaped by our prior experiences but are not doomed to stay in those experiences. We can change our perceptions and actions. This wisdom and knowledge can change our lives if we are ready and open to the possibility of healing and change.

We further explore the idea that each person's journey is their own. We are not responsible for their journey or making them see the light. We release attachment to others' actions and accept accountability and responsibility by removing *ourselves* if a situation is unhealthy.

If we are presenting the unhealthy behavior we can reach out for professional guidance and tools to reprogram unhealthy learned behavior patterns and release trauma. We are all here to learn and evolve.

What Thoughts, Behaviors, and Ideas do We Project Onto Others?

We tend to project our thoughts, behaviors, and ideas on others because we are familiar with our own experience. Familiarity creates an illusion of safety.

Many times, when someone is talking we assume that we know what they are saying because of our own experience. However, they may have a completely different meaning and experience.

So why do we jump into this mind-reading conclusion?

According to the Anti-Loneliness blog, the answer is:

Need for control. It's safer to "think you know" than to "not know at all." In other words, the script in our head goes like this:

"The other person's reaction is too vague for me. So, I will attempt to label it in my own way. In a way that I will feel I know them, and I can predict them, and at the same time I can protect myself in case they would like to hurt me."

To put it simply, other people's thought perceived opinions are a plain mirroring of our own interpretations. When the interpretations are right, we celebrate our rightness, and we feel we protected our self in the best possible way.

When the interpretations are faulty (cognitive distorted), unfortunately we'd rather believe in our own mind (e.g., looking for more proof that we are right and they are wrong), than to change our interpretations.[36]

Awareness Tool:

We'd rather believe false information than seek the truth when our interpretations and thoughts are distorted. RF

Why is It Important to Understand Our Projections?

Understanding our projections is crucial. This information and knowledge is EXTREMELY important if we want to release negativity and work toward healing trauma.

This a process, it takes commitment. We have created a simple guide to remind us of the steps to Deconstructing Trauma, by releasing chaos, pain, and negativity.

Sacred Sol Healing Institute: Guide to Deconstructing Trauma

1. **Awareness of negativity and desire to change.**
2. **Finding a solution.**
3. **Taking the first action that allows change.**
4. **Committing to repeated action to allow reprogramming.**

Awareness Tool:

_Once we have AWARENESS of a situation, we can then begin
to look for SOLUTIONS; then we MUST CHOOSE TO TAKE
ACTION if we want something to change; and finally,
WE MUST COMMIT TO REPEATED ACTION to allow
an old habit to be removed and a new one to replace it. RF_

Example 1: I can want to scratch my head; I even know how... but if I refuse to move or take any sort of action it will never happen. I can complain and be sad and affected, but again, IT WILL NOT CHANGE WITHOUT COMMITTING TO THE ACTION AND REPETITION OF THAT ACTION.

This next example has MANY layers involved and will be a much larger challenge than deciding to move my arm to scratch my head for the desired result...

Example 2: I have an aggressively strong reaction when people disagree with me. This reaction manifests because I don't feel safe in my own being, due to the extreme amount of trauma I have suffered in my life. True Story

I have two choices...

1)   I can begin to work on releasing the trauma that has brought me to a spot of not trusting myself and being threatened if someone has a different opinion than I do...

OR

2) I can continue to live in this same way, being controlling and unapproachable and projecting my pain and trauma onto others.

Eventually... I chose option one!

I now know from the YEARS of work I have put in that if someone doesn't approve of my opinion it doesn't matter (in a good way). Each of us has a right to our own opinion.

Other people's opinions don't define us unless we let them. It took a long time to understand and gain this knowledge.

This journey will look different for all of us.

All roads lead home, though...anyone that is struggling, in any way, has a compromised self-belief system. We all share the pain of feeling like we are not enough. I one hundred percent believe this is why we are here: To Learn That We Are More Than Enough.

We are challenged on this earth to learn to trust ourselves and our journey. Once we learn those things in a good way we begin to find safety within.

When we find safety within, we stop projecting our pain and trauma onto others. We begin to understand that we are capable and loved and are able to create safety for ourselves. We take accountability and charge of our own lives without having to dictate to others how to run theirs.

We learn to remove ourselves from damaging negative situations and relationships, for it is our responsibility to mitigate, or lessen, the negativity that we place ourselves around.

This process is not always fun or pretty to look at, but it is necessary to find true peace, joy, happiness, and balance in our lives.

My journey started here...
A life-changing event helped me decide to do the self-healing work and explore my trauma so it could be released in a good way, and I could move forward in joy and happiness, instead of fear, anger, and hate.

I had no idea that anything was wrong or that I could even live in a more balanced way. I had become so used to being angry and negative that it seemed normal. Everyone around me acted in the same way because that's all we had ever known. Then this life event happened that caused me to question it all. It caused me to question who I was, why this had happened, and what place I had in it. None of it made sense...

I was accused of doing something that I did not do. No one even thought about calling me and asking if it was true. What I was accused of was most certainly NOT TRUE! I had done no such thing. The part about being accused didn't bother me as bad as the fact that NOT ONE person in this dynamic circle bothered to call, text, or ask in any way if I had done this thing.

It SHOCKED me that "I wasn't worth a phone call." I didn't feel like I was worth a whole lot, but I KNEW THAT I WAS AT LEAST WORTH A PHONE CALL.

This was one of my projections: "They think I'm not worth a phone call..."

If you had asked them if I was worth a phone they all would have most certainly said yes! But because they didn't think to call me and ask if what I was accused of was true or not, my distorted thoughts took over. This thought process, however, was the catalyst for the biggest change in my life, which led to this work!

Yes, this event literally changed my life. I stepped back from all of these relationships for a year to figure out what was going on in my life and how I could change the dynamic.

This journey was such a frustrating, difficult, painful, profound, and powerful experience. I knew these tools needed to be accessible to all. I have dedicated my life and practice to education and studies in this pursuit. This process led to the creation of my company, Sacred Sol Healing Institute (SSHI), and our Trauma-Responsive Holistic Services and Resources. These holistic services and resources have allowed me and thousands of others to heal and lead healthy, cohesive, balanced lives – with lasting results!

I am here to share the ultimate goal and ways to achieve that!

Awareness Tool:

Ultimate goal: To love yourself fully and completely. This doesn't mean we become perfect; it means we are able to face our challenges in grace and love. We learn from where we've been and choose to move forward in a different way. We release ego, judgment, grief, guilt, shame, and fear; this is not who we are, just where we've been. We are not our trauma; we are not our pain; we are not our suffering. RF

How Does Our Past Trauma Play an Integral Role in Our Present Lives?

Past trauma plays an integral role in our lives because we can become threatened by others' actions and opinions. We may create a false reality and sense of security based on our environmental threats.

We project our own trauma experiences, behaviors, and ideas onto others in order to keep ourselves safe. We create false identities, false realities, and false scenarios to keep ourselves safe. We do this without even realizing it.

We have created a phenomenon of "Trauma-Related Expectations," and this becomes not only an immediate issue but has long-term toxic effects. These thought distortions lead to years, lifetimes, and generations of trauma, pain, and dysfunction.

Awareness Tool:

We are moving through the world with "Trauma-Related Expectations." We expect negative results because we have experienced those results through past trauma. These Trauma-Related Expectations will continue to harm our lives until we reprogram them and begin to heal. RF

For example: I was kidnapped, taken away from the only life I had ever known. My location, environment, and name were changed. From this trauma I developed **extreme** abandonment issues and a **major** identity crisis, which led to a huge trauma response for a large part of my life.

Most of us have had at least one, if not multiple, traumatic experiences occur in our lifetime. We can all relate to trauma on some level, and even though our trauma experiences are not exactly the same, the end results still manifest in similar ways.

A few of the ways unresolved trauma can manifest is incorrect assumptions, unrealistic self-criticisms, irrational fears, unwanted and/or repetitive thoughts, anger, resentment, insecurity, chronic fatigue, burnout, low energy, depressive states, extreme sadness, dependency, anxiousness, chronic continual illness, self-loathing, and sometimes even refusal to acknowledge the existence of external realities.

So, how do we move forward?

How do we mitigate, or lessen, the damage that occurs from our experiences?

Good news! If I can Deconstruct Trauma and Heal, anyone can!

I had no idea about trauma or the possibility it could be resolved OR that I even had a problem. I just knew that I wasn't enough; I hated myself and was extremely uncomfortable in my own skin.

So, I did what so many people in our society do – I drank ridiculous amounts of alcohol and did as many drugs as I could get my hands on to feel better inside. I didn't want to feel because it hurt too much. I didn't feel like I could talk about it because I thought I'd be a failure if I wasn't tough and able to handle what life threw at me.

My daily life was a living hell. I have never experienced so much pain, but I thought it was normal and that was just the way it was. I lived like this for twenty years straight, still working and trying to raise my daughter by myself. I was abused by others, and then I became the abuser. I abused people in many ways; the way I talked and acted and belittled them was devastating.

I physically and mentally abused my daughter. She survived this abuse by the Grace of Creator, and the strength she holds inside. There is not a day that goes by that I don't thank Creator for guiding us out of that pain.

I had little control over my anger and rage. I had blackout rage, meaning when I got extremely angry everything went dark. It was like another person was in my body and I couldn't stop myself and didn't remember many of the things that happened.

I had extreme situational OCD (obsessive-compulsive disorder). I used to fold my clothes and laundry a certain way. I would freak out and get extremely *irate* if they weren't folded EXACTLY how they "should" be. Everything had an exact place, and I would spend hours making sure it was all where it should be.

I learned through this process that I was trying to control the things in my life that I could control, because it gave me a sense of security and safety. This manifested since I had no control over keeping myself safe when I was young.

However, this was a false sense of safety and security; folding my clothes a certain way or making sure an item is in a specific place would not keep me from getting kidnapped again.

I know **now** that all of this could have been avoided if I had dealt with my trauma. Resolving my fear of being unsafe, abandoned, and learning about my identity crisis would have changed my life, my daughter's life, and so many other lives around us. But it is impossible to change something if you don't know how and have no tools to guide you.

Awareness Tool:

If we have not taken the steps to Heal, we will try to control our present surroundings because we couldn't control something that compromised us at an earlier time in our lives. RF

So, where do we go from here?
Are we doomed to live in that pain and chaos?

Absolutely not! I have healed with the tools that you are finding here! It started out as a journey to heal and understand myself. There are so many different tools and modalities available in the world, but I was not able to find them all in one spot, so that led to the creation of our program, Deconstructing Trauma™.

I quickly began to realize and understand these extremely complicated (yet somehow very simple) concepts could lead me to lifetimes of healing. I knew that others might want this information so I decided to keep track of this process so I could pass it on to the public.

This information is changing people's lives. Our exclusive Deconstructing Trauma Program has created superior results and lasting change for thousands of people. This approach can shift negative thought processes and behaviors by releasing trauma and blockages deep within the mind-body connection... through knowledge, breathwork, and intention.

The purpose of this specific format is to learn how to live daily in positivity, happiness, and joy, in spite of our challenging lives. This is attainable! If I can do it ... anyone can!

It does take effort. We must apply this wisdom and knowledge, as well as take daily action steps, to stay balanced, healthy, and whole.

Our Deconstructing Trauma Program is utilized with great success through my own practice, in many professional organizations, substance abuse treatment centers, suicide prevention events, restorative justice centers, medical clinics, community corrections, government and city organizations, and more!

Awareness Tool:

*Balance requires daily effort and action on our part.
If we don't participate and create balance in our daily lives
it won't happen. This is up to us; it is not anyone else's
responsibility to create this balance in our lives. RF*

How Do We Release Expectations and Attachment?

How do we release expectations and attachment to behaviors and situations?

This is such an intense question! It brings up so many more questions and so much invaluable information!

We release expectations and attachment by becoming the observer; we are not taking situations personally. In this way, we learn to release expectations and attachment to behaviors and situations for others, as well as for ourselves.

When we become the observer, we are not threatened by what we see in others or in ourselves. We can begin to observe situations, just like window shopping; we are not attached to any one thing. We are browsing without expectation, ego, or judgment.

We can step outside of our reactive state and wonder...
"Why did I act like that? Why did I have that strong of a reaction?"
"Why did they act like that? Why did they have that strong of
a reaction?"

Whatever answers come are okay, because we are not our experiences, we are not our pain, we are not our thoughts, we are not our emotions, we are not our trauma, and we are not our suffering.

Awareness Tool:

All of our experiences are designed to learn from;
they are not meant to torture us or others. RF

We will inadvertently outgrow relationships with ourselves and others as we shift and evolve. This is part of the process – just as our five-year-old pants don't still fit us (nor should they), many relationships and situations won't fit us either, as the lesson has been presented and no longer fits.

At this point, we can learn from these lessons and
move on to another space, or we can continue
the cycle of pain that came with the lesson.

Society has been lacking widespread general knowledge about how to learn from our lessons and not take them personally.

This has resulted in a societal epidemic that has led to an EXTREMELY dysfunctional generational "follow-the-leader." Because of huge misnomers and trauma-based standards that we have all lived with for centuries, we have both thought distortions and inappropriate assumptions that lead us to believe that if something doesn't work out...

1) "It is always my fault because I'm not good enough."

OR

2) "Nothing is ever my fault because everyone else is wrong."

Both of these thought processes are dangerous because they are laden with expectations and attachment that stem from unhealthy learned experiences and irrational false realities.

We all are reacting from past trauma that has shaped our belief system and values.

What if we were able to release that past trauma and reshape our value and worth based on healthy, balanced experiences?

Congratulations, through this space we learn to do just that!
Moving on, we dig deeper!

Once we develop a relationship of trust and safety within ourselves, we are able to have our own opinions and perceptions without having to force them on others. We can communicate our opinion and perception without getting upset or disappointed if others don't agree, just as others can have their own opinions and perceptions without us taking it personally.

People's perceptions and opinions are different because their exposure and experiences have been different. People's perceptions and opinions don't define us, just as our perceptions and opinions don't define anyone else. It's just an opinion.

*We literally live in the vibration of the reality we perceive we
are in; each person's perception of reality will be different.*

Awareness Tool:

*Our perception dictates our experience, and our past
experiences dictate our perception. Our perception will
influence our interactions with the world around us, as well as
the world inside of us. RF*

Have you ever had interactions with people and wondered...

"Why do they treat me like that? What is the matter with them?
How could they be so unkind?"

The other person may **not** have been unkind or acting in an inappropriate way, but we might have taken it that way because of our own prior experiences, past trauma, suffering, triggers, and doubts.

Awareness Tool:

*Assumptions, expectations, and attachments to persons,
places, or things lead to self-sabotage and
altered perceptions. RF*

So, with the understanding that opinions are just opinions, we can begin to untangle ourselves a bit from the attachment of our own thoughts and opinions, as well as other people's thoughts and opinions.

Why is Releasing Expectations and Attachment Important?

Releasing expectations and attachment is extremely important to not only see our own expectations, thoughts, and actions, but also to release them, because our experiences will be drastically different when we are not in a reactive state.

When we can just observe and ask ourselves, "Why is this happening?" instead of saying, "This is happening to me," we are able to release the trauma responses that no longer serve us. This allows us to process our past experiences, learn from our lessons, and move on in freedom and joy instead of living a life that is full of continual chaos and pain.

Awareness Tool:

It is extremely important for us to see and release others' expectations, thoughts, and actions, because if we don't we will end up living someone else's experience. This also will cause us to live a life that is full of continual chaos and pain. RF

With the knowledge that others' thoughts don't define us, it becomes much easier to not take others' negative views and perceptions to heart.

For Example: I am fundamentally a good person, but a lot of people are not able to understand my need for boundaries, and that my boundaries may look different from what they are used to. So, there have been times when I ended up not being able to have contact with someone because they are dangerous for me to be around.

It is not possible for that person to understand that I may have been compromised by our interaction, and I will need to shift the dynamic to keep myself safe. They can't hear this truth because it would leave the underlying message that they are not enough because of the trauma they have been through, which now shapes their version of reality. They blame the dynamic shift on me to preserve their own self-worth and value. Their psyche can't consider the option that they may have mis-stepped.

So, they end up hurt and unable to understand my truth because of their own trauma. They move forward with a skewed interpretation of events and begin to share with anyone they meet how I have wronged them. *In their mind, they are justified in their actions because this is their reality.* On the other hand, regardless of their ability or inability to understand my boundaries or my point of view, I still need to keep myself safe.

Whew, quite the predicament! What can I do?

All I can do is keep myself safe. I am responsible for my own safety and my own level of stress. We can impart our boundaries with compassion and kindness, no need to launch into a huge tirade. Making someone else feel bad does not honor a vibration of integrity.

Examples: In a professional setting, we can let them know that it would not be a good fit to continue working together and give them a referral to see someone that would be a better fit. In a personal setting, we can limit our exposure, begin to distance ourselves, or let them know that we are not available.

Granted, this may not be accepted in a good way by someone who is not able to hear another person's truth without being threatened. However, their opinion is just that – their opinion; it doesn't define us.

This is certainly uncomfortable but necessary for growth and evolvement. When we begin to understand how we need to be treated, we are then able to show the world around us how we need to be treated.

Keep in mind, this is an awesome opportunity for both parties to learn from the experience without taking anything too personally. The Universe will guide our direction, if we are open to the shifts and are able to recognize the signals, instead of letting our trauma take over.

*Our addiction to others' feedback is damaging our lives. Others'
opinions matter because it boosts our self-esteem
(not self-worth). RF*

How do We Know We are Enough?

**This is the most important factor in our lives…How do we know we
are enough?**

We know we are enough because we have been created with infinite
worth and value; there is no way we *can't* be enough. Our actions
may not always reflect infinite worth and value, but our actions do
not determine our value and worth.

**We spend most of our lives either trying to prove we
are enough or trying to escape from feeling like we are
not enough. This happens to be the biggest irony of all
because we have all been created with infinite worth and
value…YES, EVERY SINGLE ONE OF US!**

*When we peel back the layers of trauma, pain, and suffering
at the very center of our creation is love, light, and grace.
That is who you are, that's who you always have been,
and who you always will be. RF*

Our past trauma and the lack of positive information in our current
society leads us all to feel like we are not enough. How do we adjust
these deep-seated false belief systems that have been handed down
for so many generations?

Being open to a different perspective is key…

The following excerpt is from the Anti-Loneliness blog:

The Battle of a Higher "Value."

Let's talk about self-worth. Self-worth is the sense of one's own value or worth as a person. Many people use *self-worth* as a synonym for *self-esteem*. The difference between those two concepts lays on the reference point.

On the one hand, **self-worth** is something more internal. It is not about measuring yourself based on external actions or achievements, but mostly, about valuing your inherent worth as a person: *how much value you think you add to the world*. In other words, self-worth is about who you are, not about what you do.

On the other hand, **self-esteem** is the overall subjective evaluation which is mostly focused on your achievements and the satisfaction that you may or not receive through them. Nowadays, there is this trend of pushing people in developing high self-esteem.

The "trap" in this behavior is that building higher self-esteem focuses on measuring oneself against others (Social Comparison Theory, Leon Festinger), rather than paying attention to one's intrinsic value.

We are commanded by this competitive culture to be special and extraordinary in order to feel good about ourselves and at this point, "opinions" are used as a weapon in this infinite battle. In a way, by belittling someone who just happens to sit next to you, you succeed in enhancing a higher self-value. But, if you are the one standing on the opposite side of the table, you are starving for a praise which is not yet to come; therefore, your self-esteem is hitting rock bottom and **your addiction to others' feedback is making you lose your sleep.**

However, the moment you will receive some good comments, BANG! here's your reward: happiness, a sudden explosion of dopamine in the brain. You are feeling more valuable, because someone con-firmed so. *To sum up, others' opinion matters because it boosts our self-esteem (not necessarily our self-worth).*

Psychologists use the term "Cognitive Distortions" to describe irra-tional thoughts or beliefs that distort a person's perception about the world, others or ourselves. It is automatic and often turns a simple thought into a habit which makes it hard to recognize or change.[37]

Although Cognitive Distortions maybe challenging to change, it is possible!

Awareness Tool:

We can change the thought distortions that we have adopted over time through awareness and mindfulness. RF

Why is Knowing We are Enough Important?

Knowing we are enough is the most important factor of our lives. Our entire life reflects how we feel about ourselves. It is crucial to recognize when we feel like we are not enough because it can lead us to very dark places, including chaos and negativity. We will most likely exhibit one or more of these traits: anger, defensiveness, sad-ness, despair, hopelessness, and more.

Awareness Tool:

Our thought processes have been shaped by our past experiences. RF

If we feel like we are never enough that pain will be too great to sus-tain over a lifetime and we will look for ways to numb that pain and to check out from that altered reality. This false belief system can lead to drugs, alcohol, and many other addictions.

Awareness Tool:

_False beliefs and thought distortions can create chaos, pain,
and negativity in our lives, affecting how we feel about
ourselves at a fundamental level. Once our core belief
system has been compromised, we are no longer able
to access our infinite value and worth. RF_

As mentioned previously, cognitive distortions affect the way we view the world around us, as well as the world inside of us.

According to Anti-Loneliness...

It is all about thinking patterns. Psychologists use the term "cognitive distortions" to describe irrational thoughts or beliefs that distort a person's perception about the world, others or ourselves. It is automatic and often turns a simple thought into a habit which makes it hard to recognize or change.

Particularly, our brains are predisposed to form connections between thoughts, ideas, actions, and consequences in order to help us predict the future or protect ourselves in imminent dangerous situations.

However, over time, the brain may have developed some faulty or non-helpful connections where there is no true relation.

For example: a person can reject your phone call because he/she is angry with you. But also, there is the possibility that he/she is rejecting your call because he/she is busy at the moment, or sick, or has no battery. If it happens once to connect the call-rejection (action) with your own interpretation, then the feeling (anger) will be there every time this happens.

However, the truth is that we don't know the actual reason why, unless we ask them.[38]

We have been operating with only half the information...

Many times, we will adopt the false belief that we are not enough because of someone else's words or actions.

Awareness Tool:

Through our traumatic experiences we can create a false belief system based on only half of the information. That information is skewed and faulty because it comes from someone else's trauma, not from our reality. RF

**The reality is, we've always been enough!
Not performing at a certain level has no bearing on our worth or value. It is someone else's opinion.**

Fact: we can't not be enough... We have been created with infinite worth and value; no matter where we've been, no matter what we've done, no matter what has happened, we have always been and will always be more than enough.

This is a **constant,** non-changing fact. Most of us don't know this and aren't aware of how to access our value or worth, which compromises us at a fundamental level.

We end up in a constant cycle of chaos because we are always trying to prove that we are enough. This dangerous cycle leads us to compassion fatigue and burnout.

If we are convinced deep inside that we are **not** enough, we will never be able to stop the cycle of dysfunction, the cycle of putting too much on our plate, because we are trying to prove our worth and value through our actions to others rather than to ourselves.

Awareness Tool:

Attempting to find our value and worth through acts of kindness to others is inappropriate and unhealthy. RF

If we are convinced we are not enough, no amount of action will ever suffice.

Awareness Tool:

Imagine what your life would be like if you were able to move forward in your infinite worth and value without feeling compromised or upset when other people don't agree with you or don't like you. RF

Not only is this completely possible, but it is the purpose of this information!

We have been learning about awareness and trauma and what that looks like in our lives, so we can release these trauma responses and move forward without being triggered and trapped in chaos, pain, and negativity. This will allow us to build healthy relationships with ourselves and others.

Chapter 4 Summary/ Key Takeaways

What do our Personal Challenges Look Like? Why is this Important?

- *Our personal challenges* will look different for all of us. There are times throughout our lives when we can become bitter and worn out by our personal experiences. When this happens joy and enthusiasm for life seem to disappear. *Recognizing our personal challenges is important* because as we begin to see our challenges and struggles, we can then begin to address and resolve them. We are not our challenges. These challenges and experiences do not define us. We can regard them as life information to learn and grow from.

Why is Someone Else's Opinion so Important? How Do We Overcome that?

- *Other people's opinions are important because* we are social beings who are concerned about the thoughts and feelings of others; the viewpoints of others hold a great deal of weight for us. People's opinions do affect us. *Overcoming someone else's opinion is important* because opinions are formed and shaped by experiences and environment. If a person's experience and environment have not been healthy or positive they will continue to share a cycle of trauma, negativity, and destruction. This is very toxic and gets passed on just like a disease. We then end up with generational trauma that poisons us all.

How Do We Label Ourselves and Others? Why is this Important?

- *We label ourselves and others* all the time by placing judgments and projections on each other. Every time someone treats us badly, we take that as evidence that they are a bad person, and not just that they are a possibly good person who just happened to do a bad thing. *It is important to stop labeling* because labeling is destructive and unhealthy. If we were trained to understand that personality characteristics can change, we might realize that it is not appropriate to define or label ourselves or others by current behavior, as we are all learning and growing through our experiences.

What Thoughts, Behaviors, and Ideas do We Project Onto Others? Why is This Important?

- *We tend to project our thoughts, behaviors, and ideas onto others* because we are familiar with our own experience; familiarity creates an illusion of safety. Many times, we assume that we know what others are saying because of our own experience. However, they may have a completely different meaning and experience. *Understanding our projections is extremely important* to release negativity and heal trauma. This process takes commitment.

Sacred Sol Healing Institute: Guide to Deconstructing Trauma

1. Awareness of negativity and desire to change.
2. Finding a solution.
3. Taking the first action that allows change.
4. Committing to repeated action to allow reprogramming.

How Does Our Past Trauma Play an Integral Role in Our Present Lives?

- *Past trauma plays an integral role in our lives* because we can become threatened by others' actions and opinions. We may create a false reality and sense of security based on our environmental threats. We project our own trauma experiences, behaviors, and ideas onto others in order to keep ourselves safe. We create false identities, false realities, and false scenarios to keep ourselves safe. We do this without even realizing it. This in turn compromises our relationship with ourselves, with others, and the world around us, creating a life full of negativity, trauma, and chaos.

How Do We Release Expectations and Attachment? Why is This Important?

- *We release expectations and attachment* by becoming the observer; we are not taking situations personally. In this way, we learn to release expectations and attachment to behaviors and situations. When we become the observer, we are not threatened by what we see in others or in ourselves. We can begin to observe a situation and, just like window shopping, we are not attached to any one thing; we are browsing without expectation, ego, or judgment. *Releasing expectations and attachment is extremely important* to not only see our own expectations, thoughts, and actions, but also to release them, because our experiences will be drastically different when we are not in a reactive state.

How do We Know we are Enough? Why is this Important?

- *We know we are enough* because we have been created with infinite worth and value; there is no way we can't be enough. Our actions may not always reflect infinite worth and value, but our actions do not determine our value and worth. ***Knowing we are enough is the most important*** factor in our lives. Our entire life reflects how we feel about ourselves. If we feel like we are never enough that pain will be too great to sustain over a lifetime and we will look for ways to numb that pain and to check out from that altered reality. This false belief system can lead to drugs, alcohol, and many other addictions.

Reprogramming to Positive Actions is so powerful! Are you ready to continue? In the next chapter we will learn about... Healthy Relationships.

What Promotes Wellness in Your Life

Music · Food · Meditation · Relationship with Creator · Family
Best Friend · Hiking · Relaxation · Breathing Techniques · TV
Support Group · Fishing · Camping · Basketball · Sports · Food
Dirt Bike · Own Vehicle · Own Place · Traveling · Swimming
Snowsports · Video Games · Sober Friends · Working Out
Love · Meetings · Going Out · Walks · Healthy Partners · Faith
Sober Healthy Environment · Movies · Belief · Happiness · Joy
Smiles · Crying · Sharing · Caring · Jokes · Laughter · Education
N.R.A · AA Wellbriety · Teaching · Learning · Sunny Day
Animals · Kindness · Soul Friends · New Things · Festivals
Family Gatherings · Concerts · Peace · Yoga · Positivity · Kids
Unconditional Self-Love · Trust · Recovery · Nature · Hobbies
Compassion · Reliability · Candy · Dancing · Joy Rides · Jobs
Acceptance · Mindfulness · Self-Care · Gratitude · Journaling
Values · Cleanliness · Safety · Sponsors · Communication · Sleep
Independence · Spirituality · Positive Judicial Assistance · Rehab
Healing · Mental Health Therapy · Integrity · Healthy Habits
Vacations · Healthy Skills · Consistency · Priorities · Forgiveness
Giving Back · Letting Go · Structure · Accountability · Nutrition
Responsibility · No Excuses · Awareness · Reflection · Sage
Ceremony · Traditional Ways · Cooking · Sweat Lodge · Sauna

Wellness takes effort. You can change your life, one thought, one action, one day at a time. The vibration you identify with will be reflected in your life.
Begin shifting to positive thoughts and positive actions will follow!
You can do this. You are not alone!

CHAPTER 5

HEALTHY RELATIONSHIPS

In this chapter we address these questions and answers...

What are Healthy Relationships with Others? Why is this Important?

What are Healthy Relationships with Ourselves? Why is this Important?

How do We Consistently Choose and Use Boundaries? Why is this Important?

How do We Learn to Communicate without Judgment or Ego? Why is this Important?

How do We Communicate with Compassion and Kindness? Why is this Important?

Healthy Relationships

What are Healthy Relationships with Others?
Healthy relationships with others involve honesty, trust, respect, and open communication between partners and they take effort and compromise from both people. There is no imbalance of power. Partners respect each other's independence, can make their own decisions without fear of retribution or retaliation, and share decisions.[39]

Know what you want...

What are your beliefs, core values, wants, and needs out of a relationship?

Each relationship will look different, as it should. Our relationships with partners, children, parents, siblings, relatives, friends, and acquaintances – they will all be different.

Take time to understand what you want and need first, so you can communicate that when building and re-establishing healthy relationships.

Very Well Mind has a very helpful article (included below) on distinguishing healthy relationships from unhealthy ones. The information refers to partner relationships, but it can be applied to all relationships, including friend and family relationships.

How to Know If You Are In a Healthy Relationship

From VeryWellMind.. Relationships are an important part of a healthy life. Research has consistently shown that social connections are critical for both mental and physical health. People who have healthy relationships have better health outcomes, are more likely to engage in healthy behaviors, and have a decreased risk of mortality.

This article discusses some of the characteristics of a healthy relationship and how to spot the signs of potential problems. It also explores some of the steps you can take to improve the health of your relationship.

Questions to Ask Yourself

It is important to remember that there is no such thing as a perfect relationship. Every relationship has a mix of both healthy and unhealthy characteristics. What makes a bond positive is that each person recognizes that relationships take work. Each person must strive to maintain the connection and remedy problems.

People often spend a lot of time talking about how to spot a bad relationship, but not about what constitutes a healthy relationship. Consider the following:

- Do you have trust in one another?
- Do you respect each other?
- Do you support each other's interests and efforts?
- Are you honest and open with each other?
- Are you able to maintain your individual identity?
- Do you talk about your feelings, hopes, fears, and dreams?
- Do you feel and express fondness and affection?
- Is there equality and fairness in your relationship?

Every person's needs are different. For example, some people have higher needs for openness and affection than others do. In a healthy relationship, each person is able to get what they need.

Awareness Tool:

Consider your relationship health. Understanding healthy and unhealthy patterns will allow you to choose what is appropriate for you. RF

Characteristics of Healthy Relationships

While all relationships are different, there are some key characteristics that help differentiate a healthy interpersonal connection from an unhealthy one.

Trust

Trust in your partner is a key component of any healthy relationship. Research suggests that your ability to trust others is influenced by your overall attachment style. Relationships experienced early in life help shape the expectations that you have for future relationships.

If your past relationships have been secure, stable, and trusting, you are more likely to trust future partners as well. If, however, your past relationships were unstable and undependable, you may have to work through some trust issues going forward.

Trust is also established by how partners treat one another. When you see that your partner treats you well, is dependable, and will be there when you need them, you are more likely to develop this trust.

Building trust requires mutual self-disclosure by sharing things about yourself. As time passes, opportunities to test and evaluate that trust emerge. As trust grows, the relationship becomes a great source of comfort and security. If you feel that you have to hide things from your partner, it may be because you lack this essential trust.

Openness and Honesty
You should be able to feel that you can be yourself in a healthy relationship. While all couples have varying levels of openness and self-disclosure, you should never feel like you have to hide aspects of yourself or change who you are. Being open and honest with each other not only helps you feel more connected as a couple, but also helps foster trust.

Self-disclosure refers to what you are willing to share about yourself with another person. At the beginning of a relationship, you may hold back and exercise more caution about what you are willing to reveal. Over time, as the intimacy of a relationship increases, partners begin to reveal more of their thoughts, opinions, beliefs, interests, and memories to one another.

This doesn't mean that you need to share every single thing with your partner. Each individual needs their own privacy and space. What matters most is whether each partner feels comfortable sharing their hopes, fears, and feelings if they so choose. Healthy couples don't need to be together all the time or share everything.

Differences in opinion over how much honesty there should be in a relationship can sometimes cause problems, however. Fortunately, one study found that when people are unhappy with their partner's level of openness, they typically discuss the problem with their partner. This is a good example of how addressing a problem openly can help strengthen a relationship.

While your partner may have different needs than you, it is important to find ways to compromise while still maintaining your own boundaries. Boundaries are not about secrecy; they establish that each person has their own needs and expectations.

Healthy boundaries in a relationship allow you to still do the things that are important to you, such as going out with friends and maintaining privacy, while still sharing important things with your partner.

A partner who has unhealthy expectations of openness and honesty might expect to know every detail of where you are and what you're doing, restrict who you can spend time with, or demand access to your personal social media accounts.

Mutual Respect
In close, healthy relationships, people have a shared respect for one another. They don't demean or belittle one another; instead they offer support and security.

There are a number of different ways that couples can show respect for one another.

These include:

- Listening to one another
- Not procrastinating or stonewalling when your partner asks you to do something
- Being understanding and forgiving when one person makes a mistake
- Building each other up; not tearing each other down
- Making room in your life for your partner
- Taking an interest in the things your partner enjoys
- Allowing your partner to have their own individuality
- Supporting and encouraging your partner's pursuits and passions
- Showing appreciation and gratitude for one another
- Having empathy for one another

Affection

Healthy relationships are characterized by fondness and affection. Research has shown that the initial passion that marks the start of a new relationship tends to decline over time,[4] but this does not mean that the need for affection, comfort, and tenderness lessens.

Passionate love usually happens during the beginning of a relationship and is characterized by intense longing, strong emotions, and a need to maintain physical closeness. This passionate love eventually transforms into compassionate love, which is marked by feelings of affection, trust, intimacy, and commitment.

While those intense early feelings eventually return to normal levels, couples in healthy relationships are able to build progressively deeper intimacy as the relationship progresses.

However, it is important to remember that physical needs are different for each individual. There is no right amount of affection or intimacy. The key to a healthy relationship is that both partners are content with the level of affection that they share with their partner. A nurturing partnership is characterized by genuine fondness and affection for one another that is expressed in a variety of ways.

Good Communication

Healthy, long-lasting relationships, whether they are friendships or romantic partnerships, require the ability to communicate well.

One study found that a couple's communication style was more important than stress, commitment, and personality in predicting whether married couples would eventually divorce.

While it might seem like the best relationships are those that don't involve conflict, knowing how to argue and resolve differences of opinion effectively is more important than simply avoiding arguments in order to keep the peace.

Sometimes conflict can be an opportunity to strengthen a connection with your partner. Research has shown that conflict can be beneficial in intimate relationships when serious problems need to be addressed, allowing partners to make changes that benefit the future of the relationship.

When conflicts do arise, those in healthy relationships are able to avoid personal attacks. Instead, they remain respectful and empathetic of their partner as they discuss their thoughts and feelings and work toward a resolution.

Give-and-Take

Strong relationships are marked by natural reciprocity. It isn't about keeping score or feeling that you owe the other person. You do things for one another because you genuinely want to.

This also doesn't mean that the give-and-take in a relationship is always 100% equal. At times, one partner may need more help and support. In other cases, one partner may simply prefer to take more of a caregiver role. Such imbalances are fine as long as each person is ok with the dynamic and both partners are getting the support that they need.

Awareness Tool:

Trust, openness, honesty, respect, affection, communication, and equal participation are characteristics of a healthy relationship. RF

Signs of Problems in a Relationship

Relationships can change over time and not every relationship is 100% healthy all the time. Times of stress, in particular, can lead to unhealthy behaviors and coping mechanisms that can create problems. A relationship is unhealthy when the bad outweighs the good or when certain behaviors are harmful to one or both individuals.

- Attempts to control your behaviors
- Avoiding one another
- Being afraid to share your opinions or thoughts
- Being pressured to quit the things you enjoy
- Criticizing what you do, who you spend time with, how you dress, etc.
- Feeling pressured to change who you are

- Feeling that spending time together is an obligation
- Lack of fairness when settling conflicts
- Lack of privacy or pressure to share every detail of your life with your partner
- Neglecting your own needs to put your partner first
- Poor communication
- Unequal control over shared resources including money and transportation
- Yelling

Some problems may be temporary and something that you can address together, either through self-help methods or by consulting a mental health professional. When it comes to more serious problems, such as abusive behaviors, your primary concern should be on maintaining your safety and security. f you or a loved one are a victim of domestic violence, contact the National Domestic Violence Hotline at **1-800-799-7233** for confidential assistance from trained advocates.

(For more mental health resources, you call also see VeryWellMind's National Helpline Database.[40])

How to Build a Healthier Relationship

Toxic behaviors are often a sign that an unhealthy relationship should end. For other problems, there are many ways to fix weaknesses and build a healthier relationship.

Show Appreciation

Couples who feel gratitude for one another feel closer to one another and tend to be more satisfied with their relationships. One study published in the journal *Personal Relationships* found that showing gratitude for a partner can be an important way to boost satisfaction in romantic relationships.

Another study found that feeling gratitude for a romantic partner was a predictor of whether a relationship would last.

Keep Things Interesting
Keeping up with the daily grind of work and kids can sometimes cause couples to fall into the same old routine. Boredom can lead to greater dissatisfaction as a relationship goes on. Researchers have found, for example, that couples who reported feeling bored in the seventh year of their relationship were more likely to experience marital dissatisfaction nine years later.

Some things that you can do to keep the romance alive over the long term.

- Make time for one another; schedule in dates or set aside time each week to focus on one another
- Try new things together; take a class or try a new hobby that you can both enjoy
- Break out of the same old routine
- Look for ways to surprise each other
- Spend time apart once in a while
- Turn off digital devices and spend time focused only on one another
- Find time for intimacy

Recap
Steps you can take that may help make your relationship healthier include showing appreciation for your partner and finding ways to keep the relationship interesting.

When to Seek Help

All relationships are going to have their bumps in the road. Conflicts over finances, the challenges of parenting, and other differences can all create ups and downs in a long-term relationship. Even if you and your partner have a healthy relationship most of the time, problems might sometimes arise that might benefit from professional help.

If you feel like your relationship might benefit from outside help, consider talking to a counselor or therapist. A mental health professional skilled in addressing interpersonal and relationship issues can help you both learn to communicate, listen, and cope with some of the issues that might be challenging your relationship.

It is important to remember that you cannot force someone to change their behavior unless they want to. If your partner is not interested or willing in going to counseling, go on your own and focus on your own needs and wellness. Work on building your social support system outside of the relationship and consider ending a relationship if it is ultimately unhealthy.

Recap

Working with a couples therapist can be a helpful way to address issues that you might be having in your relationship.

A Word From Verywell

Even if your relationship seems healthy, it can be helpful at times to step back and look for improvements you can make together. Healthy relationships are marked by an ability to recognize problems, including your own, that might pose a threat to the long-term success of your relationship. By being willing to analyze your relationship, you can work together to build a more fulfilling partnership. [41]

Tips for Maintaing a Healthy Relationship

- Communication
- Make time for activities together
- Keep intimacy a priority
- Gratitude
- Seek therapy if helpful

verywell

Why are Healthy Relationships with Others Important?

Understanding healthy relationships with others is important because it allows us to choose if the relationships in our lives are a good fit. If they are not a good fit for us and are unhealthy, we can begin to determine what steps we need to take to begin to shift these relationships.

What are your beliefs, core values, wants, and needs out of a relationship?

For Example: Do you want someone that will be gentle and nurturing, or someone that will be spontaneous and exciting, et cetera?

Awareness Tool:

We can begin to examine our essential, fundamental desires and needs in a relationship. Taking time to create and build a structure of what we are looking for will help us discern whether our relationships are a good fit, or if it is better to move on. We have a choice. RF

It is difficult to know when to let someone go; in order to protect ourselves, we must sometimes offer love from a distance. Understanding when to leave a relationship and recognizing that the sadness will pass can frequently alleviate greater suffering in the long run.

Connections that are demanding, taxing, or imbalanced can have detrimental consequences on your health and well-being.

Common reasons for maintaining a relationship are the belief that the other person needs us or that they will ultimately change. Additionally, we may fear hurting the other person or lack confidence in our capacity to form new relationships. However, knowing when to stop a relationship and recognizing that the hurt will pass can frequently prevent greater suffering and a sense of loss in the long run.

If you're in a relationship that isn't fulfilling or has become toxic for you, instead of trying to remedy the problem or criticizing, consider what you want from the relationship. Consider whether the other person respects your emotions.

Relationships flourish on openness, communication, mutual concern, and shared time. When one or more of these qualities are absent, it is possible that the connection, regardless of how passionate, is not worth maintaining. It is preferable to quit a relationship that doesn't seem right, rather than to continue it while harboring bitterness or animosity. On the other side, moving on without conflict may open the way to a more caring relationship in the future.

If we need to do the adjusting we can look at what is going on and why. Here we begin to reprogram our behavior patterns to accommodate a healthier relationship.

If it doesn't grow our light, it doesn't belong in our lives.

Awareness Tool:

*Meeting people where they are at instead of where
we think they should be, or where we are, will change
our relationships. RF*

If the other person needs to do the adjusting but they are not open to change or working through the challenges, it would be wise to either end or create distance in that particular relationship so we can move forward with peace, respect, happiness, and joy.

It is not our job to force others to see the light or make them understand something that they are not ready for. We each have our own journey and someone else's ability to see or not see our values and beliefs does not diminish them, or us, in any way. It is just a difference of opinion and experience.

Awareness Tool:

*What is the point of challenging interactions with others?
Ultimately, our job is to learn from each situation and decide
if it is beneficial for us to continue in that relationship
or if it has run its course and it is more appropriate
to move forward in a different way.
(This applies to all relationships.) RF*

What are Healthy Relationships with Ourselves?

A healthy self-relationship is being able to value yourself as a person and accept both your strengths and weaknesses every day. This means taking care of yourself, respecting yourself, being kind to yourself, and loving yourself.

The following article by Gina Lucia of Limit Breaker provides excellent information on cultivating and maintaining this critical relationship.

How to Have a Healthy Relationship with Yourself

When did you last take some time to think about your relationship with yourself?

If you're anything like me then you might spend a lot of time thinking about your relationships with other people.

Whether it's your partner, your kids, your boss or your friends, we all know that relationships are important. We know that our words matter. That the time and energy we give to the people in our lives makes a huge difference.

And yet sometimes, in the midst of all this, we can forget the person we spend the most time with. The person who has been with us the whole way and will be with us till the end. Ourselves!

When did you last think about your own self-relationship?

Or reflect on how to have a relationship with yourself that is good and healthy?

Not recently? Don't worry, I got you.

Why should you aim to have a healthy relationship with yourself?

Your relationship with yourself is the most lasting relationship you will ever have.

We are often told to surround ourselves with positive and encouraging people and we know the impact these relationships have.

But the person that we spend the most time with, and whose voice we hear each and every day, is our own. How we speak to ourselves and the way in which we treat ourselves is key to our wellbeing.

Awareness Tool:

There is no other relationship in our lives that
has as much impact as the relationship with ourselves...
and yet our self-relationship is often the most neglected. RF

A healthy relationship with yourself

An easy way to assess your relationship with yourself is to try to notice how you speak to yourself and care for yourself over the course of a day.

- Do the things you say to yourself sound like the kind of things you would say to a friend?
- Or do you find yourself being harsh and critical?
- As you go through the day how do you treat yourself?
- Do you allow yourself time for the things that you need?
- Even something as simple as a glass of water when you feel thirsty.
- Pay attention to the things you deny yourself.

Would you ask a colleague to work through without lunch? Or refuse your child a drink? Of course, you wouldn't! And yet you may well be asking this of yourself each and every day.

It can be hard to be real with ourselves. But by asking the question, "Would I ask this of somebody else?" you can begin to come to grips with the real picture of your relationship with yourself and start to set yourself on a better course.

And getting on a better path is, after all, what allows us to continue to invest in our relationships with others. We can't give out of what we don't have.

Our self-relationship is key.

If this sounds like you then here's some suggestions to start to invest in the most important relationship in your life.

Your relationship with yourself

Get to know yourself

Given that you have spent your entire life in your own company, you might feel you know yourself pretty well. But often, in our noisy world, our own thoughts and feelings can get crowded out.

We're surrounded by other people's thoughts, feelings, wants, and desires. Even more so in the social media age.

Many of us are so used to putting other people first that our own thoughts and feelings can regularly take a back seat to the needs of others.

To have a better relationship with yourself, somewhere in your day you need to let your voice be the one that is prioritized.

And when you do take time to listen to yourself, you might be surprised by what you hear.

- You might start to recognize what you really enjoy in life and the things you find tough.

- You might realize that the path you are on isn't the one you want after all or that a surprising aspect of your work is really the one that makes your heart sing.

- Or you might discover a need you have that isn't being met or even a sadness that needs to heal.

Really listening to yourself, and getting to know yourself, is the first step in developing a healthier you and a better self-relationship.[42]

So how can you go about this?

Lucia suggests that the first step to building a healthy relationship with yourself is to get to know yourself better. Two ways we can do this is through mindfulness exercises, such as breath work and meditation, journaling, and simply asking yourself, "How are you feeling today?"

She also suggests several other simple but profound ways in which we can build this most important relationship..

Change the language you use

When you start to get more in touch with yourself and your own thoughts you might be surprised by the way in which you speak to yourself. If you hear yourself being critical or negative then you're not alone.

We all have less than positive thoughts that pop up from time to time. But when your mind strays towards thoughts that cause you to doubt your own abilities then it is worth giving this some attention.

You may notice your thoughts follow a pattern that you begin to see is causing you real difficulty. When you begin to notice this pattern, you may have stumbled across a limiting belief.

A limiting belief is a thought you have about yourself that you believe to be true but is actually holding you back.

Limiting believes run deep, they are the kind of thoughts that you just can't seem to shake, but there are things you can do to move past **them** and transform them into something that serves you better.

Allowing negative self-talk and limiting beliefs to flourish can spiral down into feelings of helplessness and depression so it's worth tackling it when you see it. Check out our guide to transforming negative self-talk to get you started.

The good news is, talking positively to yourself can have a huge impact and make you much more likely to succeed in your goals. So, when you notice yourself talking positively then celebrate it! It really does make all the difference to your relationship with yourself.

Ask yourself: what do you do that's just for you?
We know that in our relationships with other people, a major part of getting it right is planning time with them and doing things with them they enjoy.

Whether it's taking your kids to the park or your partner to their favorite restaurant, we all know that investing in a relationship means making the time for it.

But when did you last make time like this for yourself?

When did you set aside part of your day to simply do something that you love and that makes you happy?

Your relationship with yourself hinges on moments like this. Moments when you give yourself what you need rather than relying on other people to do it for you.

Consistently pushing our own needs aside and not allowing ourselves time to simply enjoy what makes us happy, can lead to life feeling like one long to-do list.

We need to break this cycle to avoid burnout and to keep ourselves able to give out to others in the way we want to.

Treat time each week for things you love just like you would any other commitment. You wouldn't cancel your precious date night with your partner to do the laundry so don't do that to yourself either.

Allow yourself those moments of joy and fun, make it a priority and your relationship with yourself will flourish.

Develop a healthy relationship with yourself
And so, if you've been feeling that you are the last person on your own list, perhaps now is the time to start addressing this.

A healthy relationship with yourself is one of the foundations of happiness and a major factor in meeting your goals. After all yours is the voice you hear each and every day, yours are the choices that affect each and every moment of your life. So, make them loving, make them kind and treat yourself well.[43]

Why are Healthy Relationships with Ourselves Important?

It is important to have a healthy relationship with yourself because if you don't, the rest of your relationships will not be healthy. We have to learn how to love ourselves first, so we can show the world how we need to be loved.

We cannot expect to be fulfilled and happy through other relationships in our lives if we have not created balance and happiness first inside of ourselves.

How do we Consistently Choose and Use Boundaries?

Choosing and using boundaries is so hard!
Consistently choosing and using boundaries takes effort, commitment, dedication, and strength. The consistency between our actions and attitudes is created by setting boundaries. Setting boundaries allows positive effects to take place in our self-esteem and mood.

Most of the time, the hardest parts of setting limits in social interactions and relationships are dealing with the stress that comes with setting a limit and telling others when that limit has been crossed. Most of the time, the stress of talking about the boundary outweighs the few benefits of doing so, since the other side rarely responds well to efforts to set boundaries.

People often give up on trying to set limits because it's stressful and doesn't generally work out well. After all, what's the point of putting yourself through the stress of setting limits if doing so doesn't lead to the results you want?

Awareness Tool:

Removing yourself from negativity, chaos, and learned behavior patterns will not only take effort; **you will also be required to choose to take action** *if you want to see and feel a change in your life. RF*

Healthy boundaries help you achieve positive emotional health. Setting boundaries is a vital component of building one's identity and is essential for health and well-being. By specifying what you will and will not be responsible for, healthy boundaries assist individuals in defining their identity.

Awareness Tool:

Setting limits is a way to be assertive and show that you respect yourself, which is good for your self-esteem and your emotional state. RF

When we create consistency between our actions and attitudes, we create internal safety and respect for ourselves. Boundaries allow a foundation of safety and respect for ourselves. We do not need anyone else's approval to move forward with this safety and respect. It is found within.

Awareness Tool:

Consistently setting and using limits teaches us to focus less on others' reactions and more on our own self-esteem and attitude. RF

Being open to examining our thoughts and possible thought distortions can help us identify why we are not able to set strong boundaries. When we do not fully believe that we are capable and loved, we will continue to look to find our value and worth through acts of kindness and service to others. Consistency of thoughts and actions is easier to attain when we are mindful of cognitive dissonance or thought distortions, as mentioned in Chapter 2. Here is a brief reminder.

In his article, "Cognitive Dissonance: What to Know!" author Alex Wilfred explores the role cognitive dissonance (or distortion) plays in our relationships with self and others. According to Wilfred,

"When our actions and beliefs contradict each other, we experience cognitive dissonance. Making sure that our actions and thoughts are in alignment can help us overcome cognitive dissonance."[44]

Cognitive Dissonance

In Chapter 2, we discussed how cognitive dissonance (or distortion) happens when there is a disconnect between a person's beliefs and their actions, or when the person's beliefs contradict each other. These beliefs can show up as false assumptions, being overly critical of self and others, and more; they can also lead to the person feeling guilty, ashamed, and anxious. These distortions can dictate a person's behavior. For example, they may avoid interactions or information that contradicts their beliefs so they can avoid the negative feelings these experiences may trigger. In this way, it becomes a vicious cycle.

The good news is that this cycle can be broken. We can examine our beliefs, become aware of where they may be distorted, and choose different behaviors that reflect our integrity and bring us into alignment, therefore reprogramming our thinking. This takes time and work, but it is worth it.

Awareness Tool:

*Your attitude toward yourself will be consistent
with your actions; if you act in a manner that shows
respect for yourself, you will begin to respect yourself,
regardless of others' behavior toward you. RF*

Setting boundaries is crucial for our own self-value and worth, and because we tend to experience better moods when we respect ourselves, setting boundaries therefore brings with it the additional benefit of positive effects on your mood.

More Consistent Boundaries

You can improve your ability to create limits by performing a "pros vs cons" evaluation.

Take into account the cost of establishing boundaries.

It takes time, effort, and conflict to bring the issue to the other party's attention. Setting limits regularly may seem counterintuitive if you solely think about the possibility of changing the other party's behavior by making them more respectful of you, even when you are aware that this may not happen.

Awareness Tool:

*Your attitude toward yourself will be negative if you act
in a way that suggests you don't respect yourself,
by neglecting to create boundaries. RF*

Awareness Tool:

*Setting boundaries regularly makes sense
when you consider the advantages to your mood
and self-esteem that you will receive from doing so,
regardless of the other party's response. RF*

Why is Consistently Choosing and Using Boundaries Important?

Creating boundaries is vital to our physical, mental, emotional, and spiritual health and well-being. When we learn how we need to be loved, we can then show the world. How else will they know?

The world will treat you the same way you perceive yourself. Our perception dictates our experience. So, if you are always being run over and giving more than receiving, it is because you have shown the world that this is how they can treat you.

> *I KNOW, what an awful thought!!! Hang on, though,*
> *it gets better! This is a bit tricky...*

The reason we act the way we do is because we are all looking for approval and love.

- The reason we give until it hurts is because we are living in the trauma of not being enough!

- The reason the other party takes until it hurts is because they are living in the trauma of not being enough!

> **It takes both sides to create the dysfunction...**
> **They couldn't take too much if we didn't give it**
> **and we couldn't give too much if they didn't take it!**

Setting boundaries is not only valid and healthy, it is completely necessary for us to live in a balanced way. ***Because we have a limit does not make us weak or selfish!*** If something feels like it is too much then it most likely is! If you are trying to walk around packing four cars on your shoulders it would obviously be too much! One car is too much! No one would expect or want you to do that because it would be harmful and dangerous to your health!

We are all walking around with too much weight on our shoulders and then wonder why we have panic, anxiousness, anger, sadness, and despair! Your body is trying to give you a signal with those symptoms!

Trying to solve our imbalances with medication will only get us so far if we are not adjusting our behavior and the stressors that brought us there in the first place.

Awareness Tool:

*If something feels like it's too much it most certainly is.
We can learn to step back and see our situation from
a less personal view, more as an observer. From that
space we can reevaluate and set reasonable goals
and values that are in alignment with our physical,
mental, emotional, and spiritual health. RF*

If you have a cup that is **100% Full** and you insist
on squeezing in *One More Drop,* what will happen?
Of course, the water will start to spill out!!!
We don't wonder why it spills; we know it is
because the cup is full. We don't think that
the water is bad or that it is a bad cup or
that there is anything wrong with the cup.
The cup is not weak, or selfish or refusing to participate....
It Is Too Full!!!

*We don't continue pouring liquid into the cup
because we know that it will continue to spill,
making a bigger mess for us to clean up!*

*Sound familiar??? We know better than to keep filling a
full glass. The end result is a bigger mess that ends up in
unhealthy consequences in one or more ways.*

So why in the world do we keep filling up our to-do list when it is already overflowing, instead of saying no or not offering in the first place???

This is why: We are trying to find our value and worth in acts of service to others, but it is not balanced or kind at all when we are compromising ourselves and the environment around us to get it done. That frenetic energy does not help anyone; it will indirectly cause negativity and more chaos.

It is like a poison or a disease; it will eat away at everything around it. I know from firsthand experience – it will make you sick, it is toxic, and it will eventually poison everything around it, driving away happiness and peace.

Generally, we will reach for an unhealthy coping mechanism (drugs, alcohol, meds, depressive states, despair, anger, et cetera) because we can't handle what is happening.

Oh Yeah, That's Because We Are Not Supposed To Handle It. It Is Too Much, The Cup Is Full!!!

So, check this out... if we communicate to the world around us that we are not able to add any additional commitments at this time, we are setting a boundary for ourselves and others. Not only will others respect you, but most importantly...

You Will Respect Yourself and won't be Full of Stress and Anxiousness!

When the cup is full, it is full.

Many of us know these things but have not resolved the trauma of not being enough. Once we are enough, we don't have to constantly overextend in our lives to feel complete and whole! So, from this place of wisdom we can begin to back off and start to keep our "cups" (or lives) at 75% full. That way, if something does come up we will have additional space in our lives to accommodate the extras.

In this way we will also reprogram ourselves to not need **every single minute** filled with some sort of forward motion. When we are comfortable in our own skin we can begin to enjoy moments of peace and relaxation, instead of blindly running from one thing to the next in a constant state of fight-or-flight.

Living in a constant state of fight-or-flight causes many disorders and diseases because the body cannot ever regain its natural homeostasis, or balance. Our fight-or-flight mechanism is meant for emergencies to keep up alive...not to live in.

That would be like constantly driving a car with the spare tire. It will cause other issues with the car because it is not the same size; it will take a toll on many different parts of the car to continue to drive it in that way forever. The spare tire is to get us through the emergency. Once the emergency has passed, we tend to the car appropriately, and purchase a tire that is the correct size because we know that by taking care of it we will increase longevity and performance.

What About Us???? This information can change our lives, but again, just knowing about it will not change anything. We have to be the change we are looking for. Knowledge without action does not facilitate change. I **know** how to scratch my head; I even **want** to scratch my head. But if I don't take the time and effort to move my hand to my head to scratch, nothing will change.

Awareness Tool:

If we do not have healthy boundaries for ourselves and the world around us we will not have a healthy, happy life. RF

How do we Learn to Communicate without Judgment or Ego?

That's a big question! Communicating without judgment or ego takes awareness, desire to change, learning trauma-sensitive dialogue and thought processes, as well as repeated action and effort. As long as we continue to diminish ourselves and those around us with ego and judgment, growth and evolvement will not be possible.

Awareness Tool:

Our perception dictates our experience, and our experiences dictate our perception. RF

First we look at why we have judgment in our communication...

Why is someone else's opinion such a threat to us? Someone else's opinion is just their opinion, it doesn't define us. So why is it so hard to hear? Why do we get upset?

When someone has a different opinion than we do it can cause a strong reaction because it might come from a different belief system than we operate from.

When someone else's morals or values are different from ours it can cause us to have a strong reaction. We have a strong reaction because we feel threatened, and it is part of fight-or-flight – our defense mechanism.

Our defense mechanism, fight-or-flight, is innate, born within us. We are mammals, so it is natural for us to feel the need to defend ourselves. The reaction to defend ourselves can be useful; it gives us information. If we have a strong reaction to something that means that it is important to us. So, in this way we can begin to decipher what we are passionate about and what we would like to defend and keep, or what might be a reaction from past trauma that we can learn from and release.

We, however, don't have to be defensive or upset if others believe in a different way than we do, because we have the ability to keep ourselves safe. Someone else's belief system is not a threat to us unless they are trying to harm us.

Awareness Tool:

We can learn to communicate without judgment
and ego by understanding our triggers, resolving
our trauma, releasing attachment to others' opinions,
and restructuring our dialogue. RF

Why is Communicating without Judgment or Ego Important?

It is important to shift ego and judgment out of our conversations with others as well as our internal dialogue, because if we are always judging and negative we will prevent ourselves and others from experiencing joy and positivity. If we have no joy or positivity in our lives we are constantly living in a state of trauma and fear.

Awareness Tool:

Do you see a person's effort? Is it ever enough?
Or are you always needing more from yourself
and others because that's what has happened to you?
Learned behavior can be unlearned. RF

Awareness Tool:

We can't expect others to fulfill our happiness.
Expectations lead straight to judgment and ego. RF

Communicating without judgment or ego can be extremely frustrating in the beginning. Many times, we explain, or apologize, over and over, because we feel guilty or obligated to please others at our own expense.

We can practice cutting off all the additional dialogue.

We don't need to over explain ourselves; we don't have to apologize constantly; we don't have to take on someone else's stuff on to make them feel better.

It is not our job to make them feel better; it actually will harm them in the long run if they are not able to feel moments of discomfort. So, by allowing people to process and have their own experience we help them in that way.

Awareness Tool:

We learn to meet people where they're at,
instead of where we think they should be.
Our opinion is just that...our opinion. RF

For example, if you speak to someone and they say they are doing well, that they are very grounded and stable, but you know they are not, it is not up to you to point that out to them. In their mind they are doing better than they were before; their version of stable is just that... *their version.* We each have our journey and we are all at different spaces within our own journey and within society. We are unique and don't all have to be in the same space of understanding.

We all have lessons to learn and are exactly where we need to be, even if that is uncomfortable for others around us. We will continue to stay in the same vibration until we learn the lessons we are meant to learn; it is not our job to criticize where others are at.

Our job is to hold space and love as they learn to walk in their own journey, just like allowing a child to gain their balance as they learn to walk. That does **not** mean everyone else is a child except for us. What it means is that we all have to achieve balance and learn lessons in our own lives. We allow each person's journey to be their own.

With that said, it is our job to decide what we allow within close proximity of ourselves. We have to learn what is safe and unsafe for us in our **own** journey. When something is unsafe we need to distance ourselves in a good kind way. We can send them love and healing from a distance.

Only through guidance and awakening can we see what is real as we shift to a higher perspective. It is no longer about proving right and wrong, it is about opening to our full potential. We learn to explore and expand rather than argue, manage, and convince.

How do we Communicate with Compassion and Kindness?

One of the best ways to communicate with compassion and kindness is to know what you want. When we have a clear idea of what we want and how we need to be treated, we are able to meet others in a space of balance and quiet strength.

We can speak our truth in a kind way for all involved; if they can't hear our truth it's okay.

It's not our job to convince anyone of anything. Our job is to speak our truth kindly for all and then decide from there where to go. Things will shift one way or another; if their behavior remains the same then the relationship either won't be a good fit moving forward, or it could need to be re-established.

An article from DailyOm gives great insight: It's common to think a relationship with an emotionally unavailable person is unhealthy. However, it may be possible that all that's needed are a few unique skills and patience to successfully navigate the complexities of the of relationship.

When you learn how to speak your truth, in a way that doesn't trigger other people to shut down, you create an environment that allows them to become comfortable being vulnerable. The more you practice, the clearer it becomes whether the relationship can grow or not.

If they are unreceptive as you communicate your needs, you will naturally grow apart. Whether you drift onto separate paths or deepen your connection together, you will experience newfound freedom and confidence, becoming healthy and emotionally available for yourself.[45]

Reprinted from DailyOM – Inspirational thoughts for a happy, healthy, and fulfilling day. Register for free at DailyOM.com. Here is the link:https://www.dailyom.com/cgi-bin/courses/courseover-view.cgi?cid=935&img=6&utm_medium=email&utm_source=excerpt

You are capable and loved; you can rely on yourself to decide what is safe for you and what is not. It will just need to play out a bit to see where the shift will come from. Because we are all human, it takes a bit of effort and awareness to consciously change learned behavior.

Why is Communicating with Compassion and Kindness Important?

Communicating with compassion and kindness is important because when we are able to communicate our needs with an honest and kind dialogue, we create safety for ourselves. When we honor each person's right to have their own opinion and their own experience, we do not need to communicate in judgment or ego, no matter what their response is.

This DailyOM article explores the role of honest communication in our well-being and our relationships with others. Sometimes we may give others excuses rather than be fully honest. We may think it is kind to tell someone we are willing to do something with them, whether work or play, but then keep putting them off. This diverts our energy into keeping the truth at a distance while continuing a falsehood.

But when we can take responsibility for our feelings and express them honestly, but gently, the other person is free to find someone who is better suited to accompany them while we are free to pursue the things we like. When we can do this, our energy can be invested in building better lives and relationships.

There's another way in which excuses rob us of energy, and that is in the power of our thoughts and words. If we find ourselves in a situation, for example, where we are being asked for a financial contribution and we use the excuse that we can't afford it, we create and attract lack and limitation into our lives. The same goes for seemingly simple things like pretending to not feel well or any other false statement. We may think that excuses make things easier, but they complicate matters with smokescreens.

When we can commit to our priorities, take responsibility for our choices, and communicate them honestly to others, there will be no need to make excuses, and we will have much more energy to dedicate to all the things we love.[46]

Reprinted from DailyOM – Inspirational thoughts for a happy, healthy, and fulfilling day. Register for free at DailyOM.com. Here is the link:https://www.dailyom.com/cgi-bin/display/articledisplay.cgi?aid=76511

Awareness Tool:

*When we think we are putting others first,
we can be disguising what **we** need, with what
we **perceive they** need. Then these illusions
that we have created become our reality. RF*

Awareness Tool:

A habit is just a habit. Habits can be changed.

Awareness Tool:

Trauma bonds can be created in all types of relationships.

Awareness Tool:

*Trauma responses happen to each of us in our
every-day experiences.*

Awareness Tool:

*The ego can be a helpful tool for us. It offers us an opportunity
to check in and see if we need to adjust a situation or if we need
to understand that the ego is just challenging us and we need
to send it for a time out and thank it for the test.*

Try Our Mindful Communication Exercise

Mindful Communication Exercise

Try this mindfulness communication exercise!

This mindfulness communication exercise is helpful for raising communication awareness between two or more people. It allows one person to talk and one person to listen and learn about their partner, family member, or friend. We don't always have to be interested in specific things people in our lives are doing. But we can support them and grow together as we share our experiences.

Mindful Communication Exercise

Two people walk for an hour. No phones, no distractions.
Each person gets to experience both the talker and the listener.
30 minutes each. One person talks, and the other person listens and acknowledges.

Example: The listener may agree with one-word responses, nod their head, or make a sound so the talker knows they are heard.

This is not an open dialogue between two people; it is a space for the talker to share information. Each time the talker is interrupted, they stop walking as a signal to the listener that it is still their turn to talk.

- When this walk starts, set a timer for 30 minutes and decide who will be the talker first. Begin walking. When the timer goes off, both parties stop walking, and the talker wraps up what they are saying.
- The timer gets set again for 30 minutes, switches, and resumes walking. When the timer goes off, both parties stop walking, and the talker wraps up what they are saying.
- There might be times during the person's 30 minutes where they do not wish to speak; at that time, there would just be a comfortable silence.

We can also apply this exercise to a family of four or more by breaking down the time frames and keeping the walk to one hour. If there were four people, each person would have 15 minutes of talk or silent time.

Shorter walk: two people could be 30 minutes total, 15 minutes each. You can also do a much less obvious version of this exercise by practicing listening in conversations throughout your day. Always modify it to best reflect your needs.

Many times, when we are talking, we get excited and want to share because something someone says engages us. You can bring a pad of paper and a pen to write down anything you would like to share later, when your role is that of the listener. Mindfulness is an acquired skill.

Chapter 5 Summary/ Key Takeaways

What are Healthy Relationships with Others? Why is this Important?

- *Healthy relationships with others* require work and compromise from both parties, as well as honesty, trust, respect, and open communication. No one is at an unfair disadvantage. Partners treat each other with mutual respect and trust, allowing each to make their own choices without fear of criticism or punishment. *Understanding healthy relationships with others is important* because it allows us to choose if the relationships in our lives are a good fit. If they are not a good fit for us and are unhealthy, we can begin to determine what steps we need to take to begin to shift these relationships.

What are Healthy Relationships with Ourselves? Why is this Important?

- *Having a healthy relationship with yourself* means being able to value yourself as a person and accept your strengths and weaknesses on a daily basis. That consideration includes self-care, self-respect, goodwill, and self-love. *It is important to have a healthy relationship with yourself* because if you don't the rest of your relationships will not be healthy. We have to learn how to love ourselves first so we can show the world how we need to be loved. We cannot expect to be fulfilled and happy through other relationships in our lives if we have not created balance and happiness first inside of ourselves.

How do We Consistently Choose and Use Boundaries? Why is this Important?

- **Consistently choosing and using boundaries** takes effort, commitment, dedication, and strength. The consistency between our actions and attitudes is created by setting boundaries. Setting boundaries allows positive effects to take place in our self-esteem and mood. When we create consistency between our actions and attitudes we create internal safety and respect for ourselves. Boundaries allow a foundation of safety and respect for ourselves. Healthy boundaries help people define their individuality by identifying what they will and will not hold themselves responsible for. **Creating boundaries is vital** to our physical, mental, emotional, and spiritual health and well-being. When we learn how we need to be loved, we can then show the world. How else will they know? The world will treat you the same way you perceive yourself. Our perception dictates our experience.

How do We Learn to Communicate without Judgment or Ego? Why is this Important?

- **Communicating without judgment or ego takes** awareness, desire to change, learning trauma-sensitive dialogue and thought processes, as well as repeated action and effort. As long as we continue to diminish ourselves and those around us with ego and judgment, growth and evolvement will not be possible. **It is important to shift ego and judgment** out of our conversations with others as well as our internal dialogue, because if we are always judging and negative, we will prevent ourselves and others from experiencing joy and positivity. If we have no joy or positivity in our lives we are constantly living in a state of negativity, trauma, and fear.

How do We Communicate with Compassion and Kindness? Why is this Important?

- *One of the best ways to communicate with compassion and kindness is* to know what you want. When we have a clear idea of what we want and how we need to be treated, we are able to meet others in a space of balance and quiet strength. We can speak our truth in a kind way for all involved; if they can't hear our truth it's okay. It's not our job to convince anyone of anything. Our job is to speak our truth kindly for all and then decide from there where to go. Things will shift one way or another; if their behavior remains the same then the relationship either won't be a good fit moving forward, or it could need to be re-established. *Communicating with compassion and kindness is important* because when we are able to communicate our needs with an honest and kind dialogue, we create safety for ourselves. When we honor each person's right to have their own opinion and their own experience, we do not need to communicate in judgment or ego, no matter what their response is.

Healthy Relationships are so powerful!
Are you ready to continue? In the next chapter
we will learn about...
Habits and Positive Phrasing.

CHAPTER 6

HABITS AND POSITIVE PHRASING

In this chapter we address these questions and answers...

What are Habits? Why are they Important?

How Long Does It Take to Form or Break a Habit?

What is the Meaning of Forgiveness? How Can Forgiveness Change Our Lives?

How do We Perform the Act of Forgiveness?

What is Positive Phrasing and Rephrasing? Why is this Important?

What is Cognitive Behavioral Therapy (CBT)? Why is this Important?

What is Mindful Behavior Modification (MBM) Dialogue? Why is this Important?

How Habits Affect Us

What are Habits?

According to Good Therapy, a habit is any conscious behavior you do on a routine basis. A habit is a learned behavior that becomes reflexive over time. The behavior is often triggered by a certain context. For example, you may automatically go brush your teeth after finishing breakfast as part of your morning routine.

A habit can be healthy, unhealthy, or neutral. A healthy habit might be stretching for ten minutes a day or meditating when you feel stressed. An unhealthy habit could be biting your nails or texting while driving. Examples of neutral habits include eating the same brand of cereal each morning or taking the same route to work.

Unconscious behaviors such as breathing, or blinking do not count as habits because they are instinctive rather than learned.[47]

Why are Habits Important?

The following article from The World Counts explains the power of habits in our lives.

Habits are important because 40 percent of your actions are not conscious decisions but habits. So, habits are a big part of your life — and a lot of the time you don't even notice it!

Habits are our brain's way of increasing its efficiency. Our brain turns daily actions and behaviors into habits, so we would do them automatically and without too much thought – thus freeing up our brainpower for other more important challenges. This strategy of our brain has wonderful benefits for us. It allows us to function better in life. Just imagine if you have to consider and ponder every single task or reaction. We'd be doing nothing else but thinking! According to neuroscientist David Eagleman in Incognito: "Brains are in the business of gathering information and steering behavior appropriately."

The 3-Step Loop of Habits

To be able to change a negative habit, we have to understand how it forms. In the 1990s, a group of researchers from the Massachusetts Institute of Technology discovered a neurological process that is at the core of every habit. This simple 3-step loop is very powerful – it is hard-wired into our brain. So, to change the rules, you have to know the rules first.

1. **Cue** – is any trigger that tells your brain when and which habit to use.
2. **Routine** – is an activity, emotion or behavior.
3. **Reward** – is how your brain determines if a loop is beneficial to you or not.

For example: Cue – You're feeling bored. Routine - You grab a bottle of wine. Reward – You feel relaxed and happy.

The cue and the reward have a very strong influence in creating habits. They are the cause of cravings and make you repeat behaviors or actions. But your innocent wine drinking can turn you into an alcoholic if you do it often enough. So, let's say you want to change that habit, what would you need to do?

If you only focused on changing the routine, like stop drinking wine, you will be unhappy. Your brain will think that the loop doesn't work, and it will reinforce your drinking habit. Our brain demands fulfillment and satisfaction. To be able to change a negative habit, you have to replace the routine in the loop with something else – which will also give you the same reward.

Instead of grabbing a bottle of wine when you feel bored, try jogging or watching a good movie. These activities will offer the same reward – you will feel relaxed afterwards. Your brain will think that this particular loop works. As you do it more often, and experience the same reward, it will replace the loop where you reach for a bottle of wine when you get bored.

This 3 step loop shows you that you have the power to change a bad habit that's causing you more harm than good.

The power of habits to create positive change

Many people have habits that they want to shake off. Smoking, for example, is a hard habit to break. People try to quit, but the cravings overwhelm them, and they fall off the wagon. It's not for lack of determination that they fail. It's lack of understanding of how habits are formed. Since you now understand how habits take hold of our life, you could start creating new loops and forming new habits that will promote positive changes. It is possible to kick whatever bad habit is holding you back.

The following steps can help manifest positive habits in your life:

1. **Examine the Routine** – This would be the behavior you want to change. If being an alcoholic is a problem, what makes you do it? What satisfaction do you get?

2. **Analyze the Reward** – Drinking gives you hangovers and breeds other problems. But obviously, you get an immediate reward when you reach for that bottle. What is the reward? Is it an escape, the immediate feeling of relaxation or the distraction? Once you know the why of the behavior, it'll be easier to find a better habit that will give you the same reward.

3. **Identify the Cue** –What compels your behavior? Triggers are stealthy so you might need to observe your own behavior and take notes. What were you doing before an unwanted act? What were you feeling? What reward were you after? Being aware of the habit and what's reinforcing it is a positive way forward and is the first step to change.[48]

How Long Does It take to Form or Break a Habit?

Establishing or breaking a habit can take anywhere from 18 to 254 days, with an average of 66 days for a new action to become automatic. Breaking or forming habits takes awareness, desire to change, repeated action, effort, commitment, dedication, realistic goals, and strength.

**Negativity seems to be at the root of all unhealthy habits.
So, how do we break the habit of negativity?**

Awareness Tool:

*A new habit takes an average of 66 days to form
and 18 to 254 days to break. We can set **realistic** goals
and understand what is keeping us from them. RF*

We tend to focus on negativity. This is a habit as well as a choice. When negativity comes, we can choose to say no and push it away. Like putting a turn signal on when changing lanes, we can shift to the positive. Try the exercise below. You can exhale anything that is bothering you and inhale a positive that you would like to shift to.

SSHI Habit-Breaking Exercise

1. Stretch your arm and hand straight out in a stopping motion; say "NO" out loud.
2. Place your other hand flat on the center of your chest or belly.
3. Close the eyes, inhale positivity to your body.
4. Exhale negativity out of the mouth like a sigh of relief.
5. Repeat 7 times.

Other options to Inhale...Exhale

Inhale: Happiness...Exhale: Sadness

Inhale: Confidence...Exhale: Doubt

Inhale: Peace...Exhale: Anger

Inhale: Courage...Exhale: Negativity

Inhale: Joy...Exhale: Grief

Inhale: Resilience...Exhale: Negativity

Inhale: Calm...Exhale: Anxiousness

Inhale: Strength...Exhale: Negativity

Inhale: Focus...Exhale: Scatter

Inhale: Freedom...Exhale: Addiction

This doesn't mean we don't allow ourselves to feel. It means that we choose what we bring in and keep; we choose what we release. We have a choice; this brings us back into empowerment. It takes practice; it takes work, just like everything else. What we feed will grow. If we feed the negative it will grow; if we feed the positive it will grow. Give yourself permission to be happy. Give yourself permission to release negativity, permission to bring in positivity. It will change your life.

Awareness Tool:

*Rather than focusing on the problem, **focus on the solution**, even if you do not know what that is yet. This will draw the solution to you rather than more blocks of the problem. RF*

Let's move on to understanding how our negative habits can be trapped by an inability to forgive. When we are not able to forgive others or ourselves fully and completely, it creates blockages of negativity that stay trapped in the mind, body, and spirit.

New Insight on How to Achieve Forgiveness

What is the Meaning of Forgiveness?

The meaning of forgiveness is to overcome negative emotions. The world has a complete misperception of forgiveness. We can change our lives by realizing that to forgive simply means to release negativity. Forgiving (releasing negativity) does not in any way condone anyone's behavior; all it does is release the negativity that keeps us trapped in the situation.

That would be a bit elusive if we didn't have our MBM (Mindful Behavior Modification) tools – oh, but we do have them! Hang tight, what comes next is amazing!

We have already learned that when negativity is trapped in the body we can release it with our breath, so why in the world are we not using that same thought process for forgiveness?

This will all begin to tie together as you read on. *First, a bit more on forgiveness...*

Forgiveness *is defined on Wikipedia* as "the intentional and voluntary process by which one, undergoes a change in feelings and attitude, and overcomes negative emotions."

To understand what forgiveness is, it is helpful to understand what forgiveness is not.

Ideas about what forgiveness is not

- Forgiveness is not condoning
- Forgiveness is not forgetting
- Forgiveness is not excusing (i.e., making reasons to explain away responsibility)
- Forgiveness doesn't have to be religious or otherworldly
- Forgiveness is not minimizing your hurt
- Forgiveness is not reconciliation (i.e., reestablishing trust in the relationship)
- Forgiveness is not denying or suppressing anger, it is healthy to acknowledge and express negative emotions before you can forgive
- Forgiveness is not ignoring accountability or justice' in particular[49]

So...Forgiveness means to let go of negative emotions.
Not condoning anyone's behavior...Hmmm.

How Can Forgiveness Change Your Life?

Forgiveness does not mean the actions are condoned. It just means that you release the negativity surrounding that situation for yourself and/or others.

When someone has harmed us, or we have harmed others, in a mighty way, forgiveness is close to impossible. People don't generally get excited about having to forgive themselves or someone else. We know we are "supposed to" forgive because it is better for us, but how do we do that when it basically feels like we are condoning the behavior? Great question! We have come up with the most effective and amazing solution you have ever heard!

I have done some terrible things in my life that I could not forgive myself for because my actions were absolutely NOT okay. I could forgive myself about 85%, but I never could figure out what to do about the remaining 15%. So, I began to research the meaning of forgiveness to dig deeper, to see what had not been discovered. There had to be more.....and there was!!!

How do we Perform the Act of Forgiveness?

We have to do more than just decide to forgive.

We can say, "Okay, I forgive you," but it is not complete because it is only a thought.

We have to follow through with actions
to receive the desired result.

Coming back to releasing negativity for a moment, we know to inhale positive and exhale negative. Why is this so effective? It is so effective because that is literally the medical purpose of the breath. We inhale for the life, or breath, that we need to stay alive, and when the body exhales, it is releasing and filtering out toxins that are not good for the body.

So, when we take the natural function of something and begin to apply it in a deeper way, the results are magnified. This is the key the world is missing. We have to use our breath to actually release the trauma, chaos, pain, and negativity from the body and mind. Otherwise, it will lay dormant and eventually reemerge, creating re-traumatization... perpetuating the cycle of trauma.

Try out the forgiveness exercise below. Stay with me, we got this!

The secret to forgiveness exercise below is one of our Mindful Behavior Modification Tools. Think of a person or situation you have had trouble forgiving (can be someone else or yourself).

The Secret to Forgiveness

1. **Take** 3 deep cleansing breaths to release pressure.

   (Inhale through nose, exhale out of mouth.)

2. **Gently** close eyes, place palms in center of the chest and lower belly.

3. **Begin** to visualize the situation you would like to forgive.

   (You don't have to see it too close if it is traumatic.)

4. **Inhale** through the nose, bring in positivity to the situation.

5. **Exhale** through the mouth, releasing negativity to the earth.

6. **Repeat** 5-10 times. Pause to feel the tension release. Feel peace.

7. **Congratulations!** You have just performed the act of forgiveness.

This will change your life. It doesn't condone any action, what has happened was not okay.

But what it does do is release the negativity that traps us in the situation so we can be free to move on. We can release trauma around the situation in this way. From this wisdom and knowledge, we heal.

<u>Awareness Tool:</u>

*We are redefining our vocabulary. We now understand
the word forgiveness means to release negativity
around a situation, person, place or thing;
no behavior or actions are condoned. RF*

Now, with this completely different perspective of forgiveness, we understand that by releasing the negativity of the situation with our breath, we can heal. The more negativity we release, the deeper our connection to the positive, opening endless opportunities to absorb the benefits and purpose of positive phrasing.

Advantages of Positive Phrasing

What is Positive Phrasing and Rephrasing?

Now, let's move on to positive phrasing and rephrasing, as explained in this article from Montessori In Town.

Positive Phrasing is aligning the emotional and verbal content of communication in positive respectful and productive ways. Positive phrasing is the art of saying what is, rather than what isn't. Positive Phrasing means our body language, facial expression, tone of voice, inflection and words all convey the same meaning and intention.

Why is positive phrasing effective?

Because it is **clear**, it is **unambiguous**, and it **invites cooperation.**

Positive Phrasing

1. **is always delivered as a statement** – avoid choice when there isn't actually a choice; avoid changing a statement into a choice by adding 'Okay?'

2. **requires a commitment** – to say what we mean and mean what we say

3. **is honest** – but also respectful and compassionate

Positive Phrasing as part of aligned communication has **four benefits**:

1. **Clarity**. The message is clear. No tricks, no confusion, no manipulation.

2. **Respect**. Others experience courteous regard for their feelings and dignity.

3. **Trust**. We say what we mean and mean what we say. Others can trust that when we say something, it happens.

4. **Modeling**. Others around us will naturally adopt and cultivate this kind of communication when this is the communication they experience and observe from others in the environment. Particularly when people that they love and admire communicate in this manner.[50]

<u>*Awareness Tool:*</u>

Positive phrasing consists of statements that are clear and encouraging. RF

Positive Rephrasing or Reframing

Positive reframing is the process of thinking about a negative or difficult circumstance in a more positive light. This could include considering an advantage or upside to a terrible scenario that you had not previously considered. It may also entail recognizing a lesson to be gained from a bad event. Finding a reason to be appreciative in the midst of a difficult situation is a form of positive reframing. For example, following a break-up you could reflect on the opportunity to meet new people, the lessons you obtained from the relationship, and your thankfulness for the time you spent with the individual.

Consider this, from "The Usual Error," on the power of our words.

Rephasing things positively

The words we use to describe our lives affect how we perceive our lives and thus the quality of our lives. You can improve the quality of your life by choosing to *rephrase things positively.*

In particular, we've found that rephrasing obligation words, limitation words, and violent words has significantly improved our happiness, and we're going to show you why and how.

Obligation words

Sometimes we enter into obligations willingly, which is fine, but often people create tons of completely unnecessary obligation, thereby burdening themselves with heavy loads of stress.

There are lots of obligation-inducing words in English.

Here are some examples:
"Should, Ought, Must, Have to, Need to,
Supposed to, Forced to"

Every time you use one of these words or phrases, you unintentionally take a little more obligation onto yourself. Why? There's so much obligation out there anyway, why choose to speak in such a way as to heap *more* of it onto yourself? It's harmful, it's completely unnecessary, and it's not even *honest.*

The truth is that any obligation you have is self-imposed, because **if you want something badly enough, you will do it. Conversely, if you don't want to do something, you'll find ways to avoid it. A feeling of "should" indicates a conflict between your wants: you want the end result**, but you don't want to go through the process of getting it.

You can rephrase this — and thereby reimagine it — by talking about it purely in terms of what you *want* to do instead of what you feel you *should* do.

Take, for example, "I should go to the store." What we actually mean is something like, "We are low on food, and I want to eat, so I'll go to the store so I can get what I want to eat."

By using "should," we're putting obligation into it, making it into something we *don't* want to do. By removing "should," we turn it into something that is good for us and therefore less of an obligation and more of a good, happy-making thing.

Feel how empowering these rephrasing's are. Instead of presenting yourself as a hapless victim of fate, you're presenting yourself as the captain of your own destiny.

You are the one making the choices, *you* are the one choosing to do what you want to do, *you* are the one choosing to do what makes you most happy.[51]

> *Goodnet has also provided specific examples on how we can use language to create change in our lives.*

How to Turn 11 Everyday Phrases From Negative to Positive

It's official: positive language can literally change your brain. Yes, that's right—positive words like "peace," "love" and "compassion" strengthen areas of the brain's frontal lobes and promote cognitive function. In simple terms, hearing and using positive language can make you feel great—physically, mentally and emotionally. On the flip side, negative language can block the brain's natural de-stress mechanisms. So, as well as adding some sparkly positive words into your everyday language—like "certainly," "great" and "definitely"— it's worth taking a look at phrases you might be using inadvertently and giving them a polish, too.

These 11 everyday phrases can easily be replaced, giving your vocabulary an instant positivity boost.

Every Day Positive Language

1. **Why not? → Sounds good**

2. **No problem → Definitely!**

3. **Can't complain → Everything's going well, thanks**

   Despite the positive intent behind these phrases, the human brain's negative biases subconsciously trigger negative thoughts, problems, or concerns when processing these words.

4. **I'm exhausted → I need to rest**

   Flipping the phrase to include a solution leaves both the speaker and the listener with a better taste in their mouths.

Positive Language at Work

1. **I forgot → I'll make sure to set a reminder**

   Again, focusing on what can be done will help the people around you expect a positive result.

2. **Unfortunately, it will be impossible to finish the project on time because of the problems some people are causing with submitting their work late. → Can everyone turn in their portion of the project by Thursday so that we can complete the work on time and hit the deadline?**

   Email culture provides the perfect opportunity to work on positive language, as you can edit your words before sending them out to colleagues and clients. Look out for negative words like "unfortunately," "impossible" and "problems" as flags for sentences to revise.

3. **Constructive criticism** → **Feedback**

   The words you use to frame your feedback can have a significant impact on how it is received. To add to the positive vibe, <u>healthy portions of compliments</u> for achievements will help your colleagues take your comments on board.

Positive Language at Home

1. **Don't throw the ball inside!** → **Please take the ball outside.**

2. **Don't …** → **I like it when..**

   Telling children (and adults, too!) what you want them to do rather than what you don't want them to do puts the focus on the desired action and ups your chances of a positive outcome.

3. **I missed you so much!** → **It's so great to see you!**

   While absence certainly does make the heart grow fonder, reunions can be a time to rejoice in the present rather than relating negative emotions from the past.

4. **No!** → **I know you like ice cream but eating too much isn't healthy.**

   Unless you're dealing with a serious safety issue, for example near a road or a swimming pool, explaining the reason behind your "no" helps children feel respected and included. As a guide, think about how you'd like your boss to speak to you.[52]

Why is Positive Phrasing and Rephrasing Important?

Positive phrasing and rephrasing is so important because it will change the dynamic of your relationships. Not only the relationships with others, but also the relationship with yourself. This type of speech and thought process is Trauma-Informed, as well as Trauma-Responsive.

When we begin to speak in truth and kindness, while releasing attachment to our experience, we are able to offer a whole new level of compassion and understanding for all involved. We are not threatened by a difference of opinion, because we have created safety through setting deliberate and intentional boundaries.

We have taken the time to consider what is appropriate for ourselves, and are not only willing to, but insist on, creating an environment that produces safety, love and joy.

Awareness Tool:

One way to stop negative behavior is by using positive affirmations. RF

Now, let's dive deeper into positive thought processes. A specific form of therapy called, Cognitive Behavioral Therapy, can be used to produce positive behavior shifts. Look for a professional licensed CBT therapist near you.

A great article from VeryWellMind, shares the following information on Cognitive Behavioral Therapy.

What is Cognitive Behavioral Therapy (CBT)

Cognitive behavioral therapy (CBT) is a type of psychotherapeutic treatment that helps people learn how to identify and change the destructive or disturbing thought patterns that have a negative influence on their behavior and emotions.

Cognitive behavioral therapy focuses on changing the automatic negative thoughts that can contribute to and worsen our emotional difficulties, depression, and anxiety. These spontaneous negative thoughts also have a detrimental influence on our mood.

Through CBT, faulty thoughts are identified, challenged, and replaced with more objective, realistic thoughts.

Types of Cognitive Behavioral Therapy
CBT encompasses a range of techniques and approaches that address our thoughts, emotions, and behaviors. These can range from structured psychotherapies to self-help practices. Some of the specific types of therapeutic approaches that involve cognitive behavioral therapy include:

- **Cognitive therapy** centers on identifying and changing inaccurate or distorted thought patterns, emotional responses, and behaviors.

- **Dialectical behavior therapy (DBT)** addresses destructive or disturbing thoughts and behaviors while incorporating treatment strategies such as emotional regulation and mindfulness.

- **Multimodal therapy** suggests that psychological issues must be treated by addressing seven different but interconnected modalities: behavior, affect, sensation, imagery, cognition, interpersonal factors, and drug/biological considerations. **Rational emotive behavior therapy (REBT)** involves identifying irrational beliefs, actively challenging these beliefs, and finally learning to recognize and change these thought patterns.

While each type of cognitive behavioral therapy takes a different approach, all work to address the underlying thought patterns that contribute to psychological distress.

Cognitive Behavioral Therapy Techniques
CBT is about more than identifying thought patterns. It uses a wide range of strategies to help people overcome these patterns. Here are just a few examples of techniques used in cognitive behavioral therapy.

Identifying Negative Thoughts

It is important to learn what thoughts, feelings, and situations are contributing to maladaptive behaviors. This process can be difficult, however, especially for people who struggle with introspection. But taking the time to identify these thoughts can also lead to self-discovery and provide insights that are essential to the treatment process.

Practicing New Skills

In cognitive behavioral therapy, people are often taught new skills that can be used in real-world situations. For example, someone with a substance use disorder might practice new coping skills and rehearse ways to avoid or deal with social situations that could potentially trigger a relapse.

Goal-Setting

Goal-setting can be an important step in recovery from mental illness, helping you to make changes to improve your health and life. During cognitive behavioral therapy, a therapist can help you build and strengthen your goal-setting skills.

This might involve teaching you how to identify your goal or how to distinguish between short- and long-term goals. It may also include helping you set SMART goals (specific, measurable, attainable, relevant, and time-based), with a focus on the process as much as the end outcome.

Problem-Solving

Learning problem-solving skills during cognitive behavioral therapy can help you learn how to identify and solve problems that may arise from life stressors, both big and small. It can also help reduce the negative impact of psychological and physical illness.

Problem-solving in CBT often involves five steps:

1. Identify the problem
2. Generate a list of potential solutions
3. Evaluate the strengths and weaknesses of each potential solution
4. Choose a solution to implement
5. Implement the solution

Self-Monitoring

Also known as diary work, self-monitoring is an important cognitive behavioral therapy technique. It involves tracking behaviors, symptoms, or experiences over time and sharing them with your therapist.

Self-monitoring can provide your therapist with the information they need to provide the best treatment. For example, for people with eating disorders, self-monitoring may involve keeping track of eating habits, as well as any thoughts or feelings that went along with consuming a meal or snack.

Additional cognitive behavioral therapy techniques may include journaling, role-playing, engaging in relaxation strategies, and using mental distractions.

What Cognitive Behavioral Therapy Can Help With

Cognitive behavioral therapy can be used as a short-term treatment to help individuals learn to focus on present thoughts and beliefs.

CBT is used to treat a wide range of conditions, including:
Addiction, Anger issues, Anxiety, Bipolar disorder, Depression, Eating disorders, Panic attacks, Personality disorders, Phobias

In addition to mental health conditions, cognitive behavioral therapy has also been found to help people cope with:

- Chronic pain or serious illnesses, Divorce or break-ups, Grief or loss, Insomnia, Low self-esteem, Relationship problems, Stress management[53]

Why is Cognitive Behavioral Therapy Important?

The following is excerpted from VeryWell.com

Benefits of Cognitive Behavioral Therapy

The underlying concept behind CBT is that thoughts and feelings play a fundamental role in behavior. For example, a person who spends a lot of time thinking about plane crashes, runway accidents, and other air disasters may avoid air travel as a result.

The goal of cognitive behavioral therapy is to teach people that while they cannot control every aspect of the world around them, they can take control of how they interpret and deal with things in their environment.

CBT is known for providing the following key benefits:

- It helps you develop healthier thought patterns by becoming aware of the negative and often unrealistic thoughts that dampen your feelings and moods.
- It is an effective short-term treatment option as improvements can often be seen in five to 20 sessions.
- It is effective for a wide variety of maladaptive behaviors.
- It is often more affordable than some other types of therapy.
- It is effective whether therapy occurs online or face-to-face.
- It can be used for those who don't require psychotropic medication.

One of the greatest benefits of cognitive behavioral therapy is that it helps clients develop coping skills that can be useful both now and in the future.

Effectiveness of Cognitive Behavioral Therapy

CBT emerged during the 1960s and originated in the work of psychiatrist Aaron Beck, who noted that certain types of thinking contributed to emotional problems. Beck labeled these "automatic negative thoughts" and developed the process of cognitive therapy.

Where earlier behavior therapies had focused almost exclusively on associations, reinforcements, and punishments to modify behavior, the cognitive approach addresses how thoughts and feelings affect behaviors.

Today, cognitive behavioral therapy is one of the most well-studied forms of treatment. It has been shown to be effective in the treatment of a range of mental conditions, including anxiety, depression, eating disorders, insomnia, obsessive-compulsive disorder, panic disorder, post-traumatic stress disorder, and substance use disorder.

- Research indicates that cognitive behavioral therapy is the leading evidence-based treatment for eating disorders.
- CBT has been proven helpful in those with insomnia, as well as those who have a medical condition that interferes with sleep, including those with pain or mood disorders such as depression.
- Cognitive behavioral therapy has been scientifically proven to be effective in treating symptoms of depression and anxiety in children and adolescents.
- A 2018 meta-analysis of 41 studies found that CBT helped improve symptoms in people with anxiety and anxiety-related

disorders, including obsessive-compulsive disorder and post-traumatic stress disorder.

- Cognitive behavioral therapy has a high level of empirical support for the treatment of substance use disorders, helping people with these disorders improve self-control, avoid triggers, and develop coping mechanisms for daily stressors.

CBT is one of the most researched types of therapy, in part, because treatment is focused on very specific goals and results can be measured relatively easily.

Verywell *Mind's Cost of Therapy Survey, which* sought to learn more about how Americans deal with the financial burdens associated with therapy, found that Americans overwhelmingly feel the benefits of therapy:

- 80% say therapy is a good investment
- 91% are satisfied with the quality of therapy they receive
- 84% are satisfied with their progress toward mental health goals

Things to Consider With Cognitive Behavioral Therapy

There are several challenges that people may face when engaging in cognitive behavioral therapy. Here are a few to consider.

Change Can Be Difficult

Initially, some patients suggest that while they recognize that certain thoughts are not rational or healthy, simply becoming aware of these thoughts does not make it easy to alter them.

CBT Is Very Structured

Cognitive behavioral therapy doesn't focus on underlying, unconscious resistance to change as much as other approaches such as psychoanalytic psychotherapy. Instead, it tends to be more structured, so it may not be suitable for people who may find structure difficult.

You Must Be Willing to Change

For cognitive behavioral therapy to be effective, you must be ready and willing to spend time and effort analyzing your thoughts and feelings. This self-analysis can be difficult, but it is a great way to learn more about how our internal states impact our outward behavior.

Progress Is Often Gradual

In most cases, CBT is a gradual process that helps you take incremental steps toward behavior change. For example, someone with social anxiety might start by simply imagining anxiety-provoking social situations. Next, they may practice conversations with friends, family, and acquaintances. By progressively working toward a larger goal, the process seems less daunting and the goals easier to achieve.

How to Get Started With Cognitive Behavioral Therapy

Cognitive behavioral therapy can be an effective treatment choice for a range of psychological issues. If you or someone you love might benefit from this form of therapy, consider the following steps:

- **Consult with your physician** and/or check out the directory of licensed therapists offered by the National Association of Cognitive-Behavioral Therapists to locate a licensed professional in your area. You can also do a search for "cognitive behavioral therapy near me" to find local therapists who specialize in this type of therapy.

- **Consider your personal preferences**, including whether face-to-face or online therapy will work best for you.

- **Contact your health insurance** to see if it covers cognitive behavioral therapy and, if so, how many sessions are covered per year.

- **Make an appointment** with the therapist you've chosen, noting it on your calendar so you don't forget it or accidentally schedule something else during that time.

- **Show up to your first session** with an open mind and positive attitude. Be ready to begin to identify the thoughts and behaviors that may be holding you back and commit to learning the strategies that can propel you forward instead.[54]

Awareness Tool:

Restructuring our negative mindset is necessary in order to facilitate positive change. There is nothing more important than releasing our negative mindset. It is toxic and unhealthy. RF

If we continue to feed the negative mindset and habits, they will continue to have a negative effect in our lives.

We have been programmed to think and perceive the world, as well as ourselves, in a negative way. This is like poison; the negativity eats away at us, and we feel like we cannot ever get ahead or do enough.

So much of the information we receive is gleaned in a nonverbal way. Our environment has a huge impact on our perception. We can learn whether we are loved or not by the simple action of someone attending or not attending to our needs. When our environment is not nurturing this creates trauma and negativity within. Perpetuating our cycle of dysfunction and chaos. We begin to live in a false reality where we are never enough. It is damaging to our mind, body, and spirit, generation after generation. We absorb our value based on our surroundings, establishing opinions of who we are based on faulty information, filled with trauma and suffering.

Awareness Tool:

*Unless we have processed and reprogrammed
our trauma it is still affecting our daily lives,
even if we don't realize it. RF*

Awareness Tool:

*We have the ability to break the cycle of toxic thoughts
and damaging self-beliefs, through awareness,
positive action, and repetition. RF*

There are many ways to restructure negative mindsets into positive ones. One of the methods we work with is a Positive Behavior Resilience™ approach, which is unique to Sacred Sol Healing Institute and is part of our Deconstructing Trauma Program.

Using a Positive Behavior Resilience approach consists of recognizing and replacing negative thoughts with positive thoughts, through awareness and breathwork, to facilitate deeper, lasting results. Recognizing that negative thoughts exist and are prevalent is key; we first have to have this awareness. Through this perspective we learn to consider options that lead to balance.

*Why are we upset and/or negative and how can we change
that?*

Positive Behavior Resilience is modality that teaches us simplicity and a new way of thinking. It requires ongoing reprogramming and perspective changes, in this way we are able to see a lasting change. Action tools are one of the best ways to facilitate this change.

Awareness Tool:

*Through Positive Behavior Resilience we can begin
to notice the distinction between healthy negative
emotions such as temporary sadness and
unhealthy negative emotions such as
deeply depressed states of despair. RF*

Positive Behavior Resilience teaches us that we can build positivity and safety inside of ourselves; we do not need others to create that space for us. We are not dependent on anyone else to create safety or happiness for us; we create this for ourselves.

"We are Capable, We are Loved."

Try our Positive Behavior Resilience™ Tracker. We utilize this tool to recognize a negative thought pattern, identify a positive thought, and reprogram through the positive reprogramming formula.

Positive Behavior Resilience Tracker   Example Sheet   Sacred Sol Healing Institute

Your Harmful Negative Thought Write Down, Say Out Loud.	Your Positive Replacement Thought Write Down, Say Out Loud.	Positive Reprogramming Formula Write Down Positive & Follow Below, Repeat at Least 3-5 Times...
*Write Down & Say Negative Pattern I am afraid of letting people down.	Write Down & Say Positive Replacement: I am working on creating safety for myself.	Place: One hand on heart, one hand on belly. Close eyes. Say Positive: *I am working on creating safety for myself.* Do: Inhale through the nose bringing in light Exhale negativity out the mouth. Say: I am capable, I am loved.
*Write Down & Say Negative Pattern I feel like I'm not good enough for anyone or anything.	Write Down & Say Positive Replacement: My value and worth feels smaller than I would like it to be. I am taking action to change that.	Place: One hand on heart, one hand on belly. Close eyes. Say Positive: *My value and worth feels smaller than I would like it to be. I am taking action to change that.* Do: Inhale through the nose bringing in light Exhale negativity out the mouth. Say: I am capable, I am loved.
*Write Down & Say Negative Pattern I feel like I can't trust my partner because of past experience.	Write Down & Say Positive Replacement: My partner is taking the steps to earn my trust. I trust myself to handle what comes my way. I am working on living in the present moment.	Place: One hand on heart, one hand on belly. Close eyes. Say Positive: *My partner is taking the steps to earn my trust. I trust myself to handle what comes my way. I am working on living in the present moment.* Do: Inhale through the nose bringing in light Exhale negativity out the mouth. Say: I am capable, I am loved.

Goal: Change your negative thought patterns!

This will help to change the negative thought patterns! Anytime you feel like you have a Negative Thought replace it with the Positive Replacement Thought and do the Positive Reprogramming Formula.
Do this as much as it comes into your head so you can reprogram it!

Goal:

Total Times Used:

Positive Behavior Resilience Tracker — Your Sheet — Sacred Sol Healing Institute

Your Harmful Negative Thought Write Down, Say Out Loud.	Your Positive Replacement Thought Write Down, Say Out Loud.	Positive Reprogramming Formula Write Down Positive & Follow Below. Repeat at Least 3-5 Times...
*Write Down & Say Negative Pattern	Write Down & Say Positive Replacement:	Place: One hand on heart, one hand on belly. Close eyes. Say Positive: Do: Inhale through the nose bringing in light Exhale negativity out the mouth. Say: I am capable I am loved.
*Write Down & Say Negative Pattern	Write Down & Say Positive Replacement:	Place: One hand on heart, one hand on belly. Say Positive: Do: Inhale through the nose bringing in light Exhale negativity out the mouth. Say: I am capable, I am loved.
*Write Down & Say Negative Pattern	Write Down & Say Positive Replacement:	Place: One hand on heart, one hand on belly. Say Positive: Do: Inhale through the nose bringing in light Exhale negativity out the mouth. Say: I am capable, I am loved.

Goal: Change your negative thought patterns!
This will help to change the negative thought patterns! Anytime you feel like you have a Negative Thought replace it with the Positive Replacement Thought and do the Positive Reprogramming Formula.
Do this as much as it comes into your head so you can reprogram it!

Total Times Used:

Goal:

Another form of positive phrasing is Mindful Behavior Modification™. This modality is also unique to Sacred Sol Healing Institute.

What is Mindful Behavior Modification (MBM) Dialogue?

Mindful Behavior Modification (MBM) dialogue consists of conversing with others, or ourselves, without our past trauma inserting itself into our interpretations of the conversation.

Our dialogue rephrasing suggestions are non-judgmental, free of ego, Trauma-Informed, Trauma-Responsive and Trauma-Sensitive, not only for others, but also for ourselves.

Awareness Tool:

If we all began to speak in a Trauma-Sensitive format it would drastically reduce challenges, misunderstandings, trauma, and pain in our lives. RF

Example:	Non-MBM Approach	MBM Approach
My partner said he doesn't want to go to the parade with me.	If he cared about me he would go. Why doesn't he love me?	He doesn't have to go with me. I can support myself by going to the parade and enjoying it.
Someone asks me to do something that is inappropriate.	I'll do it because they need help, even though it's a bad idea for me.	Speaking kindly to them: "Honesty I don't feel comfortable with that."
Someone tells me they are having a terrible day.	I'm so sorry and offer to do many things to make them feel better.	"Oh man, that sounds really tough. I will keep you in my thoughts and send positive vibes!"
Someone is mad that I didn't commit to helping them move.	"I'm so sorry, I had so many things to do, I couldn't add one more thing."	"I would have loved to help; my schedule didn't allow it. I'm glad you got into your new place."

Someone is upset; they say I never visit them.	"I'm so sorry. I will come as soon as I can." (Knowing I can't or won't go).	"I'm not able to add anything at this time. I look forward to seeing you soon, have a blessed day!"
Someone wants me to watch their children.	"Okay, I can watch them, even though now I can't do what I need to do."	"I am unavailable to watch the kids, I have prior obligations. Great to see you."
Someone does not pay me for the work I have done.	I guess it's okay. I hope I get paid next time. (Or screaming at them to pay me.)	"It is inappropriate to not pay me for a job we agreed upon. I cannot work for you."
A friend puts me in an unsafe situation.	I guess I am stuck because they are my friend, I hope everything turns out okay.	This is not appropriate for me, it feels unsafe. (Distance myself if it doesn't change.)
Someone is talking to me in an unkind way.	Ignore it because that's how they talk and there's nothing that can be done.	I politely ask them to speak to me in a kinder tone. (Remove myself if they can't hear me.)
Someone is constantly inserting their own agenda into my life.	This person will continue to manipulate me because that's what they do.	Remove this person from my life or lessen exposure. Say, "No thank you" frequently.

Awareness Tool:

One of our most effective tools in challenging conversations is to ask the other person, "What is your goal in this conversation?" RF

Labeling Rephrasing Examples:

Someone that is struggling with trauma and fear is dominant in their relationships because they are trying to find control and safety in their life. This is misdirected.

Here are some ways we can understand and shift the dynamic of labels.

The chart below only names a few but begins to give us a good idea of how we can shift to allow Trauma-Sensitive thought patterns to begin to emerge.

Trauma-sensitive means considering that the other party may not be aware that they could be suffering from negative learned behavior and feelings of inadequacy.

Label:	MBM Label Rephrase	MBM Trauma-Sensitive Awareness
Narcissist	Person living in fear because of trauma. Lacking self-worth because of trauma.	Someone that is struggling with trauma and fear of not being enough is passive-aggressive and controlling in their relationships because they are trying to trick others into loving them. They don't think they can be loved without manipulating others.
Codependents	Person living in fear because of trauma. Lacking self-worth because of trauma.	Someone that is struggling with trauma and fear of not being enough is passive in their relationships because they are trying to please others to feel good about themselves.
Control Freak	Person living in fear because of trauma. Lacking self-worth because of trauma.	Someone that is struggling with trauma and fear is dominant in their relationships because they are trying to find control and safety in their life. This is misdirected.
Addict	Person living in fear because of trauma. Lacking self-worth because of trauma.	Someone that is struggling with trauma and fear is using substances to not feel their pain because it is too much to handle.

Obsessive-compulsive	Person living in fear because of trauma. Lacking self-worth because of trauma.	Someone that is struggling with trauma and fear in their life is trying to find control and safety in their life by making sure everything is in order. This will not keep them safe.
Borderline personality disorder	Person living in fear because of trauma. Lacking self-worth because of trauma.	Someone that is struggling with trauma and fear has a hard time controlling their emotions. They do not feel safe in expressing emotions but at the same time struggles to stifle them.

Notice any patterns???
Ah, yes!

Awareness Tool:

We are ALL living in fear and lacking self-worth to some degree because of trauma we have endured. Our trauma will all look different. It comes to us all in different ways, but it is part of ALL of our lives. Our trauma doesn't have to define us. It can be a tool in which to learn from. RF

Why is MBM Dialogue Important?

Mindful Behavior Modification dialogue is important because when we are aware of the way we think, talk and act we realize it affects not only our lives, but the lives of those around us.

When we are using labels in a descriptive, balanced, and non-threatening way it is not a bad thing. If we are able to use labels in this way there is no ego, judgment, or negativity involved. We have awareness that we can utilize labels as a tool in a good way for *discernment* to understand what is healthy and what is unhealthy for our lives.

Why discernment is essential...

Wikipedia defines Discernment as the ability to obtain sharp perceptions or to judge well (or the activity of so doing). The process of discernment within judgment involves going past the mere perception of something and making nuanced judgments about its properties or qualities.

Process of Discernment

The process of individual discernment has steps that can be taken in order to achieve a level of discernment. The following actions can be made when making decisions of discernment; taking time in making decisions, using both the head and heart, and assessing important values involved in the situation.

Time has been considered necessary in the process of making a smart choice and decisions made in a hurry can be altered by lack of contemplation. When time is available to assess the situation it improves the discernment process. When time allots the tentative decision can be revisited days later and external people can be consulted to make sure that the individual is satisfied with their choice. Making decisions is involved with discernment and they require both the "head" and the "heart."

Making decisions with the "head" means to first reflect on the situation and emphasize the rational aspect of the decision making process. In order to make a decision with the "heart" the individual needs to make decisions based on feelings as well as rationality. Values in the discernment process are weighing options that decide what is most important to the individual.

Every individual's value system is different which affects each individual discernment process. Combining values, using both the head and heart, and taking sufficient time when making decisions are the main steps for a successful discernment process.

Group discernment is a separate branch of discernment. In group discernment each individual must first undergo their own discernment process. The individual must keep in mind what is best for the group as a whole as well as the individual when making a decision. The same principles of values, using the head and heart, as well as giving the decision-making process ample time all still apply in group discernment. Group discernment is different because it requires multiple people to have a unanimous decision in order to move forward. Group discernment requires discussion and persuasion between individuals to arrive at a decision.[55]

Awareness Tool:

Discernment is crucial for us to decipher what is needed and good and what is not needed and inappropriate. When we create inner balance we can act decisively. RF

Learning to rephrase our internal and external dialogue is life-changing.

It takes a lot of work and transparency to use labels successfully without bringing in judgment or ego. When we begin to rephrase the way we think about people, we are able to stop feeding negativity. This cannot happen until we heal our trauma and suffering; only then can we begin to see the pain and suffering of others without judgment and ego.

Chapter 6 Summary/ Key Takeaways

What are Habits? Why are they Important?

- *A habit is* a conscious, repetitive behavior. The behavior happens often because of a specific situation. As part of your morning routine, you might go brush your teeth after breakfast. A habit can be neutral, good for you, or bad for you. *Habits are important* because forty percent of our actions are not conscious decisions, but habits. Habits are a big part of our lives, and a lot of the time we don't even notice it! Habits are a method used by the brain to improve performance. Because the brain programs our routines into habits, we tend to carry them out without much conscious effort. This allows us to devote our cognitive resources to more pressing matters.

How Long Does It Take to Form or Break a Habit?

- *It takes 18-254 days to form or break a habit.* Breaking or forming habits takes awareness, desire to change, repeated action, effort, commitment, dedication, realistic goals and strength. Negativity seems to be at the root of all unhealthy habits, so how do we break the habit of negativity? Rather than focusing on the problem, focus on the solution even if you do not know what that is yet. This will draw the solution to you rather than more blocks of the problem.

SSHI Habit-Breaking Exercise

1. Put your hand straight out, in a stopping motion, say "NO" out loud.

2. Place your other hand flat on the center of your chest.

3. Close the eyes, inhale positivity to your body.

4. Exhale negativity out of the mouth like a sigh of relief.

5. Repeat 5-7 times.

What is the Meaning of Forgiveness? How Can Forgiveness Change Our Lives?

- **The meaning of forgiveness is** to overcome negative emotions. The world has a complete misperception of forgiveness. **Forgiveness can change our lives** because to forgive simply means to release negativity. Forgiving (releasing negativity) does not in any way condone anyone's behavior; all it does is release the negativity that keeps us trapped in the situation.

How do we Perform the Act of Forgiveness?

We perform the act of forgiveness by releasing negativity.

The Secret to Forgiveness

1. **Take** 3 deep cleansing breaths to release pressure.(Inhale through nose, exhale out mouth.)

2. **Gently** close eyes, place palms in center of the chest and lower belly.

3. **Begin** to visualize the situation you would like to forgive. (Not too close if traumatic.)

4. **Inhale** through the nose, bring in positivity to the situation.

5. **Exhale** through the mouth, releasing negativity to the earth.

6. **Repeat** 5-10 times. Pause to feel the tension release. Feel peace.

What is Positive Phrasing and Rephrasing? Why is this Important?

- **Positive Phrasing is** putting together the emotional and verbal parts of a message in a way that is positive, respectful, and helpful. Positive language is a way to say what is instead of what isn't. Positive phrasing means that our body language, facial expression, tone of voice, and words all reflect the same positive message. **Positive phrasing and rephrasing is so important** because it will change the dynamic of your relationships – not only the relationships with others but the relationship with yourself. When we begin to speak in truth and kindness while releasing attachment to our experience, we are able to offer a whole new level of compassion and understanding for all involved. We are not threatened by a difference of opinion, because we have created safety through setting deliberate and intentional boundaries.

What is Cognitive Behavioral Therapy (CBT)? Why is this Important?

- **Cognitive behavioral therapy (CBT) is** a type of psychotherapeutic treatment that helps people learn how to identify and change the destructive or disturbing thought patterns that have a negative influence on their behavior and emotions.

- **Cognitive Behavioral Therapy (CBT), is** important because it focuses on changing the automatic negative thoughts that can contribute to and worsen our emotional difficulties, depressive states, and anxiousness. These spontaneous negative thoughts also have a detrimental influence on our mood.

What is MBM Dialogue? Why is this Important?

- **Mindful Behavior Modification (MBM) dialogue** consists of conversing with others, or ourselves, without our past trauma inserting itself into our interpretations of the conversation. This dialogue is non-judgmental, free of ego, and Trauma-Sensitive – not only for others, but also for ourselves. ***Mindful Behavior Modification (MBM) dialogue is important*** because when we are aware of the way we think, talk and act, we realize it affects not only our lives but the lives of those around us. When we use labels in a descriptive, balanced, and non-threatening way it is not a bad thing. If we are able to use labels in this way there is no ego, judgment, or negativity involved. We have awareness that we can utilize as a tool in a good way for discernment to understand what is healthy and what is unhealthy for our lives.

Positive Phrasing is so powerful!
Are you ready to continue?
In the next chapter we will learn about
Daily Resilience and Balance.

DAILY RESILIENCE AND BALANCE

In this chapter we address these questions and answers...

> *What is Resilience? Why is it Important?*
>
> *How do We Balance the Body, Mind, and Spirit? Why is this Important?*
>
> *What is the Energy Body, and How do We Balance it? Why is this Important?*
>
> *What is Mindful Heart Intelligence Reprogramming™? Why is it Important?*
>
> *Why do We Resist Balance? Why do We Have to Create Balance Daily?*
>
> *What is a Wellness Plan? Why is this Important?*

The Art of Daily Resilience and Balance

What is Resilience?

According to the American Psychological Association, Resilience is the process and outcome of successfully adapting to difficult or challenging life experiences, especially through mental, emotional, and behavioral flexibility and adjustment to external and internal demands.

A number of factors contribute to how well people adapt to adversities, predominant among them are:

1. The ways in which individuals view and engage with the world
2. The availability and quality of social resources
3. Specific coping strategies

Psychological research demonstrates that the resources and skills associated with more positive adaptation (i.e., greater resilience) can be cultivated and practiced.[56]

Dr. Amit Sood has given the simplest and best definition of resilience, saying, "It's your ability to withstand adversity and bounce back and grow despite life's downturns."[57]

Why is Resilience Important?

Resilience is important because resilience empowers people to accept and adapt to situations and move forward, without becoming stuck in the experience. Focusing on resilience while reprogramming negative thought patterns and damaging core beliefs guides us to become our own best resource.

It is important to remember that being resilient requires a set of skills that can be developed through time. Developing resilience requires time, effort, and assistance from those around you; you will undoubtedly encounter setbacks along the road. It depends on both internal and environmental factors, including self-esteem and communication abilities, as well as the social support and resources available to you.

Even those who are resilient go through stress, emotional turmoil, and pain. Working through emotional pain and suffering is a sign of resilience. One of the best ways to build resilience is to take care of yourself on a daily basis, by balancing the body, mind, and spirit.

How do we Balance the Body, Mind, and Spirit?

We can balance the body, mind, and spirit in a variety of ways! Exercise, getting out in nature, meditating, eating and sleeping well, taking time to relax, connecting with a higher space, having an appropriate support team in place, et cetera. However, our breath is by far the most effective tool available to release imbalance and create balance.

Awareness Tool:

*The ultimate tool to release tension and activate balance immediately is... **our breath**. RF*

Importance of Our Breath

Our breath is our greatest tool to release stress, tension, pain, negativity, chaos, anxiousness, despair, fear, anger, doubt, and more.

Just as we would reach for a toothbrush as the most efficient tool when cleaning our teeth, we reach for the breath when needing to release tension, stress and pressure from the body, mind, and spirit. Our body is the indicator; much like a turn signal lets others know where we are headed, the body will let us know when it is in duress and uncomfortable. Our job is to learn to recognize these signals and utilize the tools that relieve this duress so we are not suffering needlessly.

The following article from DoYou.com shares simple and very effective ways to relieve stress and create balance.

Simple Ways to Balance Your Mind, Body, and Soul

When we think about health, diet and exercise are typically the first things that come to mind. However, good health isn't just about the physical body. Our mind and body are interconnected and affect each other tremendously.

For example, a stressful situation causing negative thoughts can lead to physical pain or illness. It's important to maintain a healthy balance between your mind, body, and soul by nurturing your whole self, including your physical, mental, emotional, and spiritual needs. There are many things you can do in your daily life to achieve overall wellness.

25 simple ways to begin cultivating a mind-body-soul balance.

1. Read and learn often. Your education shouldn't stop once you're out of school. Open your mind to new possibilities, beliefs, and interests by reading, taking online classes, watching documentaries, and attending workshops.

2. Meditate regularly. Meditation improves memory, attention, mood, immune system function, sleep, and creativity. All it takes is a few minutes a day to start reaping the benefits and you can begin with this free 30-Day Meditation Challenge. Guided meditation is perfect for beginners.

3. Practice yoga. Yoga is amazing for your overall health. It helps you build strength, coordination, and flexibility while calming your mind. It also encompasses the mind-body-soul connection.

4. Avoid sitting for extended periods of time. Try to stand or move around while you work, if possible. Too much sitting is linked to heart disease, diabetes, and a shortened lifespan.

5. Get at least 15 minutes of moderate to fast-paced exercise each day. Live close to work? Walk or ride your bike on nice days. Exercise is important for heart health, physical stamina, and mood.

6. Spend time outside. Now is the perfect time of year for hiking, boating, picnics, outdoor sports, foraging for wild foods, camping, and much more!

7. Add more plant-based foods to your diet. Eating lots of vegetables and fruit can help prevent chronic disease. Shop your local farmer's market for fresh, in-season produce.

8. Get involved in a volunteer organization or activism group. Use your voice or your talents to do some good in the world. We're all connected, and it's incredible to experience that connectedness when we work toward a common goal.

9. Fuel your passions. Set aside some time each day to do what makes your soul happy. Many of us work so much that we forget how great it feels to paint, dance, make music, write, garden, or swim.

10. Listen to music often. And sing along or dance!

11. Be grateful. Take some time each day to write or think about the things you're grateful for, like family, friends, pets, food, shelter, health, or the beauty of nature.

12. Be kind to everyone. This includes yourself!

13. Get enough sleep each night. And remember that you're never too old for naps.

14. Detoxify your beauty routine. Switch to natural products.

15. Get harsh chemical cleaners out of your house. Shop green cleaners or make your own.

16. Find a career path that is meaningful to you. Chase your dreams, not riches.

17. Let go of the little things. If something won't matter tomorrow, don't let it ruin today.

18. Slow down. A little rest and relaxation when you're used to spending lots of time on the go can replenish your mind and body.

19. Stop people pleasing. There's a difference between being kind and being a doormat. If you spend too much time

worrying about what others will think, you'll lose yourself and end up feeling miserable.

20. Cut major sources of stress out of your life. This includes unnecessary spending, clutter, a job you hate, or unhealthy relationships.

21. Avoid gossip and drama. Judging your neighbors and co-workers doesn't make you superior; it just makes you hard to trust.

22. Laugh often. If you take life too seriously, you're going to miss out on a whole lot of good times.

23. Travel and learn about other cultures. Do this as much as you can!

24. Forgive yourself for your past mistakes. Learn from the past, but don't let it destroy you.

25. Opt for natural remedies whenever you can. With the guidance of a holistic health practitioner, herbs, the right foods, and essential oils can be very healing and have fewer dangerous side effects than most pharmaceuticals.[58]

Why is Balancing the Body, Mind, and Spirit Important?

Awareness Tool:

It is extremely important to balance the body, mind, and spirit if we expect to live a fulfilling, happy life. Just like our vehicles, we must maintain, care for, and balance our lives to have the optimum experience. RF

An article from DailyOm gives great insight...

When we learn to let go, more energy flows and less effort is needed.

When we become overwhelmed and things are not going as planned, it is natural to hold tighter to our goals and try to force things to go our way. In the process, we tie ourselves in knots, tensing our shoulders, jaws, and muscles throughout our bodies.

Our mind tells us that this is how to get a firmer grip on a situation that feels out of control, but as we create knots in our bodies we are blocking the flow of our energy, exhausting ourselves by exerting more effort yet accomplishing less. At these times, though it may seem counterintuitive, our higher selves know it's better to let go.

This may not be quite as easy as it sounds. After the relief of our first decision to release, if we allow questions about how to get everything done to start again, the knots will be back before we know it. So, we need to be aware that this is a process to breathe through.

First, we need to let go of our idea of what the perfect outcome should be and allow the intelligence that drives the universe knows better than we do how everything fits together for the highest good. Then we might have to release our imagined consequences and realize that, in most cases, the worst that could happen really isn't that bad. We may need to remember how to relax, first by taking deep breaths, then by meditating, and then perhaps seeking help from a loved one, massage therapist, or energy healer to clear the underlying knots.

We can ease our mental stress by prioritizing what we truly want to accomplish and then delegating the rest to someone who has more enthusiasm for those things. When we relax and let life's energy flow through our minds, bodies, spirits, and lives, we will find that we can accomplish more with less effort and feel good doing it.

We don't have to tie ourselves in knots. Instead, we can let the ribbons of our energy unfurl to gracefully direct us through life's abundant flow. [59]

The following is reprinted from DailyOM – Inspirational thoughts for a happy, healthy, and fulfilling day. Register for free at DailyOM.com. View the article at https://www.dailyom.com/cgi-bin/display/articledisplay.cgi?aid=66429

Awareness Tool:

We maintain our vehicles because we know that if we do not take care of them they can't take care of us. Yet somehow we expect ourselves to operate at peak performance with little to no maintenance. It doesn't even make sense. RF

What is the Energy Body? How do we Balance it?

"*The energy body is* pathways in the body where your energy moves. The energetic body is shaped by the interactive undercurrents of breath, movement, feeling, emotion and intelligence." ~ Michele Crawford, Illinois Extension blog.[60]

According to Marlene Smith, an instructor with EhkartYoga, "It is said that we have 72,000 channels of moving energy through our system. Energy, like water, should be moving to keep it fresh, otherwise it becomes stagnant."[61]

Awareness Tool:

Energy is everywhere, it is part of all things, yet we have forgotten it exists within us and around us. Our energy needs to be balanced and maintained because it affects us at fundamental levels in our body, mind, and spirit. RF

More on energy and the energy body shared by JustBeWell:

It is widely understood that everything is composed of energy and has its own unique pattern of vibration, called frequencies. From an energetic perspective, the human body is made up of different layers of energy, called the "biofield". The frequencies of the biofield can not necessarily be seen by the physical eye thus they are also called subtle energies, however, these frequencies have been measured.

For example, magnetic pulses and electric fields produced by cells and tissues on the surface of the skin can now be detected with the use of technology such as electrocardiograms, electroencephalograms, magnetocardiography, and magnetoencephalography.

The energy of the biofield regulates the biochemical, cellular, and neurological processes of the physical body. This means that any disease you may feel such as back pain, depression, fatigue, or other life challenges are the result of a disruption in the energy body and are ultimately expressed in the physical body.[62]

Awareness Tool:

When we maintain and balance our physical, mental, and spiritual energy, we manifest positive outcomes in our experiences with ourselves and others. RF

You probably have a good idea of how much energy you have every day. People often say that they have a lot of energy or that they could use more. Are you aware of how to effectively care for your energetic body?

A balanced nervous system requires continuous maintenance. Homeostasis is the state of balance in all living things. A healthy body can easily restore equilibrium when brainwaves are engaged in difficult situations. Sometimes a deep psychological impact demands extra support to normalize energy.

*We can balance the energy bod*ies in many ways: meditation, energy healing, exercise, breath work, yoga, music, dancing, singing, drumming, playing instruments, art, gardening, gathering traditional medicines, traditional ceremonies, stretching, balancing chakras, and more.

Awareness Tool:

We can create healthy energy that will result in joy, happiness, and motivation. RF

At Sacred Sol Healing Institute, we educate extensively in understanding the energy system, how it affects our body, mind, and spirit and our daily interactions, within ourselves and in the world around us.

We have developed many formats on understanding the energy body. This particular format is an introduction, so we have kept it brief and concise for simplicity. We are honored to share our presentation below.

Sacred Sol Healing Institute – Understanding the Energy Body

Today we will be working with the chakra system. Chakras exert shared control over our every intention and motivation to action.

As a society, we are aware of three bodies – the physical, spiritual, and emotional bodies. We know we can reach out to health care providers, therapists, and spiritual advisors.

So, what about the energetic body? What is the energetic body? We are made of atoms, neutrons, protons, and electrons. We learned this at a young age in biology, but after this point we don't much think of the energetic body and how it is affected or how it can be maintained.

There are many ways to maintain the energy body. One of the most effective ways is to work with our chakras, or energy centers.

So, what are the chakras?

Energy centers (or chakras): The body contains seven main energy centers. These energy centers are located in the center of the body and run from the crown to the root.

The energy centers collect, absorb, and distribute life energies to our cells. The energy centers are much like spark plugs in a vehicle – they produce and send energy to the meridian channels, which then distribute that energy to the entire body!

This energy is then used by the body to perform actions such as pumping the heart, expanding and contracting the lungs, moving the arms and legs, et cetera. This not only relates to the physical, but also the mental aspect. Our mind has to have energy to make the connections that facilitate the body response.

For example: Our heart needs the energy to pump the blood or we will not survive, just as our mind needs the energy to fire the appropriate connection that sends that signal to the heart to pump the blood! Without this energy being distributed, our mind-body functions would not have the energy to perform the basic tasks we need to survive.

Along with disturbing this vital energy that is necessary for our survival, each energy center is also associated with a particular function in the body, with specific life issues, and the way we handle them, both inside ourselves and in our interactions with the world. Due to external life experiences and personal habits, an energy center can become deficient or excessive, therefore leading to an imbalance.

When blocks accumulate, there is a disruption in the flow of energy. When an illness manifests in a part of the body, there will be a correlated block, or weakness, in one or more of the energy centers. A deficient energy center does not receive appropriate energy, nor does it manifest its energy to the world. When this occurs, there is a sense of being physically and emotionally closed down in that area.

Each energy center (chakra) has a main emotional obstacle and a main emotional benefit. Blockages in the energy centers disrupt the natural energy flow and can present as physical complications, as well as emotional challenges. Just like when a vehicle doesn't receive the appropriate amount of energy, it doesn't run well.

We will work through the 7 Energy Centers (chakras) and their main emotional obstacles — Fear or Anger, Guilt, Shame, Grief, Lies, Illusion and Attachment — learning that for the most part these emotions are fabricated; we no longer have to identity in them.

The pain and lessons have been very real, however, but many of the emotions are a societal fabrication. We have developed false identities and beliefs from these emotional obstacles and learned behavior patterns, leading us to punish ourselves. Without even realizing it, we assume unhealthy identities and begin to compromise ourselves. This in turn promotes unhealthy behavior patterns and habits the for mind, body, and spirit.

The main emotional obstacles in the root chakra are Anger and Fear (fight-or-flight reaction). These emotions are innate and necessary, and even though we don't use them as much as the animal kingdom they are still valid and designed to keep us alive. The main emotional obstacle in the heart chakra is Grief, also innate or hardwired, and seen in the animal kingdom. We forget often, but we are mammals, so turning to the animal kingdom to guide us, we find no judgment or chaos, just wisdom and simplicity.

The other 5 emotional obstacles in our chakras or energy centers are Guilt, Shame, Lies, Illusion, and Attachment. They are human fabrications, learned behavior, and here's why. The chipmunk isn't guilting or shaming the elk because he hasn't made it to the top of the mountain yet; no one is lying to the elk, telling him he's no good because he's not at the top yet; the elk has no illusions that he's not good enough or should be there by now; and no one has any attachment to when, where, or how the elk gets to the top of the mountain!

Now, with that insight, we can move forward with a brief breakdown of each chakra.

A Brief Understanding of the 7 Main Chakras (energy centers) in the Body

Root Chakra: In the root chakra, the main obstacle is Fear or Anger. As we release fear or anger, we find safety and support. This chakra requires trust to find ultimate grounding and security. "How do we trust ourselves?" is a big question! You already literally trust yourself with your life, every time you inhale and exhale – if you didn't trust yourself you would be gasping for air with each breath. There is no bigger measure of trust. The next time you are going through a hard situation, close your eyes, come to your breath and know that whatever you are facing will be okay, because you can and do trust yourself.

Lower Belly Chakra: Within this chakra lies our physical center of gravity and internal energy. In the sacral center, or lower belly, the main obstacle is Guilt. As we release guilt, we find balance. Balance for the world inside of us, as well as the world around us, establishes discernment. **Discernment** is that feeling that helps us decipher right from wrong, so if I have an interaction with my friend and I'm mean, I have that twinge within that says, "Oh, that wasn't very nice." I then go back and apologize and, ideally learn from my behavior and move on! But as a society we instead have learned to manifest guilt and punish ourselves! In essence, it's a generational follow-the-leader. It's no one's fault, but now we are finding other ways, other options.

Solar Plexus Chakra: In this chakra, the main obstacle is Shame. As we release Shame, we find our infinite value and worth. Shame requires self-sabotage. Shame takes away our power, our will. Only we can choose to activate our self-worth. Once we choose to step into our power and are responsible for our actions, we are then able to release unhealthy learned behaviors that have manifested in the form of controlling behavior, self-sacrificing behavior, manipulating behavior and/ or addiction. Embracing the full expression of our power requires balance, response, and kindness, allowing alignment with ultimate Source.

Heart Chakra: The Heart chakra is the other energy center that is innate, because it is hardwired, born within us. The main obstacle in this space is Grief. As we release grief, we find joy. Grief is a natural response to loss. It is the emotional suffering one feels when something or someone the individual loves is taken away. This is seen in all mammals. **The animal kingdom, however, grieves and moves on, as is our nature, but we have adopted unique ways of punishing ourselves in the human race. As a society, we have achieved a remarkably high level of self-destructive behavioral traits. These judgments and egos turn basic emotions into critical, self-loathing thoughts on a regular basis.** We are unable to completely love, be loved or forgive ourselves because we at our core do not believe we are worthy of this love, so we continue the cycle, not realizing the true nature of our dysfunction. Within the balanced and whole Heart space, we are able to find happiness and joy.

Throat Chakra: In the throat chakra, the main obstacle is Lies. As we release Lies, we find truth. Digging deeper into the obstacle of Lies, we find the lies of society – lies that we need to look or act a certain way to be accepted, lies from family, friends or people close to us, and especially lies to ourselves like we aren't good enough, or we don't deserve to be happy. This energy center consists of two parts- the ears that hear the vibration and throat that speaks the vibration. These vibrations can heal or damage. The only way we can remove habits is to reprogram our reactions to responses, and that takes practice. A person's truth will change as they evolve and grow.

Life is constantly changing, situations change so, allow fluidity and compassion for yourself and others. **Vibrations are the essence of all matter, energy, and consciousness; we will always perceive the reality of the vibration we are in.**

3rd-Eye Chakra: In the third-eye chakra the main obstacle is Illusions. As we release Illusions, we find clarity. Life is full of so many Illusions. As we find clarity, we realize that other people's opinions are just that, their opinion, their opinion doesn't define us, nor does our opinion define them. This is the space where we learn to connect with and develop our intuition, our instinct, where we can rely on our inner knowing and wisdom for guidance. Through allowing our true self or "True Identity," we gain clarity of ourselves and the world around us.

Crown Chakra: In the crown chakra the main obstacle is Attachment. As we release Attachment, we find unity. Attachment stems from expectation, judgement, and ego. We've been taught to have Attachment to all things. *Addiction is another definition for Attachment; we are all addicted in some way or another.* We have Attachment to how our day should go, what we look like, how someone should respond, how we should respond, how long something should take, how something should taste, what the temperature should be, how others look, how others live, and on and on. We are all exactly right where we need to be! While this may be hard to understand, as we develop, and grow within the crown energy center, we are able to release the situation and outcome, as it doesn't apply to us.

Our job is to find safety, balance, self-worth, joy, truth, clarity, and unity within ourselves, in all situations, in all things.

Check our store for chakra videos, MHIR Videos, meditations and many more are available in video format in our store. Your Wellness Store: https://sacredsolhealing.com/ your-wellness-store/

Enjoy this Healing Meditation

In this mediation the challenge and gift presented to us is to move beyond the limits of our ego, that inner voice that likes to tell us we are not enough and to keep our guard up at all costs. Sometimes all it takes is a little shift in perspective and crown activation to realize and accept this universal truth, as we realize and accept that everything is interconnected and that we are part of the larger scheme of life, we begin to live with gratitude, faith and trust, rather than with fear and anxiousness.

I will guide us through a deep relaxation technique, evoking a conscious deep sleep, allowing relaxation and expansion of awareness. Activating the relaxation response stabilizes the sympathetic and parasympathetic nervous systems, balancing the left and right hemispheres of the brain, resulting in cell regeneration and repair, as well as decreasing anxiousness and improving overall well-being.

Gently soften the eyes as you read and take three deep cleansing breaths, inhale through the nose, exhale through the mouth, releasing tension throughout the body, relaxing the jaw, become aware of the natural flow of the breath, the rise and fall of the chest.

The body settles into a place of quiet and stillness, with every exhale allow your entire body to fully surrender to the earth, feel the weight of your body release, soften, melt, allow. The ground supports you; your skeletal frame supports you. Feel the freedom in the stillness of the body and mind.

Relax the muscles of the forehead, muscles around the eyes, between the eyes, eyelids, cheekbones, jaw, if you have trouble relaxing the jaw; run your tongue around your teeth in a circle, 3 times in both directions, it sounds weird but totally works, relax the tongue.

Allow the neck to begin to relax, releasing the muscles all the way around. Moving down the back, the spine begins to soften, the ribs in back release.

Slowly softening the shoulders, the biceps, the triceps, the elbows. The forearms release, the wrists soften, any last bit of tension begins to work its way down the hands and gently slowly slips off the fingers to the earth beneath.

The collarbones begin to soften, the chest softens, the torso softens, the internal organs soften, the hips soften. Gently working down the legs, the thighs soften, the hamstrings soften, the shins soften, the calves soften, the ankles soften.

Any last thing that no longer serves begin to work its way down the feet and gently slowly begins to slip off the feet to the earth beneath.

You are whole, You are free
You always have been, You always will be
Here we peel back the layer to access that space
Everything you need is contained within
Pause for a moment..

Slowly begin to draw your attention back into the body, without changing anything, bring your awareness to your body, feel the ground supporting you, feel your skeletal frame supporting you. Bring your awareness to the flow of the breath at the nostrils, the sensation, of the breath. Shift your focus to the space around your body, you are more than your physical body---sense this space--- feel the power of your own presence.

Begin to inhale through the nose: "I am Capable, I am Loved."
Exhale gently out of the mouth: Sending that affirmation flowing through your body, mind, and spirit.

Gently inhale positive white light through the crown (top of the head) gently, exhale through the mouth sending this light through the body, to the feet. 2 more breaths. Slowly begin to bring movement back into the fingers and toes, allow this movement to spread through the rest of the body, arms, legs, begin to awaken, maybe a tall stretch overhead.

Gently inhale bringing the arms to the sky, exhale bringing the hands to the heart center. Place one palm flat over the Heart and the other at the lower belly.

The forgotten Miracle is the body's infinite capacity for change and renewal, we are able to reinvent our body, transforming it from a material object to a dynamic flowing process, every cell is made of awareness & energy.

We'll close today, with 3 deep cleansing breaths. Inhale thru the nose, exhale through the mouth, 2 more times. Inhale bringing in safety, love, and joy, exhale releasing any last thing that no longer serves. 1 more time, Inhale and Exhale.

You are more than enough, every thing you need is contained within. Take your time coming back into the physical space, pause as long as you want, there is no rush. It is a gift to check out in a good way. Thank you so much for sharing this space with me today. Stay safe and be blessed.

Why is Balancing the Energy Body Important?

Balancing the energy body is important because it promotes general health and well-being by ensuring the free flow of life energy (also known as prana or qi) throughout the body.

Awareness Tool:

Energy affects all things. Focused energy becomes power, which can change people, circumstances, and situations worldwide. RF

What is Mindful Heart Intelligence Reprogramming™ (MHIR)?

Sacred Sol Healing Institute educates extensively in understanding the energy system, how it affects our body, mind, and spirit, and our daily interactions within ourselves and in the world around us.

We are honored to share our MHIR Training Tools below.

Mindful Heart Intelligence Reprogramming (MHIR)

Positive Behavior Resilience System.

The MHIR Positive Behavior Resilience System is trademarked and held to nondisclosure standards, acknowledged, and agreed to by all who use this program.

The MHIR System consists of simple life management tools that allow the reprogramming of learned behavior through a heart response, rather than a mind reaction. This training teaches breath-body awareness and recognition of heart-rate variance.

Utilizing the MHIR Action Tools will provide you with the ability to make cognitive decisions in stressful situations; it will build your resilience and capacity to recover from stress. Reducing stress, pain, anxiousness, and despair generates happier and healthier lives.

Through this training we will acquire tools and gain the perspective needed to reprogram learned behavior patterns that are no longer a good fit in our lives. As we navigate through daily challenges, we learn to release judgment and ego for ourselves, as well as others. This allows us to accept ourselves at a fundamental level, embracing our humanity, and revealing our true self, the purest essence that lies within us all.

The MHIR System is created through quantum physics (the energy body), applied mathematics (techniques that lower heart rate) and science-based methodology. Reaction vs response, is identified and validated.

MHIR (pronounced "Mirror") stands for Mindful Heart Intelligence Reprogramming. It is pronounced Mirror because through the MHIR System we are able to see our true self reflecting in the mirror, free of the labels and false identities we might have adopted over time.

Reasons the MHIR System works...

1. Our thoughts, feelings, emotions, and attitudes are just frequencies that we can learn to change.
2. We learn to respond from the heart rather than react from the mind.
3. We discover the value in listening and interpreting our feelings, rather than ignoring or managing them.
4. We are able to reprogram learned behavior patterns because the MHIR System is a tangible source to refer to via the MHIR Card and Chart.

Understanding the Energy Body
The energetic body can be described much like the electrical system in a vehicle – when there are blockages it cannot run at optimal

performance. Our daily lives create these blockages, just as using a vehicle daily without maintenance would take its toll! Today we will learn how to remove these blockages, through breath work and intention – cleansing, balancing, and fine-tuning our electrical system to peak performance. This reduces the stress hormone cortisol, keeps the nervous system in balance, and allows the physical, mental, and spiritual energy bodies to heal.

As a society in general we tend to live in a stressed state much of the time, which activates the flight or fight response and cortisol, the stress hormone. This results in less oxygen, higher heart rate, and blood sugar spikes. The immune system shuts down and the internal organs are put on standby, as all the energy is needed for survival. While this inborn response is valid and useful to keep us alive, it is dangerous to maintain as a daily lifestyle.

Our body cannot always tell the difference between a real and an imagined threat, so what happens to us as we adopt this way of living? Anxiousness, despair, low energy, insomnia, anger, addiction, manipulation, and more.

So, we turn to mindfulness. "Mindfulness protects us, our families and our society. When we are mindful, we can see that by refraining from doing one thing, we can prevent another thing from happening. We arrive at our own unique insight. It is not something imposed on us by an outside authority, it is our choice."[63]

> Our environment has a fundamental impact on our lives.
> What are we choosing to live in? How do we stay aware?

> **Below are 4 Mindful Awareness Tools that will help us to
> stay aware of our environment within and around us!**

#1) MHIR Awareness Tool: 30 Mins, Your Lesson

This knowledge is a good way to decipher whether interactions with others is a lesson for you or a lesson for them. If you are still thinking about a situation or interaction you had with someone 30 minutes after it has happened, it is your lesson, not theirs. While this may be frustrating, it is good knowledge to have. If the mind keeps turning, you know it is for you and not about them. This helps to stop the mind from running away with us and obsessing about interactions we have with others.

#2) MHIR Awareness Tool: Elbows by Your Side

This exercise is designed to give us insight in our interactions with the world and how we feel in situations. This shows us where our emotional, spiritual, and physical balance is and how we can adjust so it's a good fit for our life.

Stand up straight, then stretch your hands all the way out in front of you until you are ready to fall over. Ask yourself, What could I do to become physically more balanced? I could bring the weight back into my heels, I could bring my body upright, I could bring my elbows back a bit, I could keep bringing my elbows back until they are by my sides. Now I am physically balanced!

Each time I make a physical adjustment, that symbolizes an adjustment I can make in my situation to get closer to a balanced outcome.

    a. When my elbows are by my side I am completely balanced and able to give and receive equally and it is the only place my hands will cross at the heart!

    b. If someone needs me to give more (arms and body reach forward) I am not in balance. I'm over-extended. Even though I want to help, it is not a good fit if it puts me out of balance. It is their journey, not mine. (Example: elbows stay still, hands cross and hit forehead).

c. If I take too much the elbows are behind me, I'm still not in balance, because I am receiving more than I am giving. (Example: elbows stay still, hands cross and hit lower abdomen).

#3) MHIR Awareness Tool: Cups of Water

This story is important because it demonstrates how negativity affects our lives. Studies have been done with two cups of water. Identical cups and water are placed in different environments. One is placed in a nurturing environment, and one is placed in a negative environment. After a certain amount of time they pulled both cups of water and examined the molecules of each.

The water that was in the nurturing environment has actually expanded. The molecules are fuller and lighter. The water that was placed in the non-nurturing environment is actually misshapen. This is extremely important because we feel like we've been broken, we've been damaged, like we cannot repair from our negative experiences. YOU ARE NOT BROKEN; YOU HAVE NEVER BEEN BROKEN; YOU WILL NEVER BE BROKEN! Negativity is heavy, it literally weighs down the cells, but once the negativity is removed the cell is able to repair and expand!

Our bodies are over 70% water, so the same thing that happens in those cups of water is happening to us when we are in negative environments. When you feel heavy there is a reason for that, it is real! The good thing is, there are many ways to release that negativity. The MHIR Heart Breath is an efficient simple tool to release negativity and heaviness.

#4) MHIR Awareness Tool: The Heart Breath

This breath work is designed to encourage a resting heart rate.

It is a simple tool you can use to reduce stress, anxiousness and tension. It calms the mind and body, promotes full and complete breathing, increases our oxygen supply, keeps the lungs healthy, releases muscular tension, calms the nervous system, and brings awareness to the present moment.

The mind follows the breath. The slower the breath, the calmer the mind. If we are breathing more than 12-15 times a minute, we are creating stress.

The Heart Breath

To begin this exercise, gently close the eyes. Less outside stimulation allows deeper results. Take 3 deep cleansing breaths. Inhale through the nose, nice long exhale out the mouth, allowing pressure and stress to release. Bring the palms flat, one over the other, at the center of the chest. This is the heart energy center, or chakra.

We place our hands over the heart center, so it knows we are directly speaking to it, for a deeper connection. Extensive studies show that using multiple senses (sight, touch, smell, taste, hearing) allows a deeper cognitive connection and associations to be made with a concept, expanding our learning capacity. We are using sight, touch, and hearing in this exercise.

Visualize positive light at the crown or top of the head. Begin inhaling through the nose, drawing this positive light into the body, then dip the head, exhale that positive light out of the mouth to the heart.

That's all there is to this breath, it's that simple. Continue repeating that same breath pattern.

Inhale through the nose, drawing positive light, then exhale positive light out of the mouth to the heart. Let this positive light spill into the heart, filling the heart like a balloon.

Continue inhaling through the nose, bringing in this light, and exhaling through the mouth, releasing this light into the heart. The heart is beginning to fill with this white light. Relax the muscles between the eyes and around the eyes; the jaw softens. Inhale white light through the crown, exhale to the heart.

The heart is full and is starting to spillover to the inner body. We continue this same breath pattern, always exhaling to the heart; the heart is full and spilling over to the inner body. The inner body is now beginning to fill with this white light. Inhale through the nose, exhale out the mouth to the heart.

The inner body is now full and is beginning to spill to the outer body, building this glowing bubble surrounding us from the inside out. Continue the same breath pattern.

Inhale white light through the nose, exhale this white light to the heart. It flows from the heart to the inner body, to the outer body. Three more breaths, feel this light flow from the inside out, maybe smile. Everything you need is already contained inside of you, what a relief!

Bring the hands down to the lap; the breath comes easy, everything slips away.

We pause here for a few moments, getting to know this space, the more familiar we become with this space, the easier it is to get back to it. Eventually, we begin to live from this space.

Bring your attention back into the physical frame. Notice the support of the ground under you, notice the support of your skeletal frame. You are supported, you are loved, at all times.

Let's take 3 gentle, deep cleansing breaths. Inhale through the nose, exhale through the mouth, allowing anything that no longer serves you to wash through the body and release to the earth as you exhale. Relax the muscles of the forehead, relax the muscles around the eyes and between the eyes, relax the jaw.

Begin to bring movement back into the fingers and toes, noticing the sensations as you awaken into this new frame. When you are ready, slowly and gently begin to open the eyes and come back into this space. No rush, it is powerful to check out in a good way. Take your time.

You can use this Hearth Breath anytime you need, if you are stressed, have anxiousness, sleeplessness, despair, depressive states, anger, or any sort of tension. Many people have been able to reduce medications, always contingent on approval from their medical and mental health practitioners, and are happier and healthier through incorporating this breath work into their daily lives!

The reason it is so effective is because you are aligning with your true self; there is no damage or dysfunction deep at your core. This breath work allows us to peel back the layers and access that space!

We are now ready to move forward with the rest of the MHIR System, using the Card and the Chart.

The MHIR System has many options. You can reprogram negativity that you would like to release from your life, or you can also reprogram something positive you would like to bring into your life!

Sometimes you will only need the Card, other times you will need the Card and the Chart. Another way to use the MHIR System is if you notice a part in your body that is bothering you, for example, your lower abdomen. You can just go straight to the Chart and do the work in that specific area to release the blockages and bring in balance!

It sounds a bit complicated, but once you understand how to use it the whole system can be used in 11 minutes or less!

**Our goal in utilizing the MHIR Card and Chart
is to respond in a balanced, non-judgmental manner
for all involved. Be patient with yourself. It takes
time to learn Response vs. Reaction!**

We will start with the MHIR Card first.

Begin to think of a situation that has upset you; it can be recent or from a long time ago. Following the steps below will help to release anger and trauma, as well as bring in awareness and balance. See the example situation for a deeper understanding.

Learn how to use the MHIR System with our Example Situation

It always seems easier when there is an example to work with!

This example comes from a real learning experience I had with myself and my husband.

A bit of background: I work at rehabilitation treatment centers guiding women's and men's holistic trauma healing groups weekly. This work is at the center of my heart as I had been through many years of pain and addiction.

It was winter here in Oregon, and both of the groups asked me to walk in the Snowflake Parade with them and the recovery float. Even as I relate this story, my eyes fill with gratitude and joy that they asked me to walk with them in this parade proudly through our town.

So, of course I said yes, I would be honored to walk with them and the recovery float at the Snowflake Parade! I was so excited, I raced home to tell my husband! When I got home he was sitting on the couch and looking at paperwork on the coffee table.

I came skidding in soooo excited. I told him how excited and honored I was to have been asked to walk in the Snowflake Parade with my groups and how HUGE this was for me to be able to walk in the parade with the recovery float and the groups that I was now teaching at the treatment center!!!

I asked him if he would attend the parade to support me and my groups!

HE SAID, "NO," AND DIDN'T EVEN LOOK UP FROM THE COFFEE TABLE.

I was devasted. My mouth opened and closed three times, then I literally ran down the hall to my home office where I had the MHIR System. I immediately began to work with this situation and the MHIR Card first.

Mindful Heart Intelligence Reprogramming (MHIR) System

SACRED SOL HEALING INSTITUTE®
MHIR™ Card Action Tool
Response vs. Reaction

1. **MINDFUL**: Non-judgmental awareness of situation. Only the facts!
2. **HEART**: Hands flat over chest. Inhale: Positivity, Exhale: Negativity, 4x.
3. **INTELLIGENCE**: Pause. Is it still significant? No: Go to 4, Yes: Repeat 1-3.
4. **REPROGRAMMING**: Say 3 times. I Am Capable, I Am Loved. Success!

Renee Frye
Trauma Healing Holistic Specialist

Okay here we go....

Example Situation

MHIR™ Card Action Tool

#1. Mindful: Non-Judgmental Awareness of Situation. Only the Facts!
Okay so, non-judgmental awareness of the situation, only the facts...

Me: My husband hates me and won't support me, why doesn't he love me? I can't believe he thinks what I'm doing is not important when it is changing so many lives.

Me: Oh, that's not really the facts, that's just my perception and trauma talking...Crap, I so wanted to be furious with him!

- #1 Success: <u>Me</u>: I asked my husband to go to the parade. He said no. (These are the facts.)

#2. Heart: Hands flat over the chest. Inhale: Positivity, Exhale: Negativity. 4x.

- #2 Success: <u>Me</u>: I brought my shaking hands flat over my chest and inhaled positivity, then exhaled negativity. I did this five times before I stopped shaking and could find a sense of calm.

#3. Intelligence: Pause. Is it still significant? No: Go to 4, Yes: Repeat 1-3.

- #3 Success: <u>Me</u>: I paused after deciphering the facts and the calming breath work, then I asked myself if it was still significant... my answer was no. I COULDN'T BELIEVE THAT THE ANSWER WAS NO!!!!

#4. Reprogramming: Say 3 times. I Am Capable, I Am Loved. Success!

- #4 Success: <u>Me</u>: I finished the instructions on the card. I said out loud three times, "I am Capable, I am Loved."

I could not believe the shift. It was a miracle! I was able to think clearly without anger or sadness. I realized that I had never even asked him why he didn't want to go. I went into a HUGE negative dialogue that was a reflection of my own doubts and past trauma – it had nothing to do with him! Lol, Wow!!!

So, at this point I had two choices: I could ask him why or let it go… hmmm.

I was not good at letting things go without feeling sorry for myself, so I decided to try it out. I never mentioned it to him again. I went to the parade and proudly walked with my groups! We were supported by so many people. It was one of the best nights of my life!!!

There were times throughout the parade that I wished my husband was on the sidelines cheering me on, but it was okay that he wasn't because I was learning that the only person I truly need constant support from is… me!!

I never did find out why he didn't want to go; he never said, I never asked, it was fine! By the way, it WAS nineteen degrees that night – very likely why he didn't want to stand outside for two hours in the evening!

One more important note: it is fine if my partner doesn't want to go to something I am doing. That doesn't mean he doesn't support me. He supports me in so many other ways and shows up for me all the time! If he never showed up and didn't want to engage with me or my life in any way, then at that point I would need to reevaluate our compatibility, and that would be a different scenario.

WOW!!! MIND-BLOWING, RIGHT??? FOR ME TOO!!!

Moving forward, we will use this same situation
to work with the MHIR Chart

After I did the work with MHIR Card I was basically good, but I could feel a bit of heaviness at my heart. So, we will use that for the example MHIR Chart.

You can use this chart in a variety of ways. When working with a difficult situation, you can use the card first and then follow with the chart. To use the chart in this way, refer to the *first row*, identify in your body where you feel the situation, then follow the directions and work *down the correlating column*, finishing with the affirmation.

You can also use the chart to cleanse and balance all of the energy centers (chakras) in the body at any time. Starting at the first energy center, begin working down the column following the directions above the chart. Work through all the columns of the energy centers in order 1-7. Rows 1–5 are the work; everything below that is additional information for the curious at heart.

Our daily experiences affect our energy body; it needs to be cleansed and balanced regularly. General maintenance suggestion would be once a month.

I had felt a tightness in my heart when thinking of the parade situation with my husband. We will work with the heart chakra (or energy center) for the MHIR Chart example.

Example Situation

MHIR Chart Action Tool

Goal: Respond in a balanced, non-judgmental manner for all involved. Be patient with yourself. It takes time to learn Response vs. Reaction!

#1. Where do you feel this situation in your body? Place hand there. Identify Body Location on Chart. Work Down that Column using steps 2-3.

- #1 Success: <u>Me</u>: I felt the situation in my heart, placed my hand there and found the heart column (energy center 4).

#2. Inhale Color, Exhale Obstacle out the mouth. Repeat 3-6 times. Continue until you feel the Weight Lift. Pause, to become familiar with this feeling.

- #2 Success: <u>Me</u>: I inhaled green to my heart and exhaled grief out of my mouth. I repeated five times, until I felt the weight lift; there was less pressure in my chest. I paused so I could become familiar with this lighter feeling.

#3. Inhale Benefit, Exhale out the mouth. Repeat 3-6 times. Continue until you feel Content. Pause, to become familiar with this feeling.

- #3 Success: <u>Me</u>: I inhaled joy to my heart and exhaled gently out of my mouth. I repeated five times, until I felt content. I paused so I could become familiar with this feeling of contentment. The was no huge emotion, just balance.

#4. Say Affirmation 1-3 times. Notice how you feel now. Your response may be quite different. Repeat as needed.

- #4 Success: <u>Me</u>: I said the affirmation three times, "I Love, I Am Loved, I Forgive Myself." Wow, I felt good!

How do you feel after this work? It may be quite different now that we have reprogrammed and released blockages. It doesn't always happen immediately; it can take time to unwind trauma!

End result after working with the chart:
I felt so much better. I felt happy, calm, and peaceful.
I had no judgment or ego for the situation with
my husband. I was just happy to be asked and
to go to the parade. I was more than
enough for myself!!!

This shift changed my life; it can change yours too!
Try out these tools!

MHIR™ Chart Action Tool   MHIR™ Somatic Response Chart   Reprogram Behavior Patterns

1) Where do you feel this situation in your body? Place hand there. Identify Body Location on chart. Work down the column using steps 2-3.
2) Inhale Color; exhale Obstacle out of mouth 3-6 times. Continue until you feel the weight lift. Pause to become familiar with this feeling.
3) Inhale Benefit; exhale out of mouth 3-6 times. Continue until you feel content. Pause to become familiar with this feeling.
4) Say Affirmation 1-3 times. Notice how you feel now. Your response may be quite different. Repeat as needed.

CHAKRAS:	CHAKRA 1	CHAKRA 2	CHAKRA 3	CHAKRA 4	CHAKRA 5	CHAKRA 6	CHAKRA 7
Body Location	Pelvis, Hips, Root	Lower Abdomen	Solar Plexus	Heart	Throat, Ears	Forehead, Temples	Top Of Head
Color	Red	Orange	Yellow	Green	Blue	Purple	White, Iridescent
Obstacle/Block	Fear, Anger, Doubt	Guilt	Shame, Not Enough	Grief, Sadness	Lies	Illusions	Attachment
Benefit/Balance	Secure, Safe, Support	Balance, Freedom	Confidence, Value	Love, Joy	Truth	Clarity	Unity, Connection
Affirmation	I Have, I Am Safe, I Am Supported	I Can Feel, I Am Free To Be Me	I Access My Own Power; I Am Enough	I Love, I Am Loved, I Forgive Myself	I Speak, I Listen To The Inner Sounds	I See, I Rely On My Inner Guidance	I Am You; You Are Me; We Are One
Sound/Element	LAM/Earth	VAM/Water	RAM/Fire	YAM/Air	HAM/Sound	OM/Light	Silent AUM/Thought
Endocrine Gland	Adrenals	Ovaries, Testicles	Pancreas	Thymus	Thyroid	Pineal	Pituitary
Body Part	Eliminatory System, Legs, Feet	Womb, Genitals, Bladder	Digestive System, Muscles	Heart, Lungs, Arms, Hands	Ears, Mouth, Neck, Throat, Shoulders	Eyes	Cerebral Cortex, Nervous System
Food	Meats, Proteins	Liquids	Starches	Leafy Vegetables	Fruits	Iodine Rich Foods	Fasting
Exercise/Pose	Grounding, Mountain	Hip Opener, Low Lunge	Core Work, Twists	Chest Opening, Camel	Open/Close, Cat Cow	Balancing, Tree	Meditate, Savasana
Malfunction	Weight Problems, Constipation	Frigidity, Impotence, Uterine Disorders	Digestive Disorder, Nervousness	Asthma, High Blood Pressure	Colds, Sore Throat, Hearing Problems	Head & Eye Pain, Blind, Nightmares	Depression, Mental Illness, Confusion
Function	Survival, Grounding, Security	Intimacy, Desire, Pleasure	Personal Power, Will, Self-Esteem	Universal Love, Forgive, Compassion	Communicate, Inner Listening	Creative, Intuition, Perception	Understand Unity, Source Connection
Excessive Characteristics	Heavy, Overweight, Monotony, Greed	Overly Emotional, Sex Addiction, Obsessive	Control, Aggressive, Dominate, Scattered	Codependent, Poor Boundaries, Jealous	Excessive Talking, Inability To Listen	Delusions, Hallucinate	Spiritual Addiction, Confused, Dissociate
Deficient Characteristics	Fearful, Restless, Underweight, Spacey	Frigid, Impotent, Rigid, Checked Out	Weak Will & Self-Esteem, Passive	Lonely, Isolated, Critical, No Empathy	Unwilling to Speak, Poor Rhythm, Deaf	Poor Memory, Denial, Uninspired	Limited Beliefs, Materialism, Apathy
Crystal/Stone	Red Garnet, Onyx	Tiger's Eye, Sunstone	Citrine, Yellow Jasper	Rose Quartz, Jade	Lapis, Turquoise	Amethyst, Fluorite	Quartz, Selenite
Goal	Stability, Grounding, Physical Health, Prosperity, Trust	Fluidity, Pleasure, Allows Feelings, Healthy Sexuality	Vitality, Spontaneity, Purpose, Strong Self Image, Esteem & Will	Balance, Empathy, Self-Acceptance, Healthy Interactions	Creative, Diverse, Clear Speaking, Resonance	Psychic Perception, Clear & Accurate Interpretation	Wisdom, Knowledge, Consciousness, Spiritual Connection

Why is Mindful Heart Intelligence Reprogramming (MHIR) Important?

MHIR is important because this system offers us an option that allows the release of blockages, pain, and suffering from the body, mind, and spirit. Trauma from our past experiences, and the blockages that it leaves, affect us in our daily lives. It negatively affects our relationships with the world around us, but especially with the world inside of us.

We cannot live in a balanced and truly happy way until we release trauma and negativity. We are not meant to live with trauma and negativity forever; it comes to us in the way of a lesson. From there we are meant to process our experiences, realize what we can learn from them, and then utilize tools to release the rest back to earth.

Awareness Tool:

"Deconstructing Trauma" does not happen with only one modality. It is a unique experience for each of us. Utilizing physical, mental, and spiritual tools, including professional medical and mental health practitioners, is essential in understanding trauma, and releasing chaos, pain, and negativity. RF

We must make an effort to balance our lives daily or we will begin to adopt this trauma and negativity as our identity and way of life. It will poison us, as well as those around us.

Why do we Resist Balance?

We resist balance because we are addicted to negativity and chaos. When we are stressed the hormone cortisol is released and we get an adrenaline rush. So unknowingly we will continue to create negativity and chaos so we can continue to get our fix.

Many times, we are stuck in a cycle of self-sabotage. We would love for things to change but will not take the action to make that happen. We may stay in the negativity and trauma because we are used to it. Even though it is not good for us, we know what to expect and how to operate in that space, so we stay. It can seem like more of a risk to face the unknown than to stay in a damaging situation.

Choosing to do nothing can cause suffering. We suffer when we have awareness of a negative situation yet choose not to take the necessary action to change the outcome. We have choices. The choices we have may not always be the choices we like, but we always have a choice; even by not choosing, we are choosing to do nothing.

Whatever we are familiar with we will revert to easiest. Luckily, as we have been establishing, we can reprogram our tendencies to seek out negativity and chaos, but this requires action to see a different result.

Awareness Tool:

We are responsible for our own level of stress and have the ability to balance our lives. RF

See our Deconstructing Trauma Program Solutions Toolkit download your complimentary gift.. It combines the tools that have been offered throughout this book all in one convenient reference space, plus some bonus materials.

Why do we Have to Create Balance Daily?

Awareness Tool:

If we do not create daily balance in our environment, it will negatively affect our lives. Balance requires daily effort and action on our part; if we don't participate and create balance in our daily lives, it won't happen. RF

Creating balance daily allows us to maintain a fulfilled positive and happy life. This is up to us; it is not anyone else's responsibility to create balance in our lives. It may take a while to catch up with us, but if we are not creating balance eventually we will experience excessive amounts of stress, sadness, despair, anger, hopelessness, anxiousness, fear, and more.

Awareness Tool:

In a condition of fatigue, there is no hope since there is no energy to inspire and motivate. RF

When we are depressed or exhausted there is **not** a healthy energy flow in our body. We can change this by releasing negative energy and doing activities that bring in positive energy. Examples: yoga, energy healing, traditional ceremonies, singing, dancing, drumming, art, playing instruments, hiking, running, meditation, fishing, skiing, boating, family functions, sports, relaxing, sleeping, etc.

We have the power to change our circumstances.
We can create daily balance through the eight dimensions of wellness.

Identifying the Eight Dimensions of Wellness

Achieving and maintaining wellness means giving our love and attention to all aspects of our life – in other words, balancing them. How do we do this? The first step is to identify these areas, and thanks to the work of Dr. Bill Hettler this is easy to do.

After practicing medicine for decades, Dr. Hettler shifted his focus from treating sickness to creating wellness. In 1976, he co-founded the National Wellness Institute; his model includes six intercon-nected "dimensions": emotional, physical, intellectual, occu-pational, social, and spiritual. As researchers' understanding of wellness evolved, so did the model – they added financial and envi-ronmental dimensions.[64]

Awareness Tool:

Creating balance daily is vital for our physical, mental, and spiritual health. RF

One of the leading substance abuse and mental health advo-cates in the nation is Substance Abuse and Mental Health Ser-vices Administration (SAMHSA).

The Substance Abuse and Mental Health Services Administra-tion (SAMHSA) is the agency within the U.S. Department of Health and Human Services that leads public health efforts to advance the behavioral health of the nation.

SAMHSA's mission is to lead public health and service delivery efforts that promote mental health, prevent substance misuse, and provide treatments and supports to foster recovery while ensuring equitable access and better outcomes.

The Substance Abuse and Mental Health Services Administra-tion has created the following guide to show how we can inte-grate the eight dimensions into our daily lives.[65]

Also see SAMHSA's publication for more detail on the eight dimensions, https://store.samhsa.gov/sites/default/files/d7/priv/sma16-4958.pdf

How Do the Eight Dimensions of Wellness Affect Your Life?

Wellness is a term we all know and use often, but what exactly is it, and what does it mean for a person to be well? According to the Substance Abuse and Mental Health Services Administration (SAMSHA), wellness means overall well-being. It incorporates the mental, emotional, physical, occupational, intellectual, and spiritual aspects of a person's life. Each aspect of wellness can affect the overall quality of life, so it's important to consider all aspects of health. This is especially important for people with mental health and substance use conditions because wellness directly relates to the quality and longevity of your life (1).

The eight dimensions of wellness are emotional, environmental, financial, intellectual, occupational, physical, social, and spiritual. All are very important to someone's overall well-being. In the coming paragraphs, I will explain, in more detail, each dimension and also give you a few ways to make improvements in each dimension.

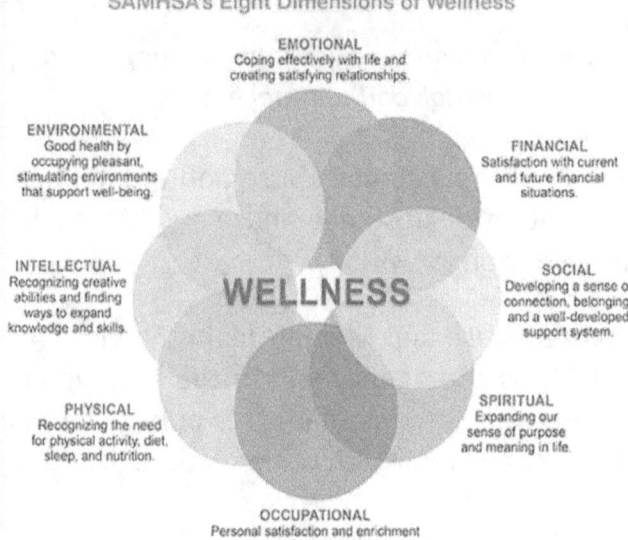

Emotional wellness is the ability to cope effectively with life and create satisfying relationships. Life has a way of throwing us curve balls, which can be very difficult at times. The relationships we create and nurture give us a shoulder to lean on when that curve ball comes our way. One way to improve emotional wellness is to put a positive spin on life situations. Try to cultivate a positive feeling even during negative times throughout your life. This is much easier said than done, but with practice, it can be achieved. You do need to be mentally aware of your emotions, and when a negative feeling arises, attempt to change it into a positive one. Playing a favorite song, chatting with a close friend, or playing with a pet are just a few examples of how to cultivate positive feelings.

Rejection and loss are two major issues that can have a big impact on our emotional well-being. It's important to recognize the feelings you have during times of rejection and loss, but it is also important not to dwell on them or remain in that negative emotional state. Remind yourself how much worth you have by listing the positive attributes you possess in the area of life in which you were rejected, whether it's your work life, dating life, social life, etc. Finding meaning in a loss can be difficult, but it can improve your emotional well-being.

You may want to develop a greater appreciation for those who are still here, reevaluate your values and ideals, or honor what or who has been lost. These are only a few examples of how to find meaning during a time of loss. Emotional wellness doesn't mean avoiding bad or difficult times; rather, it's the ability to cope effectively during them.

Environmental wellness means good health by occupying pleasant, stimulating environments that support well-being. It's important to feel good about where you live, work, play, and wherever else you may spend time. Good health for the planet is also a major part of environmental wellness. Here are a few ways to improve your environmental well-being.

Clean and organize your living space. Then clean and organize your workspace. After these two tasks are done, you should feel a greater sense of comfort and much less anxiety. This is a big boost for your environmental well-being. Now it's time to take a look at the big picture, and that's the planet we live on. Start recycling, use less water, and pick up trash when you come across it. We have to live in this environment, it's important that we do our part to keep it clean.

Financial Wellness is the satisfaction of your current and future financial situations. It's not about how much you make that makes you financially well, but rather, are you satisfied with how much you make? Someone who makes $30,000 a year could be more financially well than someone who makes $100,000 per year. It's a proven fact that those who are financially well are more productive at work. Planning is the key to attaining financial wellness. It's important to plan a budget, set goals, plan a saving strategy, and plan for retirement. These are just a few of the plans that need to be made to have financial wellness in your life. Once the planning is complete, it's time to stick to your plans and put them into action. A savings plan will create financial margins in your life for those unexpected car/house repairs or whatever else might come up that will cost you money. Taking these steps will help guide you to a financially well future.

Intellectual Wellness means recognizing creative abilities and finding ways to expand knowledge and skills. A person who is intellectually well never stops learning. They're thirsty for knowledge and recognize that there is so much more to be learned. There is a certain feeling you get when you achieve something that you have never done before. It's that positive feeling that drives us to become more intellectually well. Some ways to improve your intellectual wellness are to improve time management, remove objectivity, and improve your critical thinking. It's important to make time for reading a book or learning a new hobby. Remove objectivity by keeping an open mind about new ideas, insights, thoughts, expressions, and values. Always question and keep your brain active, and you will begin to improve your intellectual wellness.

Occupational Wellness is the personal satisfaction and enrichment of one's work. You need to feel a sense of contribution and achievement in the work that you do. Developing occupational wellness allows you to communicate your values through whatever work you choose to do. This could be paid work or unpaid work. Here are some ideas on how you can improve your occupational wellness. Start by reflecting on what occupations will leave you feeling gratified. Look into the tasks you enjoy doing. Also, think about what occupational tasks you dislike and find burdensome. Search for volunteer work that you find interesting. Also, set career goals for yourself and constantly work toward achieving those goals. Taking these steps will lead you to have more occupational wellness in your life.

Physical Wellness means recognizing the need for physical activity. Exercise offers many benefits for a person's overall well-being. It improves your chances of living longer and healthier, relieves symptoms of depression and anxiety,improves your mood, and prevents weight gain. Exercise is just one facet of being physically well. Taking care of your physical body by showering, brushing your teeth, and going to the doctor for checkups are all ways to improve your physical wellness. Treating the body with respect will ultimately lead you to be more physically well.

Social Wellness is developing a sense of connection, belonging, and a well-developed support system. This is why spending quality time with close friends is so important. One of the best things you could do to become more socially well is to become a contributing member of your community. You can volunteer, and at the same time, you will meet new people and gain new social skills. Communication is a key factor in becoming socially well. Good communication skills will allow you to resolve problems that you may have with other people that you socialize with on a day-to-day basis. These tips can improve your social wellness.

Spiritual wellness means expanding our sense of purpose and meaning in life. Spiritual wellness is unique to everyone. It's the deepest part of you that gives meaning to your life. Some ways to improve spiritual wellness are to meditate, pray, and listen to affirmations. A spiritually well person is okay with spending time alone and reflecting. It's important to take time to search for the things that provide meaning in your life. It could be your beliefs, values, and morals that give meaning to your life. Make sure that these things guide the decisions you make as you live out your life. As you practice, you will become more spiritually well.

These eight dimensions of wellness all play an important role in our lives. Focus on the areas that you are weak in and start from there; it can seem a bit overwhelming if you try to change everything at once. As you work in the areas where you're struggling the most, you will find that stress in your life will start to decrease and positive feelings will start to increase. You'll begin to produce more feel-good neurotransmitters like dopamine and serotonin. Life will surely be more enjoyable.

Awareness Tool:

We achieve daily balance in our lives by tending to all dimensions of our wellness. RF

In addition to the eight dimensions of wellness, this brief summary on self-management skills is of great value. Much of the information in our Deconstructing Trauma Program redirects our attention to the obvious and simple things we forget about in life.

Here are some quick tips from Elite Trainers on how we can more efficiently tend to these various dimensions of well.

5 Essential Self-Management Skills

Success starts with self-management. In order to be truly pro-ductive, successful and happy, you need to develop the art of self-management.

The world's greatest leaders are experts at self-management. Any position of authority or responsibility for others requires you to be able to manage yourself, before managing others.

If you can master these 5 self-management skills, you'll be on track to a happy and successful life both personally and professionally.

Positivity

You can't fake true positivity. Well, not for long anyway. Positivity must come from the inside in order to be seen on the outside.

The first step to developing a positive outlook is having long-term and short-term goals. Motivate yourself to achieve them with a constant stream of positivity. Refuse to allow negativity into your mind. As you complete your goals, you'll start to see a snowball effect.

Keep your eyes on the end-goal and do something every day to get one step closer. Don't be too hard on yourself, and always acknowledge your successes.

The thing about genuine positivity is that it's infectious. Project your positivity onto those around you and build a positive environment at work and at home.

Self-awareness

Understanding the causes of your own behavior is an incredibly important skill to have. We all know someone who is completely oblivious to their own actions, why they do them and the effect they have on others.

Learn to observe yourself from an objective standpoint. Be your own manager. Ask others to judge you. At first, you may not like what you hear. However, instead of becoming defensive, make a genuine effort to remain neutral.

Self-awareness is a valuable skill that few truly master. It takes years of effort to truly achieve, so start working on it today.

Stress management

Stress has ruined lives. If you're the type to make mountains out of molehills, you're on a fast track to an early coronary and burnout. But don't stress! There's always a solution.

Implementing effective stress techniques will allow you to be proactive in managing the things that pop up in life, rather than reacting in negative ways.

The energy that fuels impulsive behavior, such as angry outbursts, is the same energy that can be harnessed to motivate you to reach further and higher than ever before. When something stresses you out or drives you to anger, *use* that event as motivation.

The key to managing stress effectively is delaying your initial reaction and thinking about an effective way to deal with a situation. Take the time to breathe, think and relax. Only then are you in a good state of mind to make the right choices about how to move forward.

Responsibility

Taking responsibility for your actions is step one towards true self-management. From a very young age, school teaches us to take responsibility for ourselves. However, many of us never master this skill.

Prioritize your most important responsibilities. Take care of tasks as they come up, and most importantly, accept the mistakes you make. There is nothing wrong with making a mistake. There is, however, something wrong with failing to learn from a mistake.

Expanding your responsibilities is exciting. Self-development is all about expanding your horizons, and that comes with responsibility. Take it, own it, and develop yourself. When you slip up (and you *will* slip up), accept it and move forward.

Productivity

The best path toward higher productivity is to manage your down-time. Got a huge load of work to knock out in a single day? Ensure you schedule breaks and enjoy them. If you've got a big year coming up, schedule a weekend where you can relax and unwind.

It's impossible to operate at 100% capacity all of the time. Proper planning and time management are the key to getting the most out of your day.

If you're losing focus or failing to make progress, switch tasks and come back later. Don't bang your head against a wall, it never works out.[66]

<u>*Awareness Tool:*</u>

Success requires self-control. Self-management is a skill that must be learned. It is essential to succeed. RF

In alignment with self-control and self-management, we come to wellness plans and goals.

What is a Wellness Plan?

What Daily Actions are We Taking to Stay Balanced?

A wellness plan is an action-oriented program that provides tools, instructions, and resources to improve one's health and overall well-being. A wellness plan can greatly improve our chances of producing positive change and successful habits.

When we focus on communication skills, social skills, and self-management skills, we are able to strengthen our vulnerabilities by changing triggers and reinforcing a positive environment. We have a better chance of success when we recognize issues, establish a plan, put it into action, and then check in to evaluate where we are at (accountability).

Check out our wellness plan options, we have short and long versions available.

SSHI Wellness Plan

Wellness plans encourage intentional living and guide us in making life changes that reduce stress and illness while improving and maintaining our health and happiness. Intentional living will change your life.

People who are successful at making life changes release limiting beliefs, fears, and low self-esteem. They add positive beliefs, skills, and tools that allow abundance. Our Deconstructing Trauma Program shifts negative thought processes and behaviors. Discover how to reprogram to positive, healthy thoughts and behavior patterns as you learn how to identify triggers and negative learned behavior.

Decide the areas where you would like to make improvements and the areas where no improvements are needed. You are not alone. Start today! Reclaim your life, find freedom and joy, and reprogram to a positive self-belief system. Step into a happier, healthier life.

Write down, visualize, and repeat out loud your specific goals. This activates the plan of action. The moment you decide to shift your mindset from passively wanting change to actively using the tools and knowledge offered, you will see change, success, and your life will change.

List your present situation and specify your goals (what you want to accomplish).

Write down, visualize, and repeat out loud your specific goals.

Keep track of your progress. Review your goals regularly. Seek assistance from others as needed. All information below is a suggestion. Consult with your medical team to create your customized plan.

Why are Wellness Plans Important?

Wellness plans are important because life is challenging! We have to actively participate in creating and bringing positivity into our lives to manifest desired results!

It is like surfing; each wave will require a small, or sometimes large, adjustment of our weight to keep balance. Sometimes we will need more weight on the front foot, sometimes the back foot; other times we will need exactly even pressure. All situations will require a different balance. If we are not aware of this need for adjusting to life's situations, we will have a hard time finding true peace and happiness.

Awareness Tool:

Try finishing this sentence: "I participate in adding balance to my life today by..." RF

Awareness Tool:

Use a wellness plan to create one week of health and balance. From there, use each week to create a month of health and balance. RF

We have created two different wellness plans. Sometimes it is nice to have an in-depth option; other times, simple and easy is the best fit!

Daily Wellness Plan

With this daily wellness chart, we can see a simple break down of standard work and sleep hours. If we work and sleep eight hours we then have 8 hours left in a day, to clean and feed ourselves and our families, let alone sports and grocery shopping etc.

No wonder we are stressed and feel like there is not enough time in a day! The answer to this seemly overwhelming realization is to commit to daily and weekly balance. Each day we will do our standard daily needs and weave additional needs into the mix.

If you are not working the chart would be divided differently.

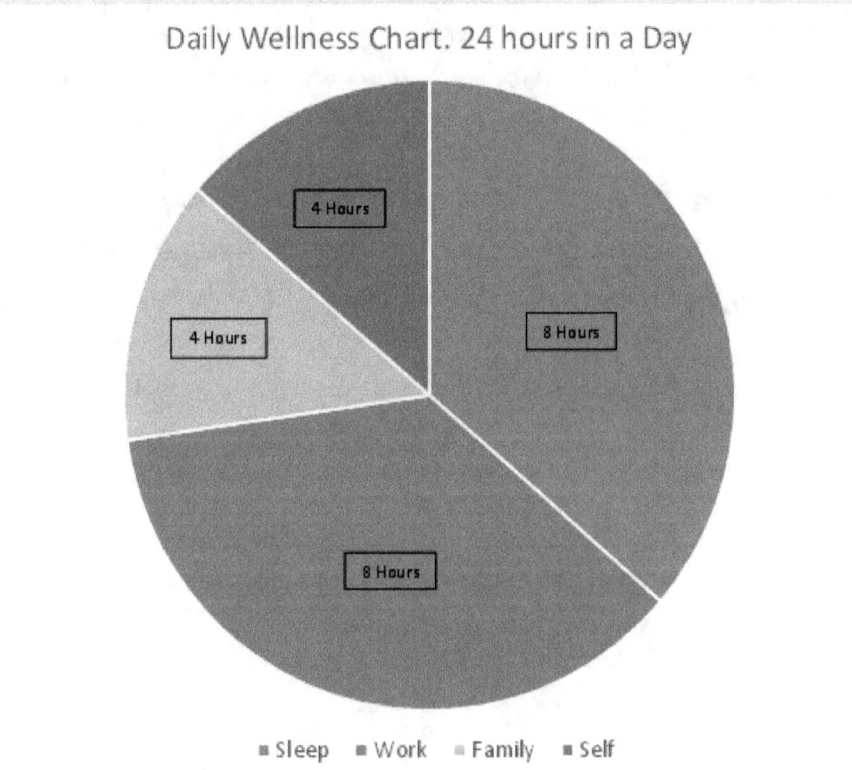

Daily Wellness Chart. 24 hours in a Day

4 Hours

4 Hours

8 Hours

8 Hours

■ Sleep   ■ Work   ■ Family   ■ Self

Daily Wellness Plan

My Health & Wellness Life Balance

Example of Daily Wellness Plan for a 24 hour period. We have modeled the daily wellness plan after the working person with children. Your daily wellness plan will shift according to work and family life. Customize your own plan below. Not every hour has to be used!

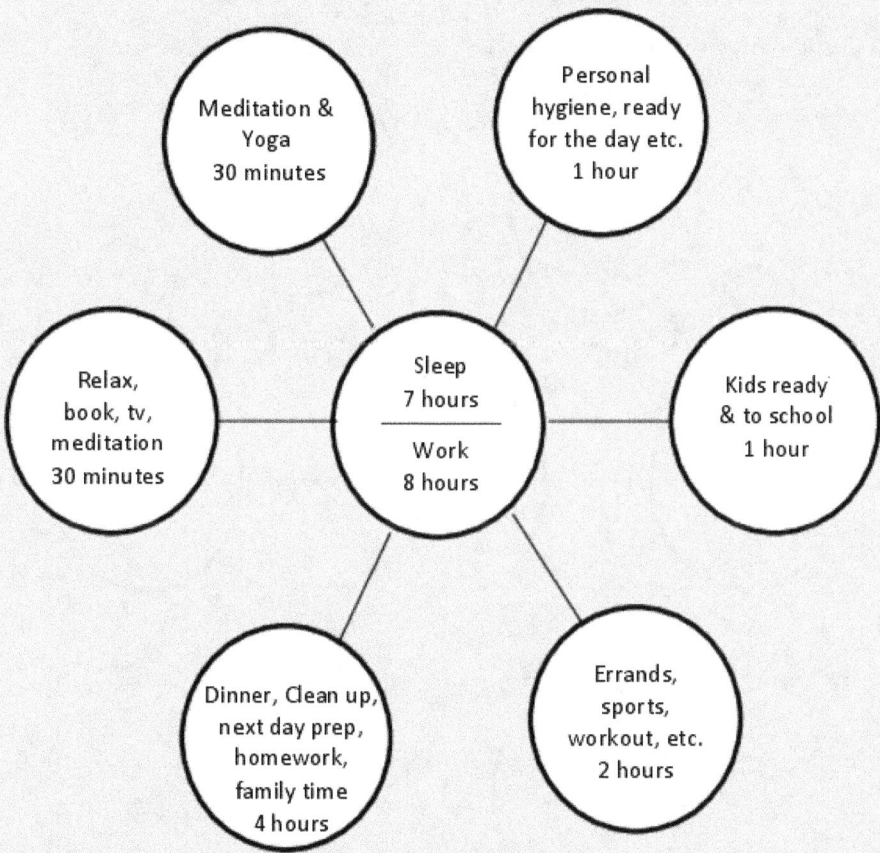

Daily Wellness Plan

My Health & Wellness Life Balance

Endless ways to use these charts! You can put yourself in the middle and use three bubbles as future goals and three as already achieved. You can put a challenge in the middle use bubbles as solutions, and or pros and cons. You can use as a hobby or recovery model, positive hobbies or actions that bring happiness to your life. Use as work/home balance three and three etc.

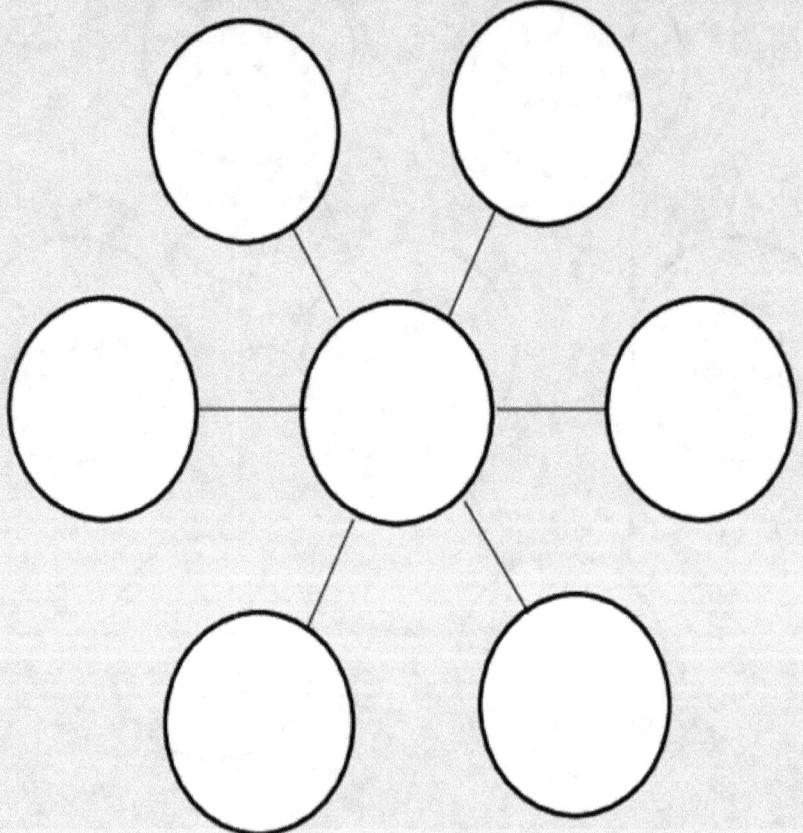

Daily Wellness Plan

My Health & Wellness Life Balance

Endless ways to use these charts! You can put yourself in the middle and use three bubbles as future goals and three as already achieved. You can put a challenge in the middle use bubbles as solutions, and or pros and cons. You can use as a hobby or recovery model, positive hobbies or actions that bring happiness to your life. Use as work/home balance three and three etc.

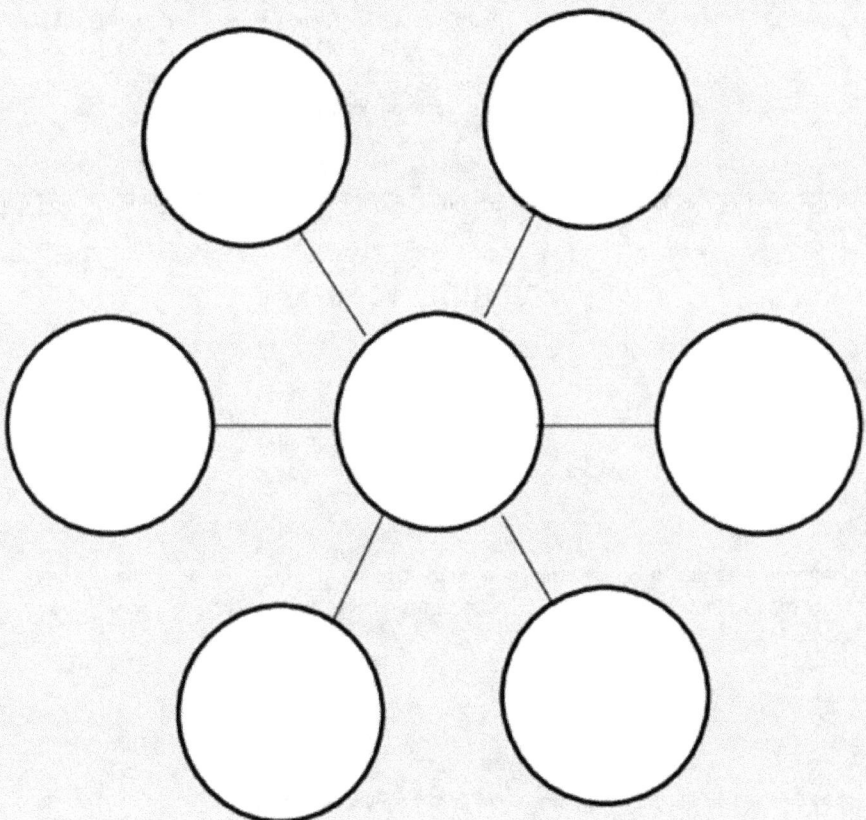

SSHI Wellness Action Plan

Wellness plans encourage intentional living and guide us in making life changes that reduce stress and illness while improving and maintaining our health and happiness. Intentional living will change your life.

People who are successful at making life changes release limiting beliefs, fears, and low self-esteem. They add positive beliefs, skills, and tools that allow abundance. Our Deconstructing Trauma Program shifts negative thought processes and behaviors. Discover how to reprogram to positive, healthy thoughts and behavior patterns as you learn how to identify triggers and negative learned behavior.

Decide the areas you would like to make improvements and the areas that no improvement is needed. You are not alone. Start today! Reclaim your life, find freedom and joy, reprogram to a positive self-belief system. Step into a happier, healthier life.

Begin with this wellness action plan; write down, visualize, and repeat out loud your specific goals. This activates the plan of action. The moment you decide to shift your mindset from passively wanting change to actively using the tools and knowledge offered, you will see change, success, and your life will change.

List your present situation and specify your goals (what you want to accomplish). Write down, visualize, and repeat out loud your specific goals.

Keep track of your progress. Review your goals regularly. Seek assistance from others as needed. All information below is a suggestion. Consult with your medical team to create your customized plan.

Your Wellness Journey

Wellness Action Plan for: _____   *Start date:* _____

(Name)

Professional Work Health: Specific things I want to do to improve my health at my place of work.
Action plan: (Reduce stress, shift work load, stress relief tools, etc....)

Healthy Eating: Specific things I want to do to improve my eating habits.
Action plan: (Reduce chemicals and carbs, eat fruits, vegetables, fiber, protein, healthy fats...)

Weight Goal : Present weight: _____   Weight goal in 3 months:_____
Action plan: (Reduce stress, exercise regularly, healthy diet, consult personal trainer, nutritionist...)

Blood Pressure (BP): Present BP: _____   BP goal in 3 months: _____
Blood Glucose (BG): Present A1C: _____   A1C goal in 3 months: _____
Action plan: (Reduce stress, exercise regularly, healthy diet, reduce sodium, sugar...)

Blood Cholesterol: Present Total cholesterol level: _____   HDL cholesterol level: _____
Present Total cholesterol level: _____   cholesterol level: _____
Action plan: (Add foods that lower LDL, avoid trans fats, reduce saturated fats, consult nutritionist...)

Physical activity: Number of days a week I currently get 30+ min of physical activity _____
Action plan: (Walking, running, swimming, hiking, strength training, biking, yoga, dance...)

Hobbies and Interests: Develop hobbies and activities that bring positivity and joy into my life:
Action plan: (Cooking classes, art, jewelry making, scrapbook, fishing, martial arts...)

Stress and Coping: Ways I can improve mental/emotional health and coping skills:
Action plan: (Heart Breath, stress relief tools, therapist, self-help, meditate, exercise, outdoors,...)

Preventive Wellness: Wellness exams and services to maintain my physical and energetic health:
Action plan: (Trauma healing, energy healing, massage, chiropractor, medical exams...)

Addictive Behaviors: Habits that damage my health and family life, that I would like to change... smoking, alcohol, drugs, gambling, binge eating, anger, arguments, excessive work , excessive screen time, etc.
Action plan: (Replace harmful habits with hobbies and interests, stress relief tools...)

Spiritual and Family Health: Values, virtues, or service to others I would like to incorporate into my life that would provide meaning, purpose, peace, and enrichment to my life and to others.
Action plan: (Activities with family, volunteer in community, attend nurturing services and meetings..)

Partner Health: Partner relationship Care. Daily Happiness. Positivity. Joy.
Action Plan: (Date night, see a movie, board games, vacation, alone time together...)

Personal Care: Personal Care, Daily Happiness. Positivity. Joy.
Action Plan: (Time for yourself, take a class, pedicure, haircut, bath, massage, energy healing...)

Empowerment Questions:

Who am I? _____   Who do I want to be? _____   Where do I want to go?_____

Do I accept me? _____ 3 things I like about me _____ 3 things I would I like to change _____

Are any of the following behaviors familiar? For more tools go to, www.sacredsolhealing.com

Is this familiar: Hopeless about my circumstances never changing, others create my problems and I am powerless to change it; life is against me, stuck in life with a negative attitude, frustrated and angry, hurt when I believe loved ones don't care, resentful of people who seem happy and successful; I am exhausted, physically sick, in depressive states, anxious, resentful, and unfulfilled much of the time.

Action plan: (explore underlying causes of symptoms, work on self-compassion, identify personal needs and goals, create a plan to achieve goals, explore reasons behind feelings of powerlessness, therapist...)

Is this familiar: I do things for people even though I don't feel appreciated; I often try to do too much, the people I spend time with make me feel bad about myself, I consistently feel dissatisfied in my job or relationships; all I do is take care of partners who do little to meet my needs; nothing I ever do is right, I am exhausted, physically sick, in depressive states, anxious, resentful, and unfulfilled much of the time.

Action plan: (avoid passive-aggressive behavior, express emotions, especially those of frustration and resentment, keep negative feelings from building up, set boundaries, time for personal care, therapist...)

Is this familiar: I am always trying to please people; people run over me and don't respect me; I take care of as many people as possible; I don't think very highly of myself; I get upset and take situations personally; it is a challenge to communicate my needs; if I am not taking care of people I feel lost and unaccomplished; I am exhausted, physically sick, in depressive states, anxious, resentful, and unfulfilled much of the time.

Action plan: (set boundaries, listen with empathy, but stop there, practice polite refusals, time for personal care, therapist. **Ask yourself:** 1.Why am I doing this 2. Do I want to or have to? 3. Will this drain any of my resources? 4. Will I still have energy to meet my own needs?...)

Ultimate goal: To love yourself fully and completely. This doesn't mean we become perfect; it means we are able to face our challenges in grace and love. We learn from where we've been and choose to move forward in a different way. We release ego, judgment, guilt, shame, and fear; this is not who we are, just where we've been. We are not our trauma; we are not our pain; we are not our actions. Our actions and behaviors can shift and change as we learn. We move forward in discernment, knowing right from wrong. As we shift our perception, our perspective will change. When we are able to view ourselves in a positive light, the rest of the world around us shifts to mirror that positive vibration. You are the miracle you've been looking for. It starts with you. Reprogram to a Positive Self-Belief System. You are not alone. Everything you need is already inside of you. "Heal Ourselves, Heal the World."

Commitment: INTENTIONAL LIVING WILL CHANGE MY LIFE. I CHOOSE to implement these wellness goals to the best of my ability. It is my choice to change my current situation. I do not expect others to be responsible for my happiness or my choices.

_____   _____   _____
(Signature)   (Date)   (Optional support signature)

Chapter 7 Summary/
Key Takeaways

What is Resilience? Why is it Important?

- *Resilience is* both the process and the result of being able to deal with hard or challenging things in life. This is done by being flexible mentally, emotionally, and behaviorally, and adjusting to both outside and inside demands. *Resilience is important* because resilience empowers people to accept and adapt to situations and move forward, reprogramming negative thought patterns and damaging core beliefs. Important to remember is that being resilient requires a set of skills that can be developed through time. Developing resilience requires time, effort, and assistance from those around you; you will undoubtedly encounter setbacks along the road. It depends on both internal and environmental factors, including self-esteem and communication abilities, as well as the social support and resources available to you).

How do We Balance the Body, Mind, and Spirit? Why is this Important?

- *We can balance the body, mind, and spirit* in a variety of ways! Exercise, getting out in nature, meditating, eating and sleeping well, taking time to relax, connecting with a higher space, et cetera. The ultimate tool to release tension and activate balance immediately is our breath. Our breath is one of the greatest tools to release stress, tension, pain, negativity, chaos, anxiousness, depressive states, fear, anger, doubt, and more. *It is extremely important to balance the body, mind, and spirit* if we expect to live a fulfilling, happy life. Just like our vehicles, we must maintain, care for, and balance our lives to have the optimum experience.

What is the Energy Body, and how do we Balance it? Why is this Important?

- *The energy body is* pathways in the body where your energy moves. The energy field controls bodily functions, including those that are biochemical, cellular, and neurological. Therefore, any illness you experience, including pain, grief, fatigue, or other problems with life, is caused by an imbalance in your energy body and is ultimately manifested in your physical form. Energy, like water, should be moving to keep it healthy; otherwise, it becomes stagnant.

- *We can balance the energy body* in many ways – meditation, energy healing, exercise, breath work, yoga, music, art, stretching, balancing chakras, and more. *Balancing the energy body is important* because it ensures life energy flow throughout the body, promoting health and well-being. Mental, emotional, and physical sickness come from energy blockages. By clearing obstructions and optimizing energy flow, you optimize body, mind, and spirit function.

What is Mindful Heart Intelligence Reprogramming (MHIR)? Why is it Important?

- *The MHIR Positive Behavior Resilience System consists* of simple life management tools that allow the reprogramming of learned behavior through a heart response, rather than a mind reaction. This training teaches breath-body awareness and recognition of heart-rate variance. MHIR stands for Mindful Heart Intelligence Reprogramming. *MHIR is important* because this system offers us options that allow the release of blockages, pain, and suffering from the body, mind, and spirit. Trauma from our past experiences, and the blockages that it leaves, affect us in our daily lives. We cannot live in a balanced and truly happy way until we release trauma and negativity.

Why do We Resist Balance? Why do We Have to Create Balance Daily?

- *We resist balance* because we are addicted to negativity and chaos. When we are stressed the hormone cortisol is released and we get an adrenaline rush. So, unknowingly, we will continue to create negativity and chaos so we can continue to get our fix. *We have to create balance daily* so we can maintain positivity and a happy fulfilled life. This is up to us; it is not anyone else's responsibility to create balance in our lives. If we do not create daily balance in our environment it will negatively affect our lives. Balance requires daily effort and action on our part. If we don't participate and create balance in our daily lives, it won't happen.

What is a Wellness Plan? Why is this Important?

- *A wellness plan is* a program that offers tools, guidelines, and resources to boost health and well-being. A wellness plan can greatly improve our chances of producing positive change and successful habits. When we focus on communication skills, social skills, and self-management skills, we are able to strengthen our vulnerabilities by changing triggers and reinforcing a positive environment. We have a better chance of success when we recognize issues, establish a plan, put it into action, and then check in to evaluate where we are at (accountability). *Wellness plans are important* because life is challenging! We have to actively participate in creating and bringing positivity into our lives to manifest desired results!

Daily Resilience and Balance is so powerful! Are you ready to continue? Here we are, the finale... You made it!!! Enjoy the Conclusion.

THE COLLECTIVE UNDERSTANDING

The Whole Picture, The Collective Understanding, Identifies Our Daily Struggle.

We Are Able To Understand The Generational Dysfunctional Follow-The-Leader.

It's Okay To Not Be Okay...We Have To Be Real To Heal...No One Else Can Do This For You.

The Collective Understanding Allows Us to Support Ourselves and Others Without Judgment or Ego.

What is the Collective Understanding?

The Collective Understanding allows us to arrive at a place of observation and acceptance for ourselves and others, without judgment or ego. In this way, we can understand why we behave the way we do and take the action steps required to "Deconstruct Trauma, Release Chaos, Pain, and Negativity."

- Where is our focus? Are we living in a truthful, authentic way?
- Where are we putting our energy? How do we spend our time?
- Are we busy feeding the chaos, triggers, and situations that we are supposed to learn from?
- Are we finding excuses to not honor what we know is right?
- What unconscious patterns or behaviors can we begin to see clearly?
- Do our thoughts, words, and body language reflect kindness and compassion for all?
- Do we really want change, or are we more comfortable in the dysfunction?
- Are we taking accountability and responsibility for our actions and choices?
- What are our goals? Do we know? How do we become aware?

These are all tough questions, but the answers that come are okay. We are extremely resistant to change because we have learned to identify ourselves in our trauma. Occasional doubt will be part of our lives. We can learn to manage our doubts, grow, and evolve from our experiences. One of the greatest skills we can learn is observing. Observing ourselves and others without judgment or ego requires awareness. We learn by making mistakes. We are not perfect; if we were perfect, we wouldn't need to be here; this is the human experience. We are here to learn.

We begin to understand that we are not defined by our mistakes, our trauma, our pain, or our suffering. It has definitely had an impact on us and others in our lives, but it does not define who we are. Just as the storm comes for the rain to manifest, the storm comes into our lives to bring about the change we need. If we were never uncomfortable, we would never evolve. These challenges come to us to teach us what is a good fit and what is not a good fit in our lives. We can change our thoughts, our behaviors, our choices, our actions, and our habits.

Awareness Tool:

We learn that everything is temporary; it's okay to be uncomfortable, and it's okay to not be okay. The key is to let it pass, and if we seem to be stuck in it, we can take action to change that! RF

Negativity and chaos can push us to a point of extreme discomfort, but in small doses, they can also serve a healthy purpose. If used in the appropriate way, as a guide or lesson, negativity and chaos can push us to the point of positive change.

The reason inappropriate behaviors are hard to change is because they are useful; they generally help us in some way. Negative environments increase these behaviors. As we begin to recognize negative patterns in our lives, we are able to unwind and heal the trauma that lies underneath the negativity. Negativity is learned behavior; we are trying to protect ourselves. When we begin to release the negativity and see what's underneath, we are able to resolve that pain and heal.

A trauma trigger is activated when we respond in aggressive, or passively aggressive, negative ways. We most likely feel unsafe, so we are lashing out in fight-or-flight in an attempt to keep ourselves safe. We are able to access a calm, balanced brain by practicing self-awareness and self-acceptance. Trauma-informed and trauma-responsive approaches allow us to explore ourselves safely and honestly. Within each challenging situation, our goal can be to learn, resolve, and move forward, so we are not repeating the same toxic cycle over and over and over. We can learn from our mistakes to create safe, healthy, and appropriate environments.

Awareness Tool:

We don't have to act on our impulses; we can observe them, discover where they come from, and allow them to inspire us to change. When we resolve the trauma surrounding them, we gain balance and peace. RF

We can "Deconstruct Trauma" through awareness and the reprogramming of negative habits. When we are stressed or unhappy, our bodies produce chemicals that are addictive and harmful. On the other hand, when we are happy and empowered, our bodies produce chemicals that make us feel good and healthy. We can release our addiction to negativity and chaos by learning from the lessons when they come and by keeping our focus on happiness and joy. Whatever we are most familiar with, we will come back to easier. When we shift our familiarity to positivity, we are able to get back to positivity easier. This creates safety and balance in all situations, even uncomfortable ones.

By applying mindfulness and trauma-responsive skills to our daily lives, we are able to live in a positive, healthy, and holistic way. Through this space, we allow the busy mind to rest easy and step into the intelligence of the heart; in this way, we release addictions, pain, trauma, and suffering. Along with growth and healing, we must leave time for integration, relaxation, and connection. Integration allows the situation, feelings, and thoughts to settle and diffuse; it may seem like we are doing nothing, but just being... is a necessary part of the process.

Awareness Tool:

How many times have we pushed through something even though all the signs told us not to, and then we were surprised when we ended up with a bad result? RF

Allow time for integration; allow time for things to settle. It's like baking a cake that needs to cook for thirty-five minutes. If we take it out at thirteen minutes, it's not done; we will not have the desired result.

Awareness Tool:

Instant gratification does not always create the desired result. Being patient with ourselves and others is one of the greatest tools of all. RF

The Deconstructing Trauma Program empowers us to change our perception—other people are not necessarily trying to harm us; it's not all about us. They are reacting the way they are because of their own blockages, their own triggers, their own issues, and their own trauma.

Awareness Tool:

We don't have to take everything so personally. We can step back and observe. It's not always about us! What a relief! RF

When we begin to give ourselves permission to feel, along with the appropriate tools to process our feelings and heal our trauma, it can change our lives. We do not have to live in certain ways because someone else thinks we should. If they do not approve of us, it is okay; we do not need anyone else's permission or approval; we only need our own. Someone's opinion is just that: their opinion. It doesn't define us, just as our opinion doesn't define anyone else. It's just an opinion.

Awareness Tool:

Our love for others does not need to compromise our safety or our relationship with ourselves. If it does, we need to readjust and find balance. It is inappropriate to compromise one thing to have another thing grow. RF

We all live with our own version of perception. People can create false realities about events that occur. For example, one person may have been completely traumatized and compromised by a shared negative, traumatic event, while the other person created an adventure and likes to reminisce. The person who downplays the event creates a false reality so they can live with what has transpired. We cannot control or force someone to see something they are not ready to see. It is their journey, and it is not appropriate for us to live it for them. However, it is also not appropriate for us to compromise ourselves through this process. If someone asked us to eat poison, we would not take it, no matter who was offering it. We are responsible for re-establishing the relationships in our lives to reflect safety and balance for ourselves.

So, what does re-establishing relationships look like? It might go from the extreme of not being able to have any sort of relationship with someone to less drastic adjustments, such as spending less time together and being more of an observer in the relationship, or being there to listen and support but not being directly involved in offering advice or sharing information.

We may feel like someone is not participating correctly in the relationship they have with us. For example, "They wouldn't treat me the way they do if they really loved me," or "They are my parents; they should take care of me and be kind."

We perceive that they are not doing what they should because they aren't giving us what we need. While this train of thought is understandable, it is not balanced or trauma-informed. Most likely, they cannot give us what we need because their own needs have not been met; they do not have the skills or tools to look past their own trauma to meet their own needs, let alone the needs of others.

Awareness Tool:

Someone may be giving their 150%. It may not be enough for us, and nowhere near our 150%, and that's okay. It doesn't

mean they are bad or that we are bad. It just means they have
no more to give; we don't have to take it personally. RF

This is frustrating but valuable information. The reason we don't receive what we need from others is not because we aren't good enough or they aren't good enough. It's because we can only give what is available. If we have not resolved our trauma, our availability to give will be greatly diminished. Therefore, we learn to adjust our relationships according to what is safe or unsafe for ourselves. We learn to be accountable for our thoughts, feelings, emotions, actions, and choices. We get to pick how we show up in the world.

Through challenging life experiences, we are meant to learn and evolve. We do not have to suffer to surrender to the lesson; we can surrender the suffering.

Awareness Tool:

It's a conscious effort to not suffer, as we are conditioned
to normalize suffering.

Suffering and negativity have become part of our lives. We have the opportunity to change these habits. We are all responsible for our own level of stress. We are not the suffering or the lesson. Discomfort can lead to growth. We don't have to suffer to heal.

Our body holds infinite wisdom and knowledge. Once we begin to unwind and understand what the body needs, we can heal in the most amazing ways. Once the physical body begins to heal, it opens pathways to healing the mind and the spirit.

Our value and worth are beyond measure. No person or thing can validate our value and worth because it already is. Just as the mountain is already a mountain, it does not need to be validated. Just as an elk is already an elk, it does not need someone to value its strength and endurance because it already is. You already are.

Awareness Tool:

Each one of us has greatness inside. We can be extraordinary. The only way we can be truly happy is if we live in our own trauma-informed and trauma-responsive truth. RF

Each one of us has been created with infinite value and infinite worth. We are love, we are light, we are grace. This is who we have always been, who we are, and who we will always be.

You are the miracle you've been looking for.

Awareness Tool:

Each one of us has greatness inside. We can be extraordinary. The only way we can be truly happy is if we live in our own trauma-informed and trauma-responsive truth. RF

You are the miracle you've been looking for.

ACKNOWLEDGMENTS

Wokhlew
We use this word as a medicine version of thank you.
It's when thank you just simply isn't enough.

I give thanks to all who have touched my life. Through all of our interactions we are presented with the gift of learning and evolving if we are open to it.

Each interaction I have ever had has brought me to this space today. Without each of you the Deconstructing Trauma Program would not have been created.

Wokhlew to my handsome husband and my beautiful Fancy Face.

I am eternally grateful. You both have been with me through the addiction, pain, suffering and dysfunction, and still stand next to me in a good way, supporting my journey and embracing me through my evolvement as I stepped into my medicine. I am able to now show the world who I was always meant to be. Wokhlew!

Wokhlew to my family and friends in Oregon and in California. Each of you is so dear and close to my heart. Your support has kept me walking in a good way and has given me much so much strength.

Wokhlew to the two most influential teachers in my life, where the world of traditional Native American medicine and energy healing intertwine.

Wokhlew to all who are remembering, learning, and living in the old ways. We give thanks to the water, to our ceremonies, to the tree, to the mineral nation, plant and tree nation, human nation, and the animal nation. Without you I would not exist.

Wokhlew soone'y yôotva
Thank you, we pray, thank you

Deconstructing Trauma

TOOLKIT

Release Chaos, Pain, and Negativity

Renee Frye

Deconstructing Trauma Toolkit

Release Chaos, Pain, and Negativity. Discover the Missing Peace.

Our Deconstructing Trauma Program Solution Toolkit combines the tools and techniques that have been offered throughout our book, all in one convenient reference space. Many additional tools that are not offered in the book have also been included in the toolkit. Please visit deconstructing-trauma.com to access your complimentary bonus gift.

The Deconstructing Trauma Program at Sacred Sol Healing Institute includes the resources and knowledge gained during at least forty Deconstructing Trauma Healing sessions, valued at over $5800. We have compiled the contents of those sessions into our guidebook, Deconstructing Trauma, in an effort to solve barriers to access and complete our mission. Our mission is to solve barriers to access by providing trauma-responsive healing resources worldwide.

Thank you for purchasing Deconstructing Trauma™. We can Deconstruct Trauma by shifting unhealthy, rigid perspectives and negative behavior patterns. Unbiased behavior exploration allows us to identify and modify negative behaviors and damaging core beliefs. Awareness of our thoughts and actions, along with simple positive mindful behavior modification techniques, can assist us in reprogramming negative patterns. Through this process, we Deconstruct Trauma.

Our programs offer new solutions as well as practical, life-changing resilience tools. Our exclusive Deconstructing Trauma™ Program has created superior results and positive, lasting change for thousands of people. This approach can shift negative thought processes and behaviors by releasing trauma and blockages deep within the mind-body connection.

This information allows us to release the preconceived notions and stigmas of society. Through this space we learn that we don't have to be afraid of what we see in the mirror. Shortcomings or faults that we experience through our interactions with ourselves, and others are opportunities to learn and grow. Our mistakes and lessons don't have to define us, they are not who we are.

Learn how to reprogram negative chaotic patterns that have occurred from trauma in your life. Discover how to love yourself fully and completely. We are all looking to be loved and accepted.

As we "Deconstruct Trauma, we Release Chaos, Pain, and Negativity." Discover the Missing Peace.

Note: The author, Renee Frye is a Trauma-Healing Holistic Specialist and the owner and founder of Sacred Sol Healing Institute®. She provides mental wellness and substance abuse recovery support resources through her deconstructing trauma program and indigenous clearing and trauma healing. She is, first and foremost, an indigenous traditional healer; her modalities are all holistic and deeply rooted in Native American teachings.

Notice: Each person's experience will be different because we are all unique. We are in no way diminishing or condoning past trauma. This is simply a different perspective, with unique opportunities to deconstruct trauma. If you are working on healing trauma, please be sure to establish a professional medical and mental health support team to guide you through that process.

We have been extremely diligent in the creation of this material. However, there is always the possibility of a missed mistake in grammar or punctuation. To that end, I pass along a teaching.

When we bead, we are taught to always add an off-color bead to our work for the following two reasons: One, we add the off-color bead to note that we are human, and mistakes will be made because they are part of life; this is how we learn. This keeps us humble and open to learning. Second, the off-color bead is a signature. We use the same color bead in all our work, and people will recognize our work and our medicine in that way.

Pay special attention to the awareness tool and mindful behavior modification techniques throughout the book. They are also gathered together at the end of this book into a simple reference resource, called the Deconstructing Trauma Toolkit, also available to download in full-size color pdf; see the next page for information. You can easily access these tools as you need them. When you are having a tough time, check out the toolkit to see what awareness tools and mindful behavior modification tools will be the best fit for your current challenge.

You can start using this information immediately by applying these techniques and tools in your daily life. Combine the Deconstructing Trauma guidebook with our interactive curriculum workbooks at https://sacredsolhealing.com/wellness-store/. The Deconstructing Trauma interactive workbook is available in two versions: the Substance Abuse Recovery Edition and the Personal Social Development Edition.

BONUS! Download our full-size, color pdf, "Deconstructing Trauma Toolkit," at https://deconstructingtrauma.com/. This is a complimentary gift for you. Our Deconstructing Trauma Toolkit combines all the tools that have been offered throughout the Deconstructing Trauma Guidebook in one convenient reference space, plus bonus material.

As we heal ourselves, the world around us begins to heal.

Embodying Grace

Grace is what emerges from the struggle... Grace is the courage to face the uncomfortable

Grace is our true raw self exposed. Not only in spite of but because of our flaws, this is how we learn. Grace allows us to take our struggles, our trials, our lessons and turn them into wisdom.

Through this Grace, we know we are not our trauma, we are not our suffering, we learn our lessons and move on. Grace allows us to separate negative feelings, triggers, and experiences from our identity.

Grace knows the struggle is real but allows us to release the struggle. We are not the struggle, we are not the pain, we are not the suffering. We are not alone.

Grace is humility in action; humility is not shame.

Being humble takes courage, strength, balance, and Grace.

Grace allows us to support and love others without controlling, manipulating, or running their lives.

Grace allows us to evolve from our trauma.

Grace allows us to let others walk their own journey, without rushing in fixing, saving, and taking away their opportunity for lessons and growth.

Grace allows us to trust others to handle their own journey, not in the way we see fit but in the way that is best served for them. They will learn their lesson... or they won't; this is not up to us. It is our responsibility to be mindful and care for ourselves by removing ourselves from unhealthy situations. It is not our responsibility to change anyone else or make them see the light.

Grace allows us to release this to a higher space, a higher presence. In this way, we learn not to take situations personally.

Grace tells us it's not always about us...What a relief!

Grace allows us to fully and completely love and accept ourselves at the most basic fundamental level.

Grace is our true self realized. Our true self is Love, Light, and Grace.

Grace Embodied...Is You.

Renee Spiritflyer Frye 2022

AN AUTOBIOGRAPHY IN FIVE CHAPTERS

Chapter 1

I walk down the street.
There is a deep hole in the sidewalk.
I fall in.
I am lost...I am helpless.
It isn't my fault.
It takes forever to find a way out.

Chapter 2

I walk down the same street.
There is a deep hole in the sidewalk.
I pretend I don't see it.
I fall in, again.
I can't believe I am in this same place.
But it isn't my fault.
It still takes a long time to get out.

Chapter 3

I walk down the same street.
There is a deep hole in the sidewalk.
I see it is there.
I fall in...it's a habit...
But, my eyes are open.
I know where I am.
It is my fault.
I get out immediately.

Chapter 4

I walk down the same street.
There is a deep hole in the sidewalk.
I walk around it.

Chapter 5

I walk down a different street.

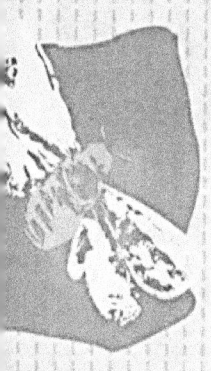

-Anonymous

YOU ARE WHOLE YOU ARE FREE

YOU ALWAYS HAVE BEEN

YOU ALWAYS WILL BE

HERE WE PEEL BACK THE LAYERS

TO ACCESS THAT SPACE

EVERYTHING YOU NEED IS

CONTAINED WITHIN

What Causes Conflict in Your Life

Anger · Neglect · Mental Abuse · Physical Abuse · Alcohol

Drugs · Criticism · Sex · Relationships · Arguing · Anxiety

Victim · Hate · Co-Dependence · Annoyances · Irritable

Addiction · Damaging Core Beliefs · Gambling · Death · Food · DHS

Lack of Self-Respect · Lies · Sexual Assault · Lack of Self-Worth

Spiritual Abuse · Abandonment · Child Abuse · Environment

Bullying · Dissociation · Belittling · Shame · Not Being Forgiven

Pride · Poor Decision-Making · Downgrading · Comparing

Resentment · Self-Blame · Ego · Lack Of Confidence · Suicide

Righteous Religion · People Pleasing · Recklessness · Labeling

No Self-Love · Depression · Lack of Approval · Boredom

Isolation · Self-Medicating · Lack of Respect · Loneliness · Spite

Lack of Responsibility · Wrath · Vengeance · Jealousy · Greed

Perfectionist · Excuses · Envy · Rage · Selfishness · Judging

Adopting Others' Opinions · Cheating · Assumptions · Bills

Self-Sabotage · Meddling · Guilt Frustration · Family · Finances

Negligence · Disappointment · Lack of Work · False Identity

Bad Choices · Assumptions · Disease · Suffering · Trauma

Negativity weighs heavy on us. If each one of these words weighed
5 pounds it would be over 400 pounds...way too much to carry.
That weight transfers to our body, mind, and sprit.
Release the negative, find positivity and hope. You are not alone!

What Promotes Wellness in Your Life

Music · Food · Meditation · Relationship with Creator · Family
Best Friend · Hiking · Relaxation · Breathing Techniques · TV
Support Group · Fishing · Camping · Basketball · Sports · Food
Dirt Bike · Own Vehicle · Own Place · Traveling · Swimming
Snowsports · Video Games · Sober Friends · Working Out
Love · Meetings · Going Out · Walks · Healthy Partners · Faith
Sober Healthy Environment · Movies · Belief · Happiness · Joy
Smiles · Crying · Sharing · Caring · Jokes · Laughter · Education
N.R.A · AA Wellbriety · Teaching · Learning · Sunny Day
Animals · Kindness · Soul Friends · New Things · Festivals
Family Gatherings · Concerts · Peace · Yoga · Positivity · Kids
Unconditional Self-Love · Trust · Recovery · Nature · Hobbies
Compassion · Reliability · Candy · Dancing · Joy Rides · Jobs
Acceptance · Mindfulness · Self-Care · Gratitude · Journaling
Values · Cleanliness · Safety · Sponsors · Communication · Sleep
Independence · Spirituality · Positive Judicial Assistance · Rehab
Healing · Mental Health Therapy · Integrity · Healthy Habits
Vacations · Healthy Skills · Consistency · Priorities · Forgiveness
Giving Back · Letting Go · Structure · Accountability · Nutrition
Responsibility · No Excuses · Awareness · Reflection · Sage
Ceremony · Traditional Ways · Cooking · Sweat Lodge · Sauna

Wellness takes effort. You can change your life, one thought, one action, one day at a time. The vibration you identify with will be reflected in your life.
Begin shifting to positive thoughts and positive actions will follow!
You can do this. You are not alone!

10 Tips To Boost
our Mental Health

- Connect with others

- Move your body

- Talk to someone

- Listen to music

- Meditate

- Schedule downtime

- Eat whole foods

- Reset when you can

- Practice setting boundaries

- Get help if you need it

MINDFUL BEHAVIOR MODIFICATION™ TOOLS AND TECHNIQUES

Positive Tools to use in Our Daily Lives

⇒ *SSHI: Guide to Deconstructing Trauma*

Release frustrations, trauma, pain, and suffering in a positive way.

SSHI: Guide to Deconstructing Trauma

1. Awareness of negativity and desire to change.
2. Finding a solution.
3. Taking the first action that allows change.
4. Committing to repeated action to allow reprogramming.

It takes practice, it takes work, just like everything else. What you feed will grow. If we feed the negative, it will grow; if we feed the positive, it will grow. Give yourself permission to be happy. Give yourself permission to release negativity, permission to bring in positivity. It will change your life.

⇒ *SSHI: Release Repeated Thought Patterns*

Release frustrations, trauma, pain, and suffering in a positive way.

To stop the mind from going round and round like a hamster on a wheel...

SSHI Habit-Breaking Exercise

1. Stretch your arm and hand straight out in a stopping motion, say, "NO," out loud.
2. Place your other hand flat on the center of your chest or belly.
3. Close the eyes, inhale positivity to your body.

4. Exhale negativity out of the mouth like a sigh of relief.

5. Repeat 7 times.

Other options to Inhale...Exhale

Inhale: Happiness...Exhale: Sadness   Inhale: Confidence...Exhale: Doubt

Inhale: Peace...Exhale: Anger   Inhale: Courage...Exhale: Negativity

Inhale: Joy...Exhale: Grief   Inhale: Resilience...Exhale: Negativity

Inhale: Calm...Exhale: Anxiousness   Inhale: Strength...Exhale: Negativity

Inhale: Focus...Exhale: Scatter   Inhale: Freedom...Exhale: Addiction

This doesn't mean we don't allow ourselves to feel. It means that we choose what we bring in and keep and what we release. We have a choice; this brings us back into empowerment. It takes practice, it takes work, just like everything else. What you feed will grow. If we feed the negative it will grow; if we feed the positive, it will grow. Give yourself permission to be happy. Give yourself permission to release negativity, permission to bring in positivity. It will change your life.

⇒ *SSHI: Self-Check-In*

Find out in a non-judgmental, balanced way where your thoughts and actions are.

Self-Check-In

1. Ask yourself this question. How do I represent myself in each situation?

When we check in with ourselves about our actions and behaviors before, during, and after a situation, we are more aware and able to understand and shift to positive behaviors.

⇒ *SSHI: Tough and Challenging Situations*

This exercise is helpful in shifting tough and challenging situations.

Tough and Challenging Situations

1. When you are having a tough day, imagine yourself stepping out of your current situation and moving forward to a space where the issue is resolved. Use your senses to see what it looks like, feels like, tastes like, smells like, and sounds like.

Continue this exercise daily until your situation has shifted; this will help you create resolutions.

⇒ *SSHI: Daily Positive Personal Social Development*

Intentionally focus on bringing in positive thoughts.

Daily Positive Personal Social Development

1. Daily, bring in one positive thought in general. And one positive thought about yourself.

This will build positivity in the environment around you as well as in the environment inside of you.

⇒ *SSHI: Relationship-Building Tool*

Build healthy relationships. Can be used with all relationships, not just partners.

Relationship-Building Tool
Daily Share:

1. The most challenging thing that happened
2. The most positive thing that happened

Weekly Share:

1. Share some news about yourself
2. Share one thing you did for personal health care

⇒ *SSHI: Irrational Venting Tool*

Build healthy relationships. Can be used with all relationships, not just partners.

To use when you have extremely negative feelings about an exchange you had with another person and know you are overreacting...

Irrational Venting Tool

1. IN PRIVATE SO NO ONE ELSE HEARS. Begin saying all the negative things out loud that come to mind after you have had a conflict with someone. As you hear yourself say some of these things you will probably start laughing. Take a couple of deep breaths, inhaling peace and releasing frustrations out of the mouth.

A lot of times when we are mad we blow things out of portion a bit. Once we get our irrational vent out it can make us feel better and then we are a bit calmer when we do talk to the person. This tool is not to be used to hurt people's feelings, it's just to get the frustration out so we can be kinder when we do talk to them.

⇒ *SSHI: Relationship-Frustration Tool*

Build healthy relationships. Can be used with all relationships, not just partners.

To use when you are having a conflict with someone...

Relationship-Frustration Tool

1. Each person has their own paper and lists three things that have upset them about the conflict, and one positive quality about the person they are having the conflict with.

2. The papers can be exchanged or read when the parties agree they are able to talk about it. It is suggested to talk about it within twenty-four hours, so it doesn't become more uncomfortable.

⇒ SSHI: Reduce Food-Binging Technique
Build healthy food relationships.

Food-binging or random overeating is very common. You are not alone. So many of us use food to cope with stress, to feel loved and satisfied. These techniques help us to find a healthy food/life balance. When tempted or triggered to eat because of a stressor, try this.

Reduce Food-Binging Technique

1. Cut up food into third, on a smaller plate. Try to leave two bites that you don't eat.

2. Right before stress eating, ask yourself, "Why am I eating? Am I hungry? Why is one bite not enough?" Say out loud, "I am going to emotionally eat." Then eat.

It sounds ridiculous, but you will eat less because you are aware of what you are doing. You don't have to hide it. There will be less tendency to overindulge. Leaving two bites will send the message we don't have to finish our food just because it's there; we can save it or recycle to the animals or compost.

⇒ SSHI: Yell Therapy
Release frustrations, trauma, pain, and suffering in a positive way.

Yell Therapy

1. In an appropriate location and timeframe, go outside, inhale a huge breath, and exhale out the mouth with a loud *haaa* sound. Repeat 5-7 times.

This releases frustration, tension, and anger. You may even end up laughing as the tension releases.

⇒ SSHI: *Burning Release*
Release frustrations, trauma, pain, and suffering in a positive way.

Burning Release

1. Write down on a piece of paper things you would like to get rid of – pain, suffering, toxicity, addiction, drugs, alcohol, guilt, shame, anger, fear, doubt, et cetera. You can write down words or even write letters to people, including yourself.

2. Once you have it written down, in a safe place you can burn the paper. As the paper burns you will feel relief.

3. Take a few deep breaths throughout this process. The deep breaths (big breaths, inhaling through the nose and out the mouth) will release negativity in the body, mind, and spirit.

⇒ SSHI: *Brush off Stress and Frustrations*
Release frustrations, trauma, pain, and suffering in a positive way.

Brush off Stress and Frustrations

1. Take 3 deep breaths, in through the nose out through the mouth.

2. Start at your head and begin to brush off your body, with your hands flat like you are dusting yourself off. Move down the head, arms, neck, chest, back, torso, hips, legs, front and back, all the way down and off of the feet. Repeat if needed.

3. Take 3 deep breaths, in through the nose out through the mouth.

You will feel relief, lighter, and calmer after this exercise. What happens is you are moving out stagnant energy, frustrations, stress, and anxiousness.

⇒ *SSHI: The Secret to Forgiveness*

This forgiveness technique is like nothing you've ever seen.

The Secret to Forgiveness

1. Take 3 deep, cleansing breaths to release pressure. (Inhale through nose, exhale out of mouth)
2. Gently close eyes, place palms in center of the chest and lower belly.
3. Begin to visualize the situation you would like to forgive. (You don't have to see it too close if it is traumatic.)
4. Inhale through the nose, bring in positivity to the situation.
5. Exhale through the mouth, releasing negativity to the earth.
6. Repeat 5-10 times. Pause to feel the tension release. Feel peace.
7. Congratulations! You have just performed the act of forgiveness.

We work with this particular definition of forgiveness...to release negativity towards a person, place, or thing. So we release that negativity from the body with our intention and our breath. That becomes the act of forgiveness, releasing negativity. It doesn't condone anyone's action; what has happened is not okay. But what it does do is release the negativity that traps us in the situation so we can be free to move on. We can release trauma around the situation in this way. From this wisdom and knowledge, we heal.

⇒ *SSHI: Personal Health Care*

Take time to take care of yourself. Balance your body, mind, and spirit.

Personal Health Care

1. Minimum of 30 minutes in the morning for meditation, exercise, et cetera.

2. Minimum of 45 minutes for personal hygiene (shower, teeth, grooming et cetera) daily.

3. Minimum of 30 minutes in the evening to relax (book, tv, hobbies).

4. Minimum of 45 minutes to eat 2-3 meals.

If within a twenty-four-hour period you are not able to find two hours and thirty minutes to meet your basic needs, there is an imbalance. Consider adjusting to accommodate more balance in your daily life. Note: 7 hours of sleep or rest is necessary; the body doesn't function appropriately without rest and rejuvenation. It is hard to take time for ourselves regularly, but once we begin to form good habits it becomes easier to reach our goals. Of course, there are exceptions; some days we will end up adjusting our time or not having it all.

⇒ *SSHI: Mindful Risk Analysis Tool*

Mindful Risk Analysis Tool. Conflict vs. Benefit Exercise

Conflict vs. Benefit Exercise

This exercise is about identifying where we are at in our lives. Is it a good fit to accept more? Or is it a better fit to not take on more at that moment? Many things that happen in life, we don't necessarily ask for. For instance, if you are already at capacity in your life, sometimes one more shift or change will throw everything else out of balance. Things come up that we can't avoid, but sometimes it is better to release an idea or a plan than to force things or take on too much.

Mindfulness teaches us that by refraining from doing one thing we are able to prevent another thing from happening. So, with this wisdom and knowledge, we can begin to make balanced choices through a risk analysis thought process. Will adding another task in your life cause conflict and additional stress? Are you able to offer more without causing conflict or chaos? If not, no might be the better option. We tend to offer too much because we care about people and want to help. However, if we are creating conflict in our own lives to help others it is not healthy. Utilizing this type of explorational thought process in our daily lives opens us to choosing the narrative rather than the narrative choosing us. When we allow ourselves to step back and pause, we can begin to identify what is a good fit, and what is not, through this risk analysis. Diving a little deeper, let's explore what this might look like. Check out the examples below.

Risk Analysis Tool. Conflict vs. Benefit Examples
Before We Commit

> *Situation: Someone is asking us to do something,*
> *or they are talking about needing help.*

- Before we commit to something, pausing, letting people know that we are not sure, but we will get back to them. This gives us time; we don't have to immediately be put on the spot to answer.

- Or, instead of us offering right away, we can wait 6-24 hours. Then check in with ourselves to see if it's still a good idea on our end to volunteer and proceed from there.

Is it a good fit to add something else to our day? Or will adding one more thing cause chaos and complications?

Example Situation for Context:
My schedule is extremely full right now in my life. I have many people that I truly cherish and would LOVE to spend time with.

They reach out and ask me to go to coffee, go out to lunch, go out to dinner, hike, ice-skate, snowshoe, and more. I LOVE that they want to spend time with me. However, by using this risk analysis I know that right now if I add anything more to my schedule I will be very scattered and won't be effective in the rest of my life. This is temporary; when I have two of my large projects finished, I will have time to accept those offers!

After We Have Committed

Situation: We have already committed to something,
but an unavoidable shift has occurred.

- After we have committed to something, and an unforeseen complication arises, we will be faced with a choice.

- At this point, we can look to find balance between our actions and keeping the integrity of our word, but also using the risk analysis tool to understand what the best fit is, and how to adjust for optimal balance in our lives.

When we allow ourselves to step back and pause, we can begin to identify what is a good fit, and what is not, through this risk analysis tool.

Example Situation for Context:

I had an appointment set to have my house cleaned and then we had a big snowstorm. My driveway is only one car wide and tricky to navigate in this kind of weather. If someone gets stuck coming in, no one else can leave. Our house care specialist was capable and willing to come and clean. However, I ended up canceling the housecleaning, and still paid her because she was willing to come, because I was not comfortable with the risk of not being able to get to work if she got stuck.

My risk analysis told me that if she got stuck in the driveway, I wouldn't be able to get to work. When I have scheduled appointments with my clients it is my responsibility to be there. Therefore, the risk of me not being able to get out of my driveway was not worth the benefit of the house being cleaned. This may sound like a waste of money to some, but I had to identify what was the bigger loss me not being able to work all day or the house cleaning fee. She was great and said we didn't have to pay, BUT the choice was mine to not take the risk, therefore I honored our appointment and paid her.

> *Only we can decide, what is best for us. There are many times we will need to say no. Not because we don't care, but because we DO care. We need to care equally for ourselves and others. So if by helping someone else we are creating chaos for ourselves, it will not be a good fit.*

> *We should not have to harm one thing to help another. The energy used in that exchange is unhealthy and inappropriate. We don't need anyone else's permission (except for our own) to create balance and peace in our lives. We are responsible for our own level of stress. We are responsible for our own level of happiness. As we begin to understand the power of identifying what is a good fit and what is not, we take responsibility for creating and maintaining balance for ourselves in this good way.*

⇒ *SSHI Heart Breath*

Take the body out of flight or fight. Activate calm.

This meditation brings in happiness and love for ourselves. We spend a lot of time trying to find happiness and love in the world around us instead of the world inside of us. This heart breath has been created specifically to be simple and effective. The reason for this simplicity is that when you are in a panic you don't need more to think about, you need less to think about! This meditation can reduce negativity, panic, stress, anxiousness, sadness, despair, depressive states, fear, anger, doubt, self-loathing, self-doubt, reoccurring mind traps, and more.

Heart Breath Exercise

Find a place to sit for a moment...

1. **Three Clearing Breaths: Inhale through the nose, let the belly and chest expand. Big exhale out the mouth, releasing pressure.**

2. **Place both palms flat on center of chest.**

   We learn at a deeper level when we incorporate one or more of our senses. (Sense used here is touch.)

3. **Gently close or soften the eyes.**

   When our eyes are wide open we are receiving information for the outside world. Here, turn inward. (Sense used here is inner sight.)

4. **Gently begin to visualize positive light at the top of the head, Inhale through the nose drawing that light into your body.**

   (Sense used here is sight.)

5. **Gently bow the head and exhale that light and positivity out the mouth letting it flow into the heart. Filling up the heart.**

   (The senses used here are sight, touch (feeling) of the breath and sound.)

6. **Continue breathing in this same way. 5-10 breaths.**

   The breath doesn't change. It is always inhaling through the nose, bringing in positive light at the top of the head, and exhaling that positive light out of the mouth and into the heart. Our heart will fill with this positive light; then it will begin to flow over from the heart to the inner body. It will continue to flow from the inner body to the outer body, eventually building a positive glowing circle of protection all the way around us, from the inside out.

7. **Pause for a few moments to enjoy this peace and safety you are creating. This is available to you at any time.**

Eventually just placing your hand on your heart (or even imagining the hand on the heart) will bring you to that peace. The more familiar we are with something the easier it is to get back to. Here we reprogram to become familiar with positivity, peace, joy, happiness, and safety.

⇒ *SSHI: Attitude Adjustment*

Adjusting negative behavior patterns. The way we can change negative behavior patterns is to investigate the purpose and reason for them.

Attitude Adjustment

1. The first step is awareness.

2. The second step is unbiased perception only the facts on both sides.

3. The third step is taking action to adjust our behaviors, regardless of the other person's response.

Not everyone will take favorably to adjustments in our behaviors. People tend to feel more comfortable when they know what to expect. This work is not to make anyone feel uncomfortable. It is simply to adjust our behaviors to be kinder and more balanced in the long run. It takes courage to follow through with this kind of action. It may be uncomfortable, especially when it's not well received by others, but these actions are necessary for change. It helps us reprogram our responses, release triggers, and identify stress. Once we have identified our stressors and why they are there, we can then take action to change. In this way, we deconstruct trauma for others as well as ourselves.

This is about how we want to present ourselves and move forward in the world. How we show up each and every day in our relationships with ourselves and others.

⇒ *Positive Phrasing and Rephrasing Tool*

*Negative words, words of obligation, and voice tones
all have an impact on us. This is one of the biggest tools
we can utilize in our daily lives.*

Positive phrasing and rephrasing will change the dynamic of your relationships, not only the relationships with others but also the relationship with yourself. This type of speech and thought process is Trauma-Informed and Trauma-Responsive. When we begin to speak in truth and kindness, while releasing attachment to our experience, we are able to offer a whole new level of compassion and understanding for all involved. We are not threatened by a difference of opinion, because we have created safety through setting deliberate and intentional boundaries. We have taken the time to consider what is appropriate for ourselves and are not only willing to, but insist upon, creating an environment that produces safety, love, and joy.

The following, from the Montessori in Town blog, explains more about positive rephrasing and how we can utilize it.

Positive Phrasing

Positive Phrasing is about aligning the emotional and verbal content of communication in positive respectful and productive ways. Positive phrasing is the art of saying what is rather than what isn't. Positive Phrasing means our body language, facial expression, tone of voice, inflection, and words all convey the same meaning and intention. Why is positive phrasing effective? Because it is clear, it is unambiguous, and it invites cooperation.

Positive Phrasing

1. is always delivered as a statement – avoid choice when there isn't actually a choice; avoid changing a statement into a choice by adding "Okay?"
2. requires a commitment – to say what we mean and mean what we say.
3. is honest – but also respectful and compassionate.

Positive Phrasing as part of aligned communication has four benefits:

1. Clarity. The message is clear. No tricks, no confusion, no manipulation.
2. Respect. Others experience courteous regard for their feelings and dignity.
3. Trust. We say what we mean and mean what we say. Others can trust that when we say something, it happens.
4. Modeling. Others around us will naturally adopt and cultivate this kind of communication when this is the communication they experience and observe from others in the environment. Particularly when people that they love and admire communicate in this manner.[1]

The following, from The Usual Error, shows us how we can change our lives by changing our words.

Obligation words

Sometimes we enter into obligations willingly, which is fine, but often people create tons of completely unnecessary obligations, thereby burdening themselves with heavy loads of stress.

---

[1] Sackett, Ginni. "Positive Phrasing for Positive Discipline." Montessori in Town. October 6, 2015. http://www.montessoriintown.com/library/2015/10/6/positive-phrasing-for-positive-discipline#:~:text=ositive%20Phrasing%20means%20our%20body,rather%20than%20the%20actual%20words

There are lots of obligation-inducing words in English.

Here are some examples: Should, ought, must, have to, need to, supposed to, forced to.

Every time you use one of these words or phrases, you unintentionally take a little more obligation onto yourself. Why? We have too much obligation already, why choose to speak in such a way that adds more? It's harmful, completely unnecessary, and not even honest.

The truth is that any obligation you have is self-imposed, because **if you want something badly enough, you will do it. Conversely, if you don't want to do something, you'll find ways to avoid it. A feeling of "should" indicates a conflict between your wants: you want the end result**, but you don't want to go through the process of getting it. By using "should," we're putting obligation into it, making it into something we *don't* want to do. By removing "should," we turn it into something that is good for us and therefore less of an obligation and more of a good, happy-making thing.

Obligation-Inducing Phrasing	Positive Rephrasing
"I need to call my friend tonight."	"I want (or am going) to call my friend tonight."
"I should get to bed by 11 tonight so I'm not sleepy and miserable all day tomorrow."	"I'd like to get to bed by 11 tonight so I'll be happy and awake tomorrow."
"I want to sleep in, but I can't because I have to go to work today."	"I am grateful to get up and go to work, so I can provide the life I would like to have."
"I should go to the store."	"We are low on food, and I want to eat, so I'll go to the store so I can get what I want to eat."

Positive Rephrasing Examples
Turn Everyday Phrases From Negative to Positive

<u>Negative</u>	<u>Positive Rephrasing</u>
Why not?	Sounds good
No problem	Definitely!
Can't complain	Everything's going well, thanks
I'm exhausted	I need to rest
I forgot	I'll make sure to set a reminder
Constructive criticism	Feedback
Don't throw the ball inside	Please take the ball outside
Don't ...	I like it when..
I missed you so much	It's so great to see you
No ice-cream	Ice cream tastes good but eating too much isn't healthy.[2]

---

[2] "Rephrasing Things Positively." *The Usual Error*. (n.d.) http://usualerror.com/e-book/rephrasing-things-positively/

SSHI Awareness Tools
The awareness tools below help us stay balanced and healthy.

The awareness tools are powerful, simple statements. They are positive affirmations and wisdom that help teach us positive behavior resilience. Reminding us how to keep a positive, balanced, and unbiased perspective in life, therefore improving our daily experiences as well as our relationships with ourselves and others.

1. When you are upset, pause, take a moment, ask yourself why. "Why am I upset?" Whatever answer you come up with is okay – sit with it. You don't have to act immediately; it will still be available at a later date and time! If it still matters at a later date and time, it can be dealt with then.

2. If you are unhappy, ask yourself why. "Why am I unhappy? Am I unhappy because of my expectations?"

3. When we expect something, we can be let down. Our expectations put limits, not only on us but the world around us. We can move forward with an idea rather than an expectation, because an idea is flexible and expectations are not.

4. Notice your breath. Take a few minutes each day to explore what the breath feels like as it enters your body – the lungs, the cells, the organs. Take note what it feels like as it releases from the body, exhaling out the mouth, releasing pressure and taking toxins away.

5. Clearing Breath: *Inhale* through the nose, let the belly and chest expand. Big *exhale* out the mouth, releasing pressure.

6. Positive Breath: *Inhale* through the nose, drawing in positivity at the top of the head, *exhale* negativity out the mouth.

7. Practice staying in the moment. When you are present, other things won't bother you that are not in this moment; allow yourself to pause.

8. When you are in a hurry, stop, take a breath, look around, and give gratitude.

9. When you are not in a hurry, stop, pause, look around you, and allow the vibrations of the earth to fill you with joy, love, and light. This fills the body, mind, and spirit.

10. Let yourself feel the vibrations of your favorite music. Become that vibration, let everything else slip away.

11. Hold an object in your hands – what does that feel like? Feel the texture, shape, and weight.

12. Notice when you walk where your weight is distributed; notice what each part of the body feels like as you move. Can you adjust to walk more peacefully? Allow a sense of ease to flow through the body.

13. What does your food taste like? What does it feel like to chew the food and swallow? Allow observation and appreciation.

14. Get out of the mind and into the heart.

15. Our daily behavior can revolve around this simple thought, balancing and showing kindness to others and ourselves in our daily life.

16. Knowing the triggers are there but staying in the present moment serves us well. We cannot control other people's actions, but *we can control our exposure.*

17. When you are tempted to go back into any sort of addiction, pause, get a pen and a piece of paper. Sit down and begin to list all of the GOOD things that will happen in your life if you start to use again. Ah yes, the empty paper says it all.

18. We can use positive affirmations to reprogram negative behavior and stop emotional complications. "I am capable, I am loved." When we add breath work and imagery with the affirmation, we will have a much deeper result.

Example:

Visualize positive light at the top of the head.
Inhale through the nose, drawing that light into your body. Gently exhale that light out the mouth, letting it flow over your body toward the earth. Say: "I am capable, I am loved." Repeat 5 times and see how you feel!
Try it out!

19. Say out loud: "I am here."

    It reinforces your strength and keeps you focused on the moment. You can use it as a directive phrase if you are side-tracked from what you are doing.

    Say out loud – "I am here" – and feel yourself paying attention to the environment around you. This phrase also announces the realization of your goals and the fulfillment of your wishes.

    Say out loud, "I arrive," and pause to see yourself accomplishing your goals, achieving the outcomes you desire.

    Close the eyes, connecting with your spirit.

    Take a few slow, deep breaths and let the words "I arrive" sink into your being.

20. When you have a moment today, pause.

    Place a hand flat over the center of the chest and one flat on the lower belly.

    Begin to Inhale Gratitude, Appreciation, and Recognition For Yourself into your heart, mind, body, and spirit.

    As you exhale, let Gratitude, Appreciation, and Recognition For Yourself flow through your heart, mind, body, and spirit. Repeat 5 times.

    Sit with the power of your own presence for a moment.

    Allow yourself to feel and see how much you are, and how much you do.

21. Awareness allows us to understand that we are not our thoughts, we are not our feelings, we are not our emotions, we are not our trauma, we are not our suffering.

22. If you are still thinking about something 30 minutes after it happened, there is a lesson in there for you.

23. The greatest journey starts with the first step.

    The first step is awareness. Through this awareness we can access understanding and knowledge that we can then place into action to facilitate change.

    Through this awareness, we can step back and observe. When we observe we don't have to take things personally. We can see each part in an interaction without judgment or ego.

    Yes, This Takes A Lot Of Practice, But It Is So Worth It!!!

    Awareness allows us to see why we might have an issue, how we are acting, and why we are acting that way. It also allows us to see why others might have an issue, how they are acting, and why they are acting that way.

24. Becoming aware of trauma can lead to healing.

25. We have been passing on EXTREMELY dangerous information for decades. When we don't allow others or ourselves to process feelings and emotions, we are denying an inborn human response.

26. Our emotions and trauma *will* come to the surface. We can't stop it; it will happen eventually, and most likely in a very damaging way, if it has been stuffed down and ignored.

27. There are times when we can become bitter about life and worn out by our personal experiences. When this happens, joy and enthusiasm for life seem to disappear.

28. We are not our trauma. We are not our pain. We are not our suffering.

29. ACEs are relevant because they may have long-lasting, negative impacts on health, happiness, and may reduce options

for education and employment. The ACEs Study: Adverse Childhood Experiences. It is important because this study can help us identify trauma that has occurred in our lives. The ACEs we have experienced growing up will continue to have negative impacts on the rest of our lives, until we resolve that trauma.

30. We are not placing blame or passing off our current actions because we are identifying our past trauma. Through this experience we are learning more about our challenges so we can identify, resolve, and evolve!

31. If you feel frustrated, take a deep breath in through the nose, out through the mouth, and begin to sweep your hands over your body from head to toe. Brushing off negativity, anxiousness, stress, sadness, tension, and/or anger.

32. We have already started to resolve our trauma, by learning and raising our awareness! Continuing to learn will manifest knowledge and awareness. It will set us free.

33. We live in a re-traumatized state to some extent until we are able to release our trauma and start reprogramming negative learned behavior.

34. The knowledge that... We Are Not Our Trauma... is a lifesaving tool.

35. "Each person is acting appropriately for their level of trauma." ~Andrea Kremko

36. We are not responsible for other people's actions, but we are responsible for changing our actions, releasing trauma, and healing from the past.

37. We are infinite beings. We are not meant to suffer; we are meant to learn evolve and pass healing information on from one cell to the next.

38. Repeated unhealthy, negative patterns can occur from our past trauma, and can jeopardize our ability to live a healthy, happy life.

39. We all struggle with our mental health at one time or another in our lives. This is not because we are weak or should be ashamed, but because we are human, and this is how we learn.

40. Reaching out for assistance and support of our mental health takes courage and strength. We ALL need mental support. You are not alone!

41. People engage in physically or emotionally self-destructive behaviors to get an unconscious hormone response. This is why we are addicted to negativity.

42. Pain and unpleasant emotions stimulate the brain's reward pathways, resulting in unconscious addiction to these negative feelings.

43. Good news!!! You are not your thoughts, your emotions, or your feelings! You can learn to identify and reprogram negative patterns.

44. A thought distortion occurs when harmful, negative thought patterns occur on a regular basis

45. You can help yourself by learning to recognize attitudes and mental habits as they occur and stop them before they lead to a negative place.

46. Negativity weighs heavy... If you feel like something's too much it's because it is!

47. The greatest show of strength is honesty with oneself. Rather than searching to fix or heal those around us, we start with what's inside – no illusions, no judgment, no ego, only facts.

48. "Mindfulness protects us, our families and our society. When we are Mindful, we can see that by refraining from

doing one thing, we can prevent another thing from happening. We arrive at our own unique insight. It is not something imposed on us by an outside authority, it is our choice." ~ *Thich Nhat Hanh*

49. Ask Yourself Daily: "What am I thinking, what am I speaking, what am I doing, what do I mean, how do I feel?"

50. What is the difference between mindfulness and awareness? Mindfulness is directing our attention to the present moment. Awareness is knowledge or perception of a situation or fact. Combining mindfulness and awareness can change our perception, ultimately changing our lives.

51. An emotional trigger is anything – a memory, an experience, or an event – that causes a strong emotional reaction, regardless of your current state of mind. Observing the circumstances under which you experience intense emotions is crucial for identifying your triggers.

52. We close up to keep ourselves safe. No one can put shame or guilt on us unless we accept it. Just like someone throwing a ball, we don't have to reach out and grab it; we can just sidestep and let the ball go on by.

53. Moving past the negativities and the fears from our past and learning to love ourselves fully and completely is attainable. As we learn how to love ourselves, we can then show the world how we need to be loved.

54. A great response in a challenging situation: "Honesty, I don't feel comfortable with that."

55. It is extremely important to balance the body, mind, and spirit if we expect to live a fulfilling, happy life. Just like our vehicles, we must maintain, care for, and balance our lives to have the optimum experience.

56. We maintain our vehicles because we know that if we do not take care of them, they can't take care of us. Yet somehow we expect ourselves to operate at peak performance with little to no maintenance. It doesn't even make sense!

57. It is important not to assume that you understand the emotional response of someone who has been triggered or suggest that someone who has been triggered is overreacting, being "too sensitive" or being irrational, even if the trigger may seem insignificant to you.

58. Awareness of your daily emotions is the first step to managing triggers.

59. Mindfulness and awareness can change our lives in a positive way.

60. The brain frequently stores sensory stimuli from a stressful event in memory. People can still link the triggers to the trauma even if they come across the identical stimuli in a different setting.

61. A sensory trigger can cause a person to feel sad or angry before they even know why. Triggering also has a lot to do with how habits are formed. People do the same things in the same ways most of the time. When you stick to the same patterns, your brain doesn't have to decide what to do.

62. The five senses are frequently the source of emotional triggers, so pay attention to what you see, hear, smell, taste, and touch as these could cause an emotion or a behavioral reaction.

63. Understanding your emotional triggers (and how to manage them) is essential for maintaining good emotional health.

64. We have the ability to reprogram and modify our behaviors. We are not helpless and can take action.

65. Negative and positive behaviors are a result of our experience. Whatever we are familiar with will continue to manifest. We will seek out the same negativity and chaos that destroys us because it is what we are used to. We can change our experience and release the negative patterns that have been a continued cycle in our lives.

66. Constant exposure to negativity can significantly deplete our positivity, causing us to either become negative (doubtful, anxious, and distrustful), indifferent, uncaring, or even cruel.

67. Negative people demand the respect and love of others and strive for control because they don't feel sufficiently respected and loved and in control of their own lives.

68. People who are constantly negative and angry are trying to protect themselves or fit in. Recognizing one's negativity is helpful, but for lasting change we must reprogram the subconscious thought patterns, the underlying negative belief system.

69. People who are truly content rarely engage in negative talk. It is not appealing for them to talk negatively.

70. Negative self-talk is thinking that undermines our ability to make positive shifts in our lives. Negative self-talk is stressful and limits our success, self-confidence, and potential.

71. It is not as important to remind someone how to do something as it is to let them know that they are doing a good job and that others have noticed.

72. Our expectations are based on our prior experiences. Others will have different experiences, and therefore have different expectations. It is inappropriate to base the value of a relationship on a difference of opinion; we each have our own needs.

73. Critical thoughts of self and others keep us in a constant state of fight-or-flight.

74. We react instead of respond because we feel threatened and are trying to keep ourselves safe.

75. We can begin to examine situations that upset us to determine if the threat is real or perceived. From this perspective, we can change our lives drastically by reducing stress and anger.

76. The reality we perceive ourselves to be in is the truth and reality we will live in. We have become used to chaos, but we have the ability to change that. Whatever we are most familiar with is what we automatically go back to.

77. We are each playing a role in every situation. What can you learn? What is your lesson? We don't have to take experiences personally.

78. We are each responsible for learning our own lessons. It is not our job to make sure others learn their lessons.

79. Labels are dangerous and defeatist. They can lead to addictions, anger, fear, disorders, despair, health issues, and more.

80. Narcissism is a disorder that hinders healthy, satisfying relationships. Narcissists have lower life satisfaction and quality. Trauma and fear dominate their relationships, causing anger.

81. Codependency is a disorder that hinders healthy, satisfying relationships. Codependency, also called "relationship addiction," is marked by one-sided, abusive, or emotionally abusive relationships.

82. We can find compassion for people that are suffering instead of labeling them. If you come across a person with unsafe

qualities... remove yourself from the situation, send them positivity, and let them continue on their journey. When we label people it keeps us trapped in that negative energy and vibration.

83. Mental health is a serious issue, and we can ALL make a huge impact by not labeling each other. Whether there is a diagnosis or not, it is not appropriate for us to engage in that diagnosis, unless we are the person with the diagnosis.

84. The world is suffering with so much trauma and pain. You are not your diagnosis. You are not your pain; you are not your suffering. There is hope. You are not alone.

85. When we label or are labeled, we view ourselves as separate. This affects us at a fundamental level. If we are separate there is no harmony. We feel like we don't belong.

86. You are whole. You are free. You always have been, and you always will be. Here we peel back the layers to access that space. Everything you need is contained within. (RF)

87. The more familiar we are with something, the easier it is to get back to. Even if something is uncomfortable and negative, if we are more familiar with it we will gravitate toward it.

88. We'd rather believe false information than seek the truth when our interpretations and thoughts are distorted.

89. Once we have AWARENESS of a situation, we can then begin to look for SOLUTIONS, then we MUST CHOOSE TO TAKE ACTION if we want something to change, and finally, WE MUST COMMIT TO REPEATED ACTION to allow an old habit to be removed and a new one to replace it.

Sacred Sol Healing Institute: Guide to Deconstructing Trauma

- The first step is awareness of negativity and desire to change.

- The second step is finding a solution.
- The third step taking the first action that allows change.
- The fourth step is committing to repeated action to allow reprogramming.

90. Ultimate goal: To love yourself fully and completely. This doesn't mean we become perfect; it means we are able to face our challenges in grace and love. We learn from where we've been and choose to move forward in a different way. We release ego, judgment, grief, guilt, shame, and fear; this is not who we are, just where we've been. We are not our trauma; we are not our pain; we are not our suffering.

91. If we have not taken the steps to heal, we will try to control our present surroundings because we couldn't control something that comprised us at an earlier time in our lives.

92. Balance requires daily effort and action on our part. If we don't participate and create balance in our daily lives, it won't happen. This is up to us. It is not anyone else's responsibility to create this balance in our lives.

93. All of our experiences are designed to learn from; they are not meant to torture us or others.

94. Our perception dictates our experience, and our past experiences dictate our perception. Our perception will influence our interactions with the world around us, as well as the world inside of us. (RF)

95. Assumptions, expectations, and attachments to persons, places, or things lead to self-sabotage and altered perceptions.

96. Our addiction to others' feedback is damaging our lives. Others' opinions matter because it boosts our self-esteem (not self-worth).

97. When we peel back the layers of trauma, pain, and suffering at the very center of our creation is love, light, and grace. That's who you are, that's who you always have been, and who you always will be. (RF)

98. We can change the thought distortions that we have adopted over time through awareness and mindfulness

99. Our thought processes have been shaped by our past experiences.

100. Through our traumatic experiences we can create a false belief system based on only half the information. That information is skewed and faulty because it comes from someone else's trauma, not from our reality.

101. Imagine what your life would be like if you were able to move forward in your infinite worth and value without feeling compromised or upset when other people don't agree with you or don't like you.

102. Consider your relationship health. Understanding healthy and unhealthy patterns will allow you to choose what is appropriate for you.

103. Trust, openness, honesty, respect, affection, communication, and equal participation are characteristics of a healthy relationship.

104. We can begin to examine our essential, fundamental desires and needs in a relationship. Taking time to create and build a structure of what we are looking for will help us discern whether our relationships are a good fit, or if it is better to move on. We have a choice.

105. Meeting people where they are at, instead of where we think they should be, or where we are, will change our relationships.

106. What is the point of challenging interactions with others? Ultimately, our job is to learn from each situation and decide if it is beneficial for us to continue in that relationship or if it has run its course and it is more appropriate to move forward in a different way. (This applies to all relationships.)

107. There is no other relationship in our lives that has as much impact as the relationship with ourselves… and yet our self-relationship is often the most neglected.

108. Removing yourself from negativity, chaos, and learned behavior patterns will not only take effort; you will also be required to choose to take action if you want to see and feel a change in your life.

109. Consistently setting and using limits teaches us to focus less on others' reactions and more on our own self-esteem and attitude.

110. Setting limits is a way to be assertive and show that you respect yourself, which is good for your self-esteem and your emotional state.

111. Your attitude toward yourself will be consistent with your actions. If you act in a manner that shows respect for yourself, you will begin to respect yourself, regardless of others' behavior toward you.

112. Your attitude toward yourself will be negative if you act in a way that suggests you don't respect yourself, by neglecting to create boundaries.

113. Setting boundaries regularly makes sense when you consider the advantages to your mood and self-esteem that you will receive from doing so, regardless of the other party's response.

114. If something feels like it's too much it most certainly is. We can learn to step back and see our situation from a less personal view, more as an observer. From that space we can reevaluate and set reasonable goals and values that are in alignment with our physical, mental, emotional, and spiritual health.

115. If we do not have healthy boundaries for ourselves and the world around us we will not have a healthy, happy life.

116. Our perception dictates our experience, and our experiences dictate our perception.

117. We can learn to communicate without judgment and ego by understanding our triggers, resolving our trauma, releasing attachment to others' opinions, and restructuring our dialogue.

118. Do you see a person's effort? Is it ever enough? Or are you always needing more from yourself and others because that's what has happened to you? Learned behavior can be unlearned.

119. We can't expect others to fulfill our happiness. Expectations lead straight to judgment and ego.

120. We learn to meet people where they're at, instead of where we think they should be. Our opinion is just that...our opinion.

121. When we think we are putting others first, we can be disguising what we need, with what we perceive they need. Then these illusions that we have created become our reality

122. A new habit takes an average of 66 days to form and 18 to 254 days to break. We can set realistic goals and understand what is keeping us from them.

123. Rather than focusing on the problem, **focus on the solution,** even if you do not know what that is yet. It will draw the solution to you, rather than more blocks of the problem.

124. We are redefining our vocabulary. We now understand the word forgiveness means to release negativity around a situation, person, place, or thing; no behavior or actions are condoned.

125. One way to stop negative behavior is by using positive affirmations.

126. Through Positive Behavior Resilience™ we can begin to notice the distinction between healthy negative emotions such as temporary sadness and unhealthy negative emotions such as deeply depressed states of despair

127. Restructuring our negative mindset is necessary in order to facilitate positive change. There is nothing more important than releasing our negative mindset. It is toxic and unhealthy.

128. If we all began to speak in a Trauma-Sensitive format it would drastically reduce challenges, misunderstandings, trauma, and pain in our lives.

129. One of our most effective tools in challenging conversations is to ask the other person, "What is your goal in this conversation?"

130. Unless we have processed and reprogrammed our trauma, it is still affecting our daily lives, even if we don't realize it.

131. Discernment is crucial for us to decipher what is needed and good and what is not needed and inappropriate. When we create inner balance, we can act decisively.

132. It is extremely important to balance the body, mind, and spirit if we expect to live a fulfilling, happy life. Just like our vehicles, we must maintain, care for, and balance our lives to have the optimum experience.

133. We maintain our vehicles because we know that if we do not take care of them they can't take care of us. Yet somehow we

expect ourselves to operate at peak performance with little to no maintenance. It doesn't even make sense.

134. In a condition of fatigue, there is no hope since there is no energy to inspire and motivate.

135. Energy affects all things. Focused energy becomes power, which can change people, circumstances, and situations worldwide.

136. We are responsible for our own level of stress and have the ability to balance our lives.

137. If we do not create daily balance in our environment, it will negatively affect our lives. Balance requires daily effort and action on our part. If we don't participate and create balance in our daily lives, it won't happen.

138. In a condition of fatigue, there is no hope since there is no energy to inspire and motivate.

139. Try finishing this sentence: "I participate in adding balance to my life today by..."

140. What is your tone? Can you hear how your tone sounds to others?

141. If we do not feel our emotions, we will not be able to learn how to process life experiences.

142. Being open to the possibility of change requires awareness.

143. Clinging to a negative mental position robs us of our strength.

144. Extreme reactions come from feeling threatened, physically, mentally, emotionally, or spiritually.

145. We aren't able to process what we don't understand.

146. When we accept something that we don't understand, it skews our set of values.

147. If you're in a repeated pattern in your life, it is an opportunity to learn a lesson and move forward. This will break the repeated cycle.

148. Make sure to take time and thank yourself. In this journey we thank others all the time; it is important to acknowledge and thank ourselves as well for the effort and work we put in.

149. We can learn to discern between the energies and desires we project and those we receive.

150. When we are re-establishing relationships, we can still show compassion in love without completely being involved in someone's life.

151. As we align our purpose, behaviors, and surroundings with our development and growth, we will evolve and mature. Our morals, values, and ethical code will deepen and expand.

152. We don't have to take things personally. Each person has their own needs; we can all have our own opinion and our own needs without it needing to "crush" anyone.

153. How do your actions and reactions shift the world around you? Everything we do affects everything around us. It's not just the words that are said, but the tone that makes them harmful.

154. Situation: "I am trying to control someone's behavior. It is not a problem at this point, nobody is being hurt, nothing bad is happening. I want to control the situation because of my own manipulation and trauma."

155. "Who am I? Who do I want to be? What are my goals: physically, mentally, emotionally, and spiritually?"

156. Impulse control: Impulses are bound to happen from our environment, but we do not have to act on those impulses.

157. It is inappropriate to compromise one thing to have another thing grow.

158. We release attachment to the outcome of other people's lives.

159. Within each situation we face, a goal will keep us focused and balanced, allowing intentional living.

160. When living in trauma and toxic stress, we are not comfortable looking at ourselves because we are not practicing self-awareness or self-acceptance.

161. Reactivity is not intentional living; looking to others to meet our needs is inappropriate and dangerous for all involved.

162. We usually think of sight and hearing as our main senses, but what we smell has the strongest impact on our emotions. The olfactory receptors in our brain connect directly to the limbic system, where emotions begin.

163. Use positive affirmations to reprogram negative behavior.

164. Decision fatigue is the deteriorating quality of decisions made by an individual after a long session of decision-making. The quality of our choices deteriorates because we are fatigued.

165. We become aware by paying attention to our interactions with ourselves and others – noticing how we talk, think, sound, and act, as well as how others talk, think, sound, and act. No judgment or ego, just observing. From this observation, we can assess the whys of our actions, as well as other people's actions. Once we have the whys for ourselves, we can begin to release the negativity around the behavior and heal the trauma that led us there, by using the Deconstructing Trauma Program awareness tools. It is

not our job to make others understand their journey, but we can lead by example. At a fundamental level, we all want to be happy.

166. The collective understanding is arriving at a place of observation and acceptance, for ourselves and others, without judgment or ego. In this way we can understand why we behave the way we do and take the action steps required to "Deconstruct Trauma."

167. We don't have to act on our impulses; we can observe them, discover where they come from, and allow them to inspire us to change. When we resolve the trauma surrounding them we gain balance and peace.

168. The Deconstructing Trauma Program allows us to change our perception. Other people are not necessarily trying to harm us; it's not all about us. They are reacting the way they are because of their own blockages, their own triggers, their own issues, their own trauma.

169. When we begin to give ourselves permission to feel, along with the appropriate tools to process our feelings and heal our trauma, it can change our lives.

170. Our love for others does not need to compromise our safety or our relationships with ourselves. If it does, we need to readjust and find balance. It is inappropriate to compromise one thing to have another thing grow.

171. When others cannot give us what we need, it is because their own needs have not been met. They do not have the skills or tools to look past their own trauma to meet the needs of others.

172. The reason we don't receive what we need from others is not because we aren't good enough or they aren't good enough. It's because we can only give what is available. If we have not resolved our trauma, our availability to give will be diminished.

173. When other people's decisions, or lack of decisions, begin to affect your life, you can continue in the relationship or decide if the risk factor is too great and adjust as needed.

174. Stay in the present moment. Life is busy, we panic when we have a lot to do. If you have a big day, try focusing on one hour at a time; it will reduce the panic.

175. When someone is set on being negative, we can use reflective listening. Repeating back to them what they have said will make them feel heard and can reduce the intensity of the negativity.

176. We can listen to a conversation without inserting our opinion. Sometimes just being present is enough. We don't always have to fix or solve something. Sometimes people just need to vent.

177. When we are overstimulated our minds jump frantically from one thing to the next. We can reduce being scattered and frantic by allowing the mind to soften. Utilizing the breath work tools, will calm the mind and body, reducing overstimulation.

178. Balance requires actively participating in our personal health care. What are you doing each week to support your physical, mental, emotional, and spiritual health?

179. Our body needs to stretch, to move, to build strength, so it can support us in a good way. Exercising 20 minutes, 3 times a week, can change your life. You will be stronger, more

fit and flexible, with less pain. You will feel better about yourself.

180. Abundance is a choice. We can choose to bring in daily abundance with our daily action tools.

181. Societal fear is increasing because we are not using healthy tools to take our bodies out of flight or fight.

182. We have become so out of balance that we expect the world around us to provide an environment that we find favorable.

183. The experience of chaos, pain, and negativity stimulates the brain's reward centers, which in turn leads to an unconscious addiction to chaos, pain, and negativity.

184. Learning to spot and stop negative thoughts and attitudes can help you prevent negative outcomes.

185. Through mindfulness, we develop the ability to observe and accept what is happening in the mind in each moment, while letting it go without criticism or malice. We use awareness to be aware of the thoughts, feelings, and sensations that come to mind.

186. Understanding the emotions we encounter on a daily basis is the first step in learning how to deal with triggers.

187. Triggers can teach us how to manage our reactions before they become problematic. We can stop triggers. Good emotional health requires knowing and managing your emotional triggers.

188. Many times, the world around us, accompanied with our past traumatic experiences, will send us into a space of unsafety. Learning the skills and tools to return yourself to a state of safety can change your life.

189. We are moving through the world with "Trauma-Related Expectations." We expect negative results because we have experienced those results through past trauma. These Trauma-Related Expectations will continue to harm our lives until we reprogram them and begin to heal.

190. It is extremely important for us to see and release others' expectations, thoughts, and actions because if we don't we will end up living someone else's experience. This also will cause us to live a life that is full of continual chaos and pain.

191. False beliefs and thought distortions can create chaos, pain, and negativity in our lives, affecting how we feel about ourselves at a fundamental level. Once our core belief system has been compromised, we are no longer able to access our infinite value and worth.

192. Attempting to find our value and worth through acts of kindness to others is inappropriate and unhealthy.

193. Positive phrasing consists of statements that are clear and encouraging.

194. We have the ability to break the cycle of toxic thoughts and damaging self-beliefs, through awareness, positive action, and repetition.

195. We are ALL living in fear and lacking self-worth to some degree because of trauma we have endured. Our trauma will all look different. It comes to us all in different ways, but it is part of ALL of our lives. Our trauma doesn't have to define us. It can be a tool in which to learn from.

196. The ultimate tool to release tension and activate balance immediately is...**our breath**.

197. Energy is everywhere, it is part of all things, yet we have forgotten it exists within us and around us. Our energy needs to

be balanced and maintained because it affects us at fundamental levels in our body, mind, and spirit.

198. When we maintain and balance our physical, mental, and spiritual energy, we manifest positive outcomes in our experiences with ourselves and others.

199. We can create healthy energy that will result in joy, happiness, and motivation.

200. "Deconstructing Trauma" does not happen with only one modality. It is a unique experience for each of us. Utilizing physical, mental, and spiritual tools, including professional medical and mental health practitioners, is essential in understanding trauma, and releasing chaos, pain, and negativity. (RF)

201. We achieve daily balance in our lives by tending to all dimensions of our wellness.

202. Success requires self-control. Self-management is a skill that must be learned. It is essential to succeed.

203. Use a wellness plan to create one week of health and balance. From there, use each week to create a month of health and balance.

204. Everything is temporary; it's okay to be uncomfortable and it's okay to not be okay. The key is to let it pass and, if we seem to be stuck in it, to take action to change that!

205. How many times have we pushed through something even though all the signs told us not to, and then we were surprised when we ended up with a bad result?

206. Someone may be giving their 150%. It may not be enough for us, and nowhere near our 150%, and that's okay. It doesn't mean they are bad, or that we are bad. It just means they have no more to give; we don't have to take it personally.

207. It's a conscious effort to not suffer, as we are conditioned to normalize suffering.

208. We don't have to take everything so personally. We can step back and observe. It's not always about us! What a relief!

209. Instant gratification does not always create the desired result. Being patient with ourselves and others is one of the greatest tools of all.

210. A habit is just a habit. Habits can be changed.

211. Trauma bonds can be created in all types of relationships.

212. Trauma responses happen to each of us in our every-day experiences.

213. The ego can be a helpful tool for us. It offers us an opportunity to check in and see if we need to adjust a situation or if we need to understand that the ego is just challenging us and we need to send it for a time out and thank it for the test.

214. Each one of us has greatness inside. We can be extraordinary. The only way we can be truly happy is if we live in our own trauma-informed and trauma-responsive truth.

215. Before we ask someone for their opinion, consider whether or not we are willing and able to hear any answer they may respond with. "Am I okay with what they might say?" What if they say something that I don't want to hear or can't hear? We can choose not to ask the question if we think the answer might hurt us or be something we're not ready for yet.

216. A great method for releasing trauma and tension is TRE®. TRE is an innovative series of exercises that assist the body in releasing deep muscular patterns of stress, tension and

trauma. TRE is designed to be a self-help tool. https://trauma-prevention.com/. Renee Frye of Sacred Sol Healing Institute is a TRE trained provider.

217. You are love, light, and grace. That's who you are, who you have always been, and who you will always be. You are the miracle you've been looking for. (RF)

Quick Reference: My Favorite Awareness Tools.

Write down the numbers of your favorite Awareness Tools, so you can easily reference them! Example: #86, 92, 95, 210.

Mindful Communication Exercise

Try this mindfulness communication exercise!

This mindfulness communication exercise is helpful for raising communication awareness between two or more people. It allows one person to talk and one person to listen and learn about their partner, family member, or friend. We don't always have to be interested in specific things people in our lives are doing. But we can support them and grow together as we share our experiences.

Mindful Communication Exercise

Two people walk for an hour. No phones, no distractions.
Each person gets to experience both the talker and the listener.
30 minutes each. One person talks, and the other person listens and acknowledges.

Example: The listener may agree with one-word responses, nod their head, or make a sound so the talker knows they are heard.

This is not an open dialogue between two people; it is a space for the talker to share information. Each time the talker is interrupted, they stop walking as a signal to the listener that it is still their turn to talk.

- When this walk starts, set a timer for 30 minutes and decide who will be the talker first. Begin walking. When the timer goes off, both parties stop walking, and the talker wraps up what they are saying.
- The timer gets set again for 30 minutes, switches, and resumes walking. When the timer goes off, both parties stop walking, and the talker wraps up what they are saying.
- There might be times during the person's 30 minutes where they do not wish to speak; at that time, there would just be a comfortable silence.

We can also apply this exercise to a family of four or more by breaking down the time frames and keeping the walk to one hour. If there were four people, each person would have 15 minutes of talk or silent time.

Shorter walk: two people could be 30 minutes total, 15 minutes each. You can also do a much less obvious version of this exercise by practicing listening in conversations throughout your day. Always modify it to best reflect your needs.

Many times, when we are talking, we get excited and want to share because something someone says engages us. You can bring a pad of paper and a pen to write down anything you would like to share later, when your role is that of the listener. Mindfulness is an acquired skill.

SELF-CRITICAL THOUGHT RECORD

SITUATION-TRIGGER:

EMOTIONS:

PHYSICAL SENSATIONS:

SELF-CRITICAL THOUGHTS:

ALTERNATIVE POSITIVE THOUGHTS:

HOW COULD THIS HAVE CHANGED YOUR OUTCOME:

Positive Behavior Resilience Tracker — Example Sheet — Sacred Sol Healing Institute

Your Harmful Negative Thought Write Down, Say Out Loud.	Your Positive Replacement Thought Write Down, Say Out Loud.	Positive Reprogramming Formula Write Down Positive & Follow Below, Repeat at Least 3-5 Times..
*Write Down & Say Negative Pattern: I am afraid of letting people down.	Write Down & Say Positive Replacement: I am working on creating safety for myself.	Place: One hand on heart, one hand on belly. Close eyes. Say Positive: *I am working on creating safety for myself.* Do: Inhale through the nose bringing in light. Exhale negativity out the mouth. Say: I am capable I am loved.
*Write Down & Say Negative Pattern I feel like I'm not good enough for anyone or anything.	Write Down & Say Positive Replacement: My value and worth feels smaller than I would like it to be. I am taking action to change that.	Place: One hand on heart, one hand on belly. Close eyes. Say Positive: *My value and worth feels smaller than I would like it to be. I am taking action to change that.* Do: Inhale through the nose bringing in light. Exhale negativity out the mouth. Say: I am capable, I am loved.
*Write Down & Say Negative Pattern I feel like I can't trust my partner because of past experience.	Write Down & Say Positive Replacement: My partner is taking the steps to earn my trust. I trust myself to handle what comes my way. I am working on living in the present moment.	Place: One hand on heart, one hand on belly. Close eyes. Say Positive: *My partner is taking the steps to earn my trust. I trust myself to handle what comes my way. I am working on living in the present moment.* Do: Inhale through the nose bringing in light. Exhale negativity out the mouth. Say: I am capable, I am loved.

Goal: Change your negative thought patterns!
This will help to change the negative thought patterns! Anytime you feel like you have a Negative Thought replace it with the Positive Replacement Thought and do the Positive Reprogramming Formula.
Do this as much as it comes into your head so you can reprogram it!

Goal:

Total Times Used:

Positive Behavior Resilience Tracker   Your Sheet   Sacred Sol Healing Institute

Your Harmful Negative Thought — Write Down, Say Out Loud.	Your Positive Replacement Thought — Write Down, Say Out Loud.	Positive Reprogramming Formula — Write Down Positive & Follow Below, Repeat at Least 3-5 Times...
*Write Down & Say Negative Pattern	Write Down & Say Positive Replacement:	**Place:** One hand on heart, one hand on belly. Close eyes. **Say Positive:** **Do:** Inhale through the nose bringing in light. Exhale negativity out the mouth. **Say:** I am capable I am loved.
*Write Down & Say Negative Pattern	Write Down & Say Positive Replacement:	**Place:** One hand on heart, one hand on belly. **Say Positive:** **Do:** Inhale through the nose bringing in light. Exhale negativity out the mouth. **Say:** I am capable, I am loved.
*Write Down & Say Negative Pattern	Write Down & Say Positive Replacement:	**Place:** One hand on heart, one hand on belly. **Say Positive:** **Do:** Inhale through the nose bringing in light. Exhale negativity out the mouth. **Say:** I am capable, I am loved.

Total Times Used:

Goal: Change your negative thought patterns!
This will help to change the negative thought patterns! Anytime you feel like you have a Negative Thought replace it with the Positive Replacement Thought and do the Positive Reprogramming Formula.
Do this as much as it comes into your head so you can reprogram it!

Goal:

Mindful Heart Intelligence Reprogramming™, MHIR

The MHIR Positive Behavior Response System consists of simple life management tools that allow the reprogramming of learned behavior through a heart response, rather than a mind reaction. This training teaches breath-body awareness and recognition of heart-rate variance. MHIR stands for Mindful Heart Intelligence Reprogramming.

MHIR is important because this system offers us options that allow the release of blockages, pain, and suffering from the body, mind, and spirit. Trauma from our past experiences, and the blockages that it leaves, affect us in our daily lives. We cannot live in a balanced and truly happy way until we release trauma and negativity.

See our MHIR™ Card and Chart below.
for detailed instructions refer to the book, pages 157-167

SACRED SOL HEALING INSTITUTE®
MHIR™ Card Action Tool
Response vs. Reaction

1. <u>MINDFUL</u>: Non-judgmental awareness of situation. Only the facts!
2. <u>HEART</u>: Hands flat over chest. Inhale: Positivity, Exhale: Negativity, 4x.
3. <u>INTELLIGENCE</u>: Pause. Is it still significant? No: Go to 4, Yes: Repeat 1-3.
4. <u>REPROGRAMMING</u>: Say 3 times. I Am Capable, I Am Loved. Success!

Renee Frye
Trauma Healing Holistic Specialist

MHIR™ Chart Action Tool   MHIR™ Somatic Response Chart   Reprogram Behavior Patterns

1) Where do you feel this situation in your body? Place hand there. Identify Body Location on chart. Work down the column using steps 2-3.
2) Inhale Color; exhale Obstacle out of mouth 3-6 times. Continue until you feel the weight lift. Pause to become familiar with this feeling.
3) Inhale Benefit; exhale out of mouth 3-6 times. Continue until you feel content. Pause to become familiar with this feeling.
4) Say Affirmation 1-3 times. Notice how you feel now. Your response may be quite different. Repeat as needed.

CHAKRAS:	CHAKRA 1	CHAKRA 2	CHAKRA 3	CHAKRA 4	CHAKRA 5	CHAKRA 6	CHAKRA 7
Body Location	Pelvis, Hips, Root	Lower Abdomen	Solar Plexus	Heart	Throat, Ears	Forehead, Temples	Top Of Head
Color	Red	Orange	Yellow	Green	Blue	Purple	White, Iridescent
Obstacle/Block	Fear, Anger, Doubt	Guilt	Shame, Not Enough	Grief, Sadness	Lies	Illusions	Attachment
Benefit/Balance	Secure, Safe, Support	Balance, Freedom	Confidence, Value	Love, Joy	Truth	Clarity	Unity, Connection
Affirmation	I Have, I Am Safe, I Am Supported	I Can Feel, I Am Free To Be Me	I Access My Own Power; I Am Enough	I Love, I Am Loved, I Forgive Myself	I Speak, I Listen To The Inner Sounds	I See, I Rely On My Inner Guidance	I Am You; You Are Me; We Are One
Sound/Element	LAM/Earth	VAM/Water	RAM/Fire	YAM/Air	HAM/Sound	OM/Light	Silent AUM/Thought
Endocrine Gland	Adrenals	Ovaries, Testicles	Pancreas	Thymus	Thyroid	Pineal	Pituitary
Body Part	Eliminatory System, Legs, Feet	Womb, Genitals, Bladder	Digestive System, Muscles	Heart, Lungs, Arms, Hands	Ears, Mouth, Neck, Throat, Shoulders	Eyes	Cerebral Cortex, Nervous System
Food	Meats, Proteins	Liquids	Starches	Leafy Vegetables	Fruits	Iodine Rich Foods	Fasting
Exercise/Pose	Grounding, Mountain	Hip Opener, Low Lunge	Core Work, Twists	Chest Opening, Camel	Open/Close, Cat Cow	Balancing, Tree	Meditate, Savasana
Malfunction	Weight Problems, Constipation	Frigidity, Impotence, Uterine Disorders	Digestive Disorder, Nervousness	Asthma, High Blood Pressure	Colds, Sore Throat, Hearing Problems	Head & Eye Pain, Blind, Nightmares	Depression, Mental Illness, Confusion
Function	Survival, Grounding, Security	Intimacy, Desire, Pleasure	Personal Power, Will, Self-Esteem	Universal Love, Forgive, Compassion	Communicate, Inner Listening	Creative, Intuition, Perception	Understand Unity, Source Connection
Excessive Characteristics	Heavy, Overweight, Monotony, Greed	Overly Emotional, Sex Addiction, Obsessive	Control, Aggressive, Dominate, Scattered	Codependent, Poor Boundaries, Jealous	Excessive Talking, Inability To Listen	Delusions, Hallucinate	Spiritual Addiction, Confused, Dissociate
Deficient Characteristics	Fearful, Restless, Underweight, Spacey	Frigid, Impotent, Rigid, Checked Out	Weak Will & Self-Esteem, Passive	Lonely, Isolated, Critical, No Empathy	Unwilling to Speak, Poor Rhythm, Deaf	Poor Memory, Denial, Uninspired	Limited Beliefs, Materialism, Apathy
Crystal/Stone	Red Garnet, Onyx	Tiger's Eye, Sunstone	Citrine, Yellow Jasper	Rose Quartz, Jade	Lapis, Turquoise	Amethyst, Fluorite	Quartz, Selenite
Goal	Stability, Grounding, Physical Health, Prosperity, Trust	Fluidity, Pleasure, Allows Feelings, Healthy Sexuality	Vitality, Spontaneity, Purpose, Strong Self Image, Esteem & Will	Balance, Empathy, Self-Acceptance, Healthy Interactions	Creative, Diverse, Clear Speaking, Resonance	Psychic Perception, Clear & Accurate Interpretation	Wisdom, Knowledge, Consciousness, Spiritual Connection

Daily Wellness Plan

With this daily wellness chart, we can see a simple break down of standard work and sleep hours. If we work and sleep eight hours we then have 8 hours left in a day, to clean and feed ourselves and our families, let alone sports and grocery shopping etc.

No wonder we are stressed and feel like there is not enough time in a day! The answer to this seemly overwhelming realization is to commit to daily and weekly balance. Each day we will do our standard daily needs and weave additional needs into the mix.

If you are not working the chart would be divided differently.

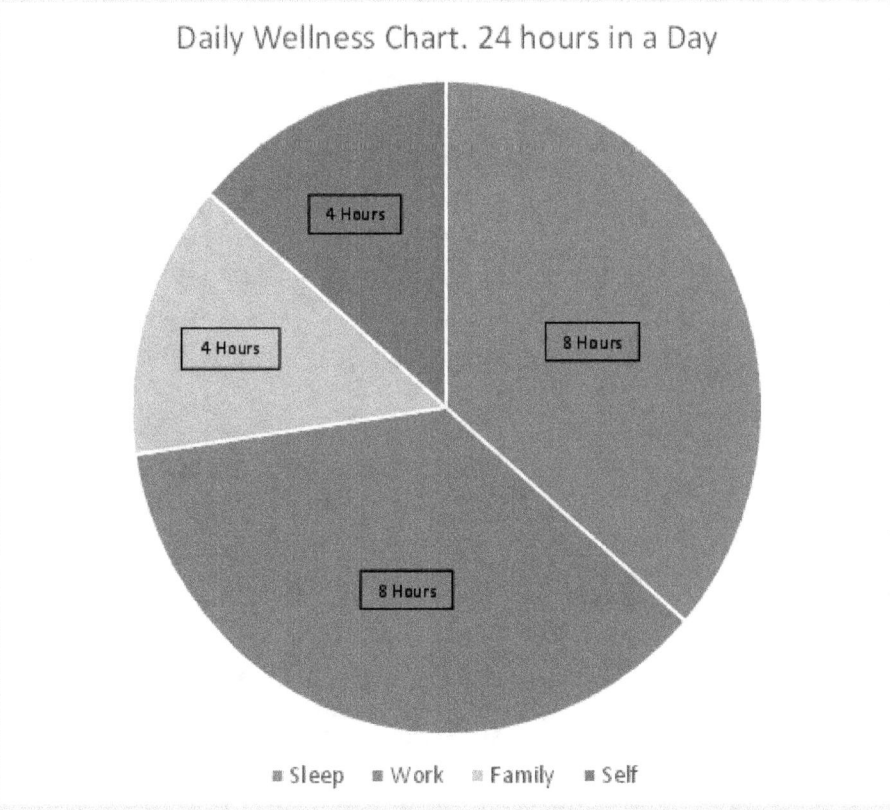

Daily Wellness Chart. 24 hours in a Day

4 Hours

4 Hours

8 Hours

8 Hours

■ Sleep   ■ Work   ■ Family   ■ Self

Daily Wellness Plan

My Health & Wellness Life Balance

Example of Daily Wellness Plan for a 24 hour period. We have modeled the daily wellness plan after the working person with children. Your daily wellness plan will shift according to work and family life. Customize your own plan below. Not every hour has to be used!

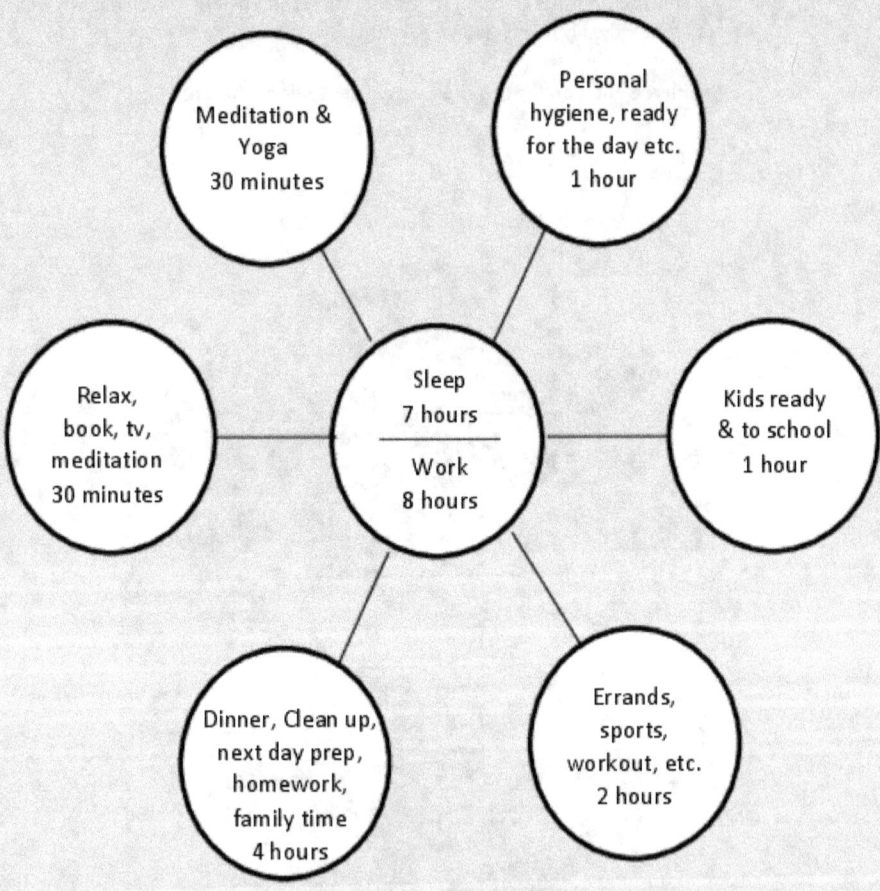

Daily Wellness Plan

My Health & Wellness Life Balance

Endless ways to use these charts! You can put yourself in the middle and use three bubbles as future goals and three as already achieved. You can put a challenge in the middle use bubbles as solutions, and or pros and cons. You can use as a hobby or recovery model, positive hobbies or actions that bring happiness to your life. Use as work/home balance three and three etc.

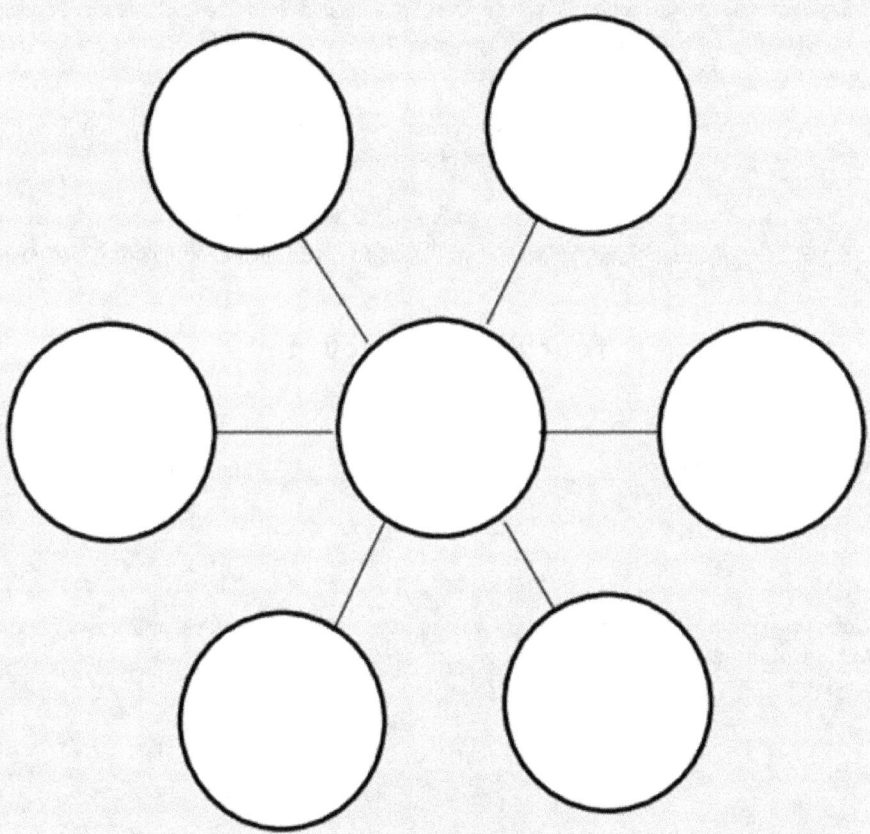

SSHI Wellness Action Plan

Wellness plans encourage intentional living and guide us in making life changes that reduce stress and illness while improving and maintaining our health and happiness. Intentional living will change your life.

People who are successful at making life changes release limiting beliefs, fears, and low self-esteem. They add positive beliefs, skills, and tools that allow abundance. Our Deconstructing Trauma Program shifts negative thought processes and behaviors. Discover how to reprogram to positive, healthy thoughts and behavior patterns as you learn how to identify triggers and negative learned behavior.

Decide the areas you would like to make improvements and the areas that no improvement is needed. You are not alone. Start today! Reclaim your life, find freedom and joy, reprogram to a positive self-belief system. Step into a happier, healthier life.

Begin with this wellness action plan; write down, visualize, and repeat out loud your specific goals. *This activates the plan of action. The moment you decide to shift your mindset from passively wanting change to actively using the tools and knowledge offered, you will see change, success, and your life will change.*

List your present situation and specify your goals (what you want to accomplish). Write down, visualize, and repeat out loud your specific goals.

Keep track of your progress. Review your goals regularly. Seek assistance from others as needed. All information below is a suggestion. Consult with your medical team to create your customized plan.

Your Wellness Journey

Wellness Action Plan for: _____   **Start date:** _____
(Name)

Professional Work Health: Specific things I want to do to improve my health at my place of work.
Action plan: (Reduce stress, shift work load, stress relief tools, etc.…)

Healthy Eating: Specific things I want to do to improve my eating habits.
Action plan: (Reduce chemicals and carbs, eat fruits, vegetables, fiber, protein, healthy fats…)

Weight Goal : Present weight: _____   Weight goal in 3 months:_____
Action plan: (Reduce stress, exercise regularly, healthy diet, consult personal trainer, nutritionist...)

Blood Pressure (BP): Present BP: _____   BP goal in 3 months: _____
Blood Glucose (BG): Present A1C: _____   A1C goal in 3 months: _____
Action plan: (Reduce stress, exercise regularly, healthy diet, reduce sodium, sugar...)

Blood Cholesterol: Present Total cholesterol level: _____   HDL cholesterol level: _____
Present Total cholesterol level: _____   cholesterol level: _____
Action plan: (Add foods that lower LDL, avoid trans fats, reduce saturated fats, consult nutritionist...)

Physical activity: Number of days a week I currently get 30+ min of physical activity _____
Action plan: (Walking, running, swimming, hiking, strength training, biking, yoga, dance...)

Hobbies and Interests: Develop hobbies and activities that bring positivity and joy into my life:
Action plan: (Cooking classes, art, jewelry making, scrapbook, fishing, martial arts...)

Stress and Coping: Ways I can improve mental/emotional health and coping skills:
Action plan: (Heart Breath, stress relief tools, therapist, self-help, meditate, exercise, outdoors,...)

Preventive Wellness: Wellness exams and services to maintain my physical and energetic health:
Action plan: (Trauma healing, energy healing, massage, chiropractor, medical exams...)

Addictive Behaviors: Habits that damage my health and family life, that I would like to change... smoking, alcohol, drugs, gambling, binge eating, anger, arguments, excessive work , excessive screen time, etc.
Action plan: (Replace harmful habits with hobbies and interests, stress relief tools...)

Spiritual and Family Health: Values, virtues, or service to others I would like to incorporate into my life that would provide meaning, purpose, peace, and enrichment to my life and to others.
Action plan: (Activities with family, volunteer in community, attend nurturing services and meetings..)

Partner Health: Partner relationship Care. Daily Happiness. Positivity. Joy.
Action Plan: (Date night, see a movie, board games, vacation, alone time together...)

Personal Care: Personal Care, Daily Happiness. Positivity. Joy.
Action Plan: (Time for yourself, take a class, pedicure, haircut, bath, massage, energy healing...)

Empowerment Questions:

Who am I? _____   Who do I want to be? _____   Where do I want to go?_____

Do I accept me? _____ 3 things I like about me _____ 3 things I would I like to change _____

Are any of the following behaviors familiar? For more tools go to, www.sacredsolhealing.com

Is this familiar: Hopeless about my circumstances never changing, others create my problems and I am powerless to change it; life is against me, stuck in life with a negative attitude, frustrated and angry, hurt when I believe loved ones don't care, resentful of people who seem happy and successful; I am exhausted, physically sick, in depressive states, anxious, resentful, and unfulfilled much of the time.
Action plan: (explore underlying causes of symptoms, work on self-compassion, identify personal needs and goals, create a plan to achieve goals, explore reasons behind feelings of powerlessness, therapist...)

Is this familiar: I do things for people even though I don't feel appreciated; I often try to do too much, the people I spend time with make me feel bad about myself, I consistently feel dissatisfied in my job or relationships; all I do is take care of partners who do little to meet my needs; nothing I ever do is right, I am exhausted, physically sick, in depressive states, anxious, resentful, and unfulfilled much of the time.
Action plan: (avoid passive-aggressive behavior, express emotions, especially those of frustration and resentment, keep negative feelings from building up, set boundaries, time for personal care, therapist...)

Is this familiar: I am always trying to please people; people run over me and don't respect me; I take care of as many people as possible; I don't think very highly of myself; I get upset and take situations personally; it is a challenge to communicate my needs; if I am not taking care of people I feel lost and unaccomplished; I am exhausted, physically sick, in depressive states, anxious, resentful, and unfulfilled much of the time.
Action plan: (set boundaries, listen with empathy, but stop there, practice polite refusals, time for personal care, therapist. **Ask yourself:** 1.Why am I doing this 2. Do I want to or have to? 3. Will this drain any of my resources? 4. Will I still have energy to meet my own needs?...)

Ultimate goal: To love yourself fully and completely. This doesn't mean we become perfect; it means we are able to face our challenges in grace and love. We learn from where we've been and choose to move forward in a different way. We release ego, judgment, guilt, shame, and fear; this is not who we are, just where we've been. We are not our trauma; we are not our pain; we are not our actions. Our actions and behaviors can shift and change as we learn. We move forward in discernment, knowing right from wrong. As we shift our perception, our perspective will change. When we are able to view ourselves in a positive light, the rest of the world around us shifts to mirror that positive vibration. You are the miracle you've been looking for. It starts with you. Reprogram to a Positive Self-Belief System. You are not alone. Everything you need is already inside of you. "Heal Ourselves, Heal the World."

Commitment: INTENTIONAL LIVING WILL CHANGE MY LIFE. I CHOOSE to implement these wellness goals to the best of my ability. It is my choice to change my current situation. I do not expect others to be responsible for my happiness or my choices.

_____   _____   _____
(*Signature*)   (*Date*)   (*Optional support signature*)

How Do the Eight Dimensions of Wellness Affect Your Life?

Wellness is a term we all know and use often, but what exactly is it, and what does it mean for a person to be well? According to the Substance Abuse and Mental Health Services Administration (SAMSHA), wellness means overall well-being. It incorporates the mental, emotional, physical, occupational, intellectual, and spiritual aspects of a person's life. Each aspect of wellness can affect the overall quality of life, so it's important to consider all aspects of health. This is especially important for people with mental health and substance use conditions because wellness directly relates to the quality and longevity of your life (1).

The eight dimensions of wellness are emotional, environmental, financial, intellectual, occupational, physical, social, and spiritual. All are very important to someone's overall well-being. In the coming paragraphs, I will explain, in more detail, each dimension and also give you a few ways to make improvements in each dimension.

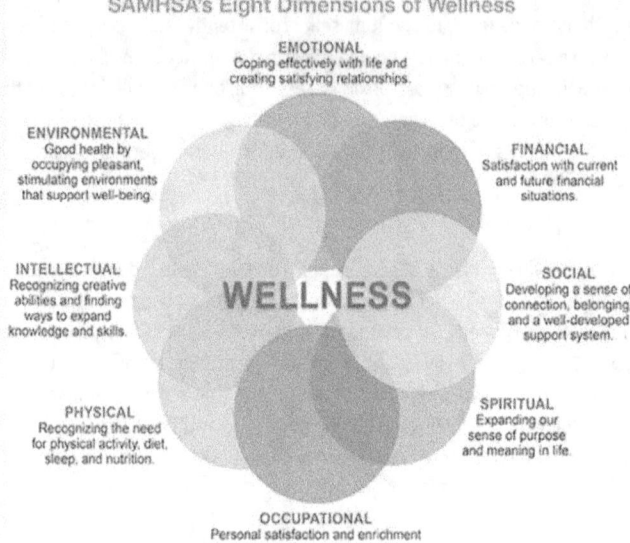

SAMHSA's Eight Dimensions of Wellness

EMOTIONAL
Coping effectively with life and creating satisfying relationships.

ENVIRONMENTAL
Good health by occupying pleasant, stimulating environments that support well-being.

FINANCIAL
Satisfaction with current and future financial situations.

INTELLECTUAL
Recognizing creative abilities and finding ways to expand knowledge and skills.

WELLNESS

SOCIAL
Developing a sense of connection, belonging, and a well-developed support system.

PHYSICAL
Recognizing the need for physical activity, diet, sleep, and nutrition.

SPIRITUAL
Expanding our sense of purpose and meaning in life.

OCCUPATIONAL
Personal satisfaction and enrichment derived from one's work.

<u>Emotional wellness</u> is the ability to cope effectively with life and create satisfying relationships. Life has a way of throwing us curve balls, which can be very difficult at times. The relationships we create and nurture give us a shoulder to lean on when that curve ball comes our way. One way to improve emotional wellness is to put a positive spin on life situations. Try to cultivate a positive feeling even during negative times throughout your life. This is much easier said than done, but with practice, it can be achieved. You do need to be mentally aware of your emotions, and when a negative feeling arises, attempt to change it into a positive one. Playing a favorite song, chatting with a close friend, or playing with a pet are just a few examples of how to cultivate positive feelings.

Rejection and loss are two major issues that can have a big impact on our emotional well-being. It's important to recognize the feelings you have during times of rejection and loss, but it is also important not to dwell on them or remain in that negative emotional state. Remind yourself how much worth you have by listing the positive attributes you possess in the area of life in which you were rejected, whether it's your work life, dating life, social life, etc. Finding meaning in a loss can be difficult, but it can improve your emotional well-being.

You may want to develop a greater appreciation for those who are still here, reevaluate your values and ideals, or honor what or who has been lost. These are only a few examples of how to find meaning during a time of loss. Emotional wellness doesn't mean avoiding bad or difficult times; rather, it's the ability to cope effectively during them.

<u>Environmental wellness</u> means good health by occupying pleasant, stimulating environments that support well-being. It's important to feel good about where you live, work, play, and wherever else you may spend time. Good health for the planet is also a major part of environmental wellness. Here are a few ways to improve your environmental well-being.

Clean and organize your living space. Then clean and organize your workspace. After these two tasks are done, you should feel a greater sense of comfort and much less anxiety. This is a big boost for your environmental well-being. Now it's time to take a look at the big picture, and that's the planet we live on. Start recycling, use less water, and pick up trash when you come across it. We have to live in this environment, it's important that we do our part to keep it clean.

Financial Wellness is the satisfaction of your current and future financial situations. It's not about how much you make that makes you financially well, but rather, are you satisfied with how much you make? Someone who makes $30,000 a year could be more financially well than someone who makes $100,000 per year. It's a proven fact that those who are financially well are more productive at work. Planning is the key to attaining financial wellness. It's important to plan a budget, set goals, plan a saving strategy, and plan for retirement. These are just a few of the plans that need to be made to have financial wellness in your life. Once the planning is complete, it's time to stick to your plans and put them into action. A savings plan will create financial margins in your life for those unexpected car/house repairs or whatever else might come up that will cost you money. Taking these steps will help guide you to a financially well future.

Intellectual Wellness means recognizing creative abilities and finding ways to expand knowledge and skills. A person who is intellectually well never stops learning. They're thirsty for knowledge and recognize that there is so much more to be learned. There is a certain feeling you get when you achieve something that you have never done before. It's that positive feeling that drives us to become more intellectually well. Some ways to improve your intellectual wellness are to improve time management, remove objectivity, and improve your critical thinking. It's important to make time for reading a book or learning a new hobby. Remove objectivity by keeping an open mind about new ideas, insights, thoughts, expressions, and values. Always question and keep your brain active, and you will begin to improve your intellectual wellness.

Occupational Wellness is the personal satisfaction and enrichment of one's work. You need to feel a sense of contribution and achievement in the work that you do. Developing occupational wellness allows you to communicate your values through whatever work you choose to do. This could be paid work or unpaid work. Here are some ideas on how you can improve your occupational wellness. Start by reflecting on what occupations will leave you feeling gratified. Look into the tasks you enjoy doing. Also, think about what occupational tasks you dislike and find burdensome. Search for volunteer work that you find interesting. Also, set career goals for yourself and constantly work toward achieving those goals. Taking these steps will lead you to have more occupational wellness in your life.

Physical Wellness means recognizing the need for physical activity. Exercise offers many benefits for a person's overall well-being. It improves your chances of living longer and healthier, relieves symptoms of depression and anxiety,improves your mood, and prevents weight gain. Exercise is just one facet of being physically well. Taking care of your physical body by showering, brushing your teeth, and going to the doctor for checkups are all ways to improve your physical wellness. Treating the body with respect will ultimately lead you to be more physically well.

Social Wellness is developing a sense of connection, belonging, and a well-developed support system. This is why spending quality time with close friends is so important. One of the best things you could do to become more socially well is to become a contributing member of your community. You can volunteer, and at the same time, you will meet new people and gain new social skills. Communication is a key factor in becoming socially well. Good communication skills will allow you to resolve problems that you may have with other people that you socialize with on a day-to-day basis. These tips can improve your social wellness.

Spiritual wellness means expanding our sense of purpose and meaning in life. Spiritual wellness is unique to everyone. It's the deepest part of you that gives meaning to your life. Some ways to improve spiritual wellness are to meditate, pray, and listen to affirmations. A spiritually well person is okay with spending time alone and reflecting. It's important to take time to search for the things that provide meaning in your life. It could be your beliefs, values, and morals that give meaning to your life. Make sure that these things guide the decisions you make as you live out your life. As you practice, you will become more spiritually well.

These eight dimensions of wellness all play an important role in our lives. Focus on the areas that you are weak in and start from there; it can seem a bit overwhelming if you try to change everything at once. As you work in the areas where you're struggling the most, you will find that stress in your life will start to decrease and positive feelings will start to increase. You'll begin to produce more feel-good neurotransmitters like dopamine and serotonin. Life will surely be more enjoyable.

From SAMHSA, The Substance Abuse and Mental Health Services Administration https://store.samhsa. gov/sites/default/files/d7/priv/sma16-4958.pdf

RESOURCES

I am infinitely grateful to my editor, Dana Micheli, and my publisher, Shanda Trofe. They have both guided me through the process of creating a masterpiece. The results I wanted would not have been possible without them. Thank you!

Editor: Dana Micheli, editor.writeword@gmail.com

Publisher: Transcendent Publishing, www.transcendentpublishing.com

CHAPTER 1

1   "Awareness." *Neo-Ren: A Celebration of the New Renaissance Happening Today*. (n.d.) https://neo-ren.com/consciousness/awareness/

2   Forsey, Caroline. "The True Meaning of Self-Awareness (& How to Tell if You Are Actually Self-Aware)." *Hubspot*. May 11, 2018. https://blog.hubspot.com/marketing/self-awareness#:~:text=Self%2Dawareness%20is%20the%20ability,correctly%20how%20others%20perceive%20you

3   Euich, Tasha. "What Self-Awareness Really Is (& How to Cultivate It). It's Not Just About Introspection" *Harvard Business Review*. January 4, 2018. https://hbr.org/2018/01/what-self-awareness-really-is-and-how-to-cultivate-it

4   Betz, Meredith. "What is Self-Awareness and Why Is It Important?" *BetterUp*. September 14, 2022. https://www.betterup.com/blog/what-is-self-awareness

5   Oxford Languages. "Trauma." Google. https://www.google.com/search?q=trauma+definition&rlz=1C1VDKB_enUS955US955&oq=trauma+&aqs=chrome.1.69i57j0i67i433j0i67i131i433j0i67j46i512j0i67i131i433j46i512j69i65.3891j0j7&sourceid=chrome&ie=UTF-8

6   "Trauma-Informed Care in Behavioral Health Services. *U.S. Department of Health and Human Services.* (n.d.) https://store.samhsa.gov/sites/default/files/d7/priv/sma14-4816_litreview.pdf

7   "Translating Trauma-Informed Principles into Trauma-Informed Practices." *The Institute for Child and Family Well-Being* (n.d.) https://uwm.edu/icfw/translating-trauma-informed-principles-into-trauma-responsive-practices/

8   "Fast Facts: Preventing Adverse Childhood Experiences" *Centers for Disease Control and Prevention.* (n.d.) https://www.cdc.gov/violenceprevention/aces/fastfact.html#:~:text=ACEs%20are%20common.,or%20more%20types%20of%20ACEs

9   http://www.odmhsas.org/picis/TraningInfo/ACE.pdf

10 "The Consequences of Childhood Trauma." *Bryon Clinic.* (n.d.) https://byronclinic.com/finding-your-ace-score/

11 Zgoda, Karen; Shelly, Pat; Hitzel, Shelley. "Preventing Retraumatization: A Macro Social Work Approach to Trauma-Informed Practices & Policies." *The New Social Worker.* https://www.socialworker.com/feature-articles/practice/preventing-retraumatization-a-macro-social-work-approach-to-trauma-informed-practices-policies/#:~:text=Retraumatization%20is%20a%20conscious%20or,safety)%20of%20the%20original%20trauma

12 Andrea Kremko, C.M.Ht., D.D. is a Hypnotherapist; Reiki Master/Teacher; Jikiden Reiki Practitioner; Spiritual Coach. https://www.facebook.com/EnlightenedLivingFaire/posts/andrea-kremko-cmht-ddorganizer-of-the-enlightened-living-faire-hypnotherapist-re/1143376329008118/

CHAPTER 2

13 McCleary, Michelle. "Scientists Finally Show How Your Thoughts Can Cause Specific Molecular Changes to Your Genes." MIJN Reis Naar Heling. December 16, 2011. https://www.michellemcleary. nl/coaching/scientists-finally-show-thoughts-change-genes/

14 "Breaking the Cycle: Negative Thought Patterns." *Sage Neuroscience Center.* November 19, 2021. https://sageclinic. org/blog/negative-thoughts-depression/

15 "Breaking the Cycle: Negative Thought Patterns." *Sage Neuroscience Center.* November 19, 2021. https://sageclinic. org/blog/negative-thoughts-depression/

16 "Breaking the Cycle: Negative Thought Patterns." *Sage Neuroscience Center.* November 19, 2021. https://sageclinic. org/blog/negative-thoughts-depression/

17 Hanh, Thich Nhat. (2009). *Happiness - Essential Mindfulness Practices.* Parallax Press.

CHAPTER 3

18 Ball, Alexander. "Understanding Mental Illness Triggers." NAMI San Diego. January 26.2022. https://cyfliaison.namisandiego. org/2022/01/26/understanding-mental-illness-triggers/

19 Good Therapy. "Trigger." *[blog].* Last updated, May 2,2018. https://www.goodtherapy.org/blog/psychpedia/trigger

20 Raghunathan, Raj. PhD. "Dealing with Negative People: Why dealing with others' negativity may involve dealing with your own." *Psychology Today; Sapient Nature [blog].* March 19, 2013.   https://www.psychologytoday.com/us/blog/sapient-nature/201303/dealing-negative-people

21 Raghunathan, Raj. PhD. "Dealing with Negative People: Why dealing with others' negativity may involve dealing with your

own." *Psychology Today; Sapient Nature [blog].* March 19, 2013.   https://www.psychologytoday.com/us/blog/sapient-nature/201303/dealing-negative-people

22 Scott, Elizabeth, PhD. "The Toxic Effects of Negative Self-Talk." verywellmind [blog]. May 24, 2022.   https://www.verywellmind.com/negative-self-talk-and-how-it-affects-us-4161304#:~:text=Basically%2C%20negative%20self%2Dtalk%20is,in%20yourself%20to%20do%20so

23 Schimelpfening, Nancy, PhD. "Symptoms of Clinical Depression." Verywellmind [blog]. Updated September 10, 2022. https://www.verywellmind.com/top-depression-symptoms-1066910

24 Scott, Elizabeth, PhD. "Reduce Stress and Improve Your Life with Positive Self-Talk." verywellmind [blog]. Updated May 24, 2022. https://www.verywellmind.com/how-to-use-positive-self-talk-for-stress-relief-3144816

25 Star, Katharina, PhD. "Using Visualization to Reduce Anxiety Symptoms." verywellmind [blog]. Updated March 10, 2022.   https://www.verywellmind.com/visualization-for-relaxation-2584112

26 Scott, Elizabeth, PhD. "The Toxic Effects of Negative Self-Talk." verywellmind [blog]. May 24, 2022.   https://www.verywellmind.com/negative-self-talk-and-how-it-affects-us-4161304#:~:text=Basically%2C%20negative%20self%2Dtalk%20is,in%20yourself%20to%20do%20so

CHAPTER 4

27 https://www.higherawareness.com/know-yourself/life-challenges.html

28 Campbell-Meiklejohn, D. K., Bach, D. R., Roepstorff, A., Dolan, R. J., & Frith, C. D. (2010). How the opinion of others affects our

valuation of objects. *Current biology : CB, 20*(13), 1165–1170. https://doi.org/10.1016/j.cub.2010.04.055

29 https://en.wikipedia.org/wiki/Narcissistic_personality_disorder

30 "Narcissistic Personality Disorder." Cleveland Clinic. June 19, 2020. https://my.clevelandclinic.org/health/diseases/9742-narcissistic-personality-disorder

31 "Treating Narcissistic Personality Disorder with CBT." Avalon Malibu [blog]. December 1, 2015. https://www.avalonmalibu.com/blog/treating-narcissistic-personality-disorder-with-cbt/

32 "Co-Dependency." MentalHealthAmerica(n.d.)https://www.mha national.org/co-dependency#:~:text=It%20is%20an%20 emotional%20and,emotionally%20destructive%20 and%2For%20abusive

33 "Co-Dependency." MentalHealthAmerica(n.d.)https://www.mha national.org/co-dependency#:~:text=It%20is%20an%20 emotional%20and,emotionally%20destructive%20 and%2For%20abusive

34 "What is Co-Dependency Treatment?" River Oaks Treatment Center (n.d.) https://riveroakstreatment.com/relationships-and-substance-abuse/codependency-treatment/

35 "Mental Health Conditions." National Alliance on Mental Illness (NAMI). (n.d.) https://www.nami.org/about-mental-illness/mental-health-conditions#:~:text=1%20in%205%20U.S.%20 adults,and%2075%25%20by%20age%2024

36 Kanaloupiti, Foteini. "Mirror, Mirror, On the Wall": Why people's opinions matter so much?" Anti-loneliness [Blog]. December 29, 2018. https://www.antiloneliness.com/self-development/mirror-mirror-on-the-wall-why-other-peoples-opinion-matters-so-much#:~:text=To%20sum%20up%2C%20others'%20

opinion%20matters%20because%20it's%20our%20way,be%20
affected%20by%20others'%20views

37 Kanaloupiti, Foteini. "Mirror, Mirror, On the Wall": Why people's opinions matter so much?" Anti-loneliness [Blog]. December 29, 2018. https://www.antiloneliness.com/self-development/ mirror-mirror-on-the-wall-why-other-peoples-opinion-matters-so-much#:~:text=To%20sum%20up%2C%20others'%20 opinion%20matters%20because%20it's%20our%20way,be%20 affected%20by%20others'%20views

38 Kanaloupiti, Foteini. "Mirror, Mirror, On the Wall": Why people's opinions matter so much?" Anti-loneliness [Blog]. December 29, 2018. https://www.antiloneliness.com/self-development/ mirror-mirror-on-the-wall-why-other-peoples-opinion-matters-so-much#:~:text=To%20sum%20up%2C%20others'%20opinion%20 matters%20because%20it's%20our%20way,be%20affected%20 by%20others'%20views

CHAPTER 5

39 "What Does a Healthy Relationship Look Like?" New York State. (n.d.) https://www.ny.gov/teen-dating-violence-awareness-and-prevention/what-does-healthy-relationship-look#:~:text=Healthy%20relationships%20involve%20 honesty%2C%20trust,or%20retaliation%2C%20and%20 share%20decisions

40 Team VeryWellMind. "National Helpline Database." VeryWellMind. Updated March 24, 2020 https://www. verywellmind.com/national-helpline-database-4799696

41 Cherry, Kendra. "How to Know If You are in a Healthy Relationship." VeryWellMind [blog[. February 21, 2022. https://www. verywellmind.com/all-about-healthy-relationship-4774802

42 Lucia, Gina. "How to Have a Healthy Relationship with Yourself." Limit Breaker. July 14,2021. https://limitbreaker.co/healthy-relationship-with-yourself/

43 Lucia, Gina. "How to Have a Healthy Relationship with Yourself." Limit Breaker. July 14,2021. https://limitbreaker.co/healthy-relationship-with-yourself/

44 Alex, Wilfred. "Cognitive Dissonance: What to Know!" {LinkedIn page}. August 15, 2022. https://www.linkedin.com/pulse/cognitive-dissonance-what-know-wilfred-alex/?trk=pulse-article_more-articles_related-content-card

45 "Dealing With An Emotionally Unavailable Partner." Daily Om (course). https://www.dailyom.com/courses/dealing-with-emotionally-unavailable-partners/?cid=935&img=6&utm_medium=email&utm_source=excerpt

46 Taylor, Madisyn. "Making Excuses." DailyOm. (n.d.) https://www.dailyom.com/inspiration/giving-excuses-1/?aid=76511

CHAPTER 6

47 "Habit." Good Therapy. (n.d.) https://www.goodtherapy.org/blog/psychpedia/habit

48 "Psychology of Habits: the key to sustaining positive change is to turn each desired action into a habit." The World Counts. (n.d.) https://www.theworldcounts.com/purpose/psychology-of-habits

49 "Forgiveness." Wikipedia. https://en.wikipedia.org/wiki/Forgiveness

50 Sackett, Ginni. "Positive Phrasing for Positive Discipline." *Montessori In Town*. October 6, 2015. http://www.montessoriintown.com/library/2015/10/6/positive-phrasing-for-positive-discipline#:~:text=Positive%20Phrasing%20means%20our%20body,rather%20than%20the%20actual%20words

51 "Rephrasing Things Positively." *The Usual Error*. (n.d.) http://usualerror.com/e-book/rephrasing-things-positively/

52 "How to Turn 11 Everyday Phrases From Negative to Positive." *Goodnet: Gateway to Doing Good*. September 16, 2015. https://www.goodnet.org/articles/how-to-turn-11-everyday-phrases-from-negative-positive

53 Cherry, Kendra. "What is Cognitive Behavioral Therapy (CBT)?" VeryWellMind. Updated August 10, 2022. https://www.verywellmind.com/what-is-cognitive-behavior-therapy-2795747

54 Cherry, Kendra. "What is Cognitive Behavioral Therapy (CBT)?" VeryWellMind. Updated August 10, 2022. https://www.verywellmind.com/what-is-cognitive-behavior-therapy-2795747

CHAPTER 7

55 "Discernment."   Wikipedia.   https://en.wikipedia.org/wiki/Discernment

56 "Resilience." American Psychological Association. (n.d.) https://www.apa.org/topics/resilience

57 Hurley, Katie. "What is Resilience? Your Guide to Facing Life's Challenges, Adversities, and Crises." *Everyday Health*. July 14,2022. https://www.everydayhealth.com/wellness/resilience/

58 Howlett, Alex. "25 Simple Ways to Balance Your Mind, Body, and Soul." *DoYou* [blog}. https://www.doyou.com/25-simple-ways-to-balance-your-mind-body-and-soul-17694/

59 Taylor, Madisyn. "The Journey of Release." DailyOm. (n.d.) https://www.dailyom.com/inspiration/the-journey-of-release-1/?aid=66429

60 Crawford, Michele. "Taking Care of Your Energy Body." Illinois Extension. March 10, 2021. https://extension.illinois.edu/

blogs/refill-your-cup-self-care/2021-03-10-taking-care-your-energy-body#:~:text=The%20energetic%20body%20is%20more,%2C%20feeling%2C%20emotion%20and%20intelligence

61 Smits, Marlene. "The Energy Body in Yoga." EkhartYoga. (n.d.) https://www.ekhartyoga.com/articles/practice/the-energy-body-in-yoga#:~:text=The%20energy%20body%20%E2%80%93%20pathways%20and%20roundabouts&text=These%20pathways%20are%20a%20complex,ll%20create%20a%20stagnant%20swamp

62 "What is the Energy Body?" *JustBeWell*. (n.d.). https://justbewell.info/what-is-the-energy-body/

63 "The Five Mindfulness Trainings." Still Water [blog[. (n.d.). https://www.stillwatermpc.org/practice-resources/the-five-mindfulness-trainings/

64 Better Help Editorial Team. "The Eight Dimensions of Wellness: Learning Balance in Life." Updated February 13, 2023. https://www.betterhelp.com/advice/mindfulness/the-eight-dimensions-of-wellness-learning-balance-in-life/?utm_source=AdWords&utm_medium=Search_PPC_c&utm_term=PerformanceMax&utm_content=&network=x&placement=&target=&matchtype=&utm_campaign=19080252225&ad_type=responsive_pmax&adposition=&kwd_id=&gclid=CjwKCAiAqt-dBhBcEiwATw-ggAy773B0kH9MmEvVHn5chylvJ8JTJw-hN4ubVflxwkx0p--MFlD2-xoC73gQAvD_BwE

65 "How Do The Eight Dimensions of Wellness Affect Your Life?" Substance Abuse and Mental Health Services Administration. (n.d.) https://www.goiam.org/wp-content/uploads/2017/01/New-Eight-Dimensions-of-Wellness.pdf

66 "5 Essential Self-Management Skills." Elite Trainers. (n.d.) https://app.muscle.fi/v10102/?app=1&ofs=12&page=shownews&newsid=13

ABOUT THE AUTHOR

You Can Add Positive Beliefs, Skills, And Tools That Allow Abundance. Heal Your Relationships With Others And With Yourself.

Reclaim Your Life, Find Freedom And Joy, Reprogram To A Positive Self-Belief System. Step Into A Happier, Healthier Life.

You are whole, You are free, You always have been, and you always will be. Here we peel back the layers to access that space. Everything you need is contained within. RF

Renee Frye

Renee Frye is a Trauma-Healing Holistic Specialist and the owner and founder of Sacred Sol Healing Institute® in Klamath Falls, Oregon. She is first and foremost, an indigenous traditional healer; her modalities are all holistic and deeply rooted in Native American teachings.

She provides mental wellness and substance abuse recovery support resources through her deconstructing trauma program and indigenous clearing and trauma healing. Renee is an Oregon certified peer support specialist in adult addictions and mental health, a certified QPR instructor, a certified recovery mentor, a healing-centered life wellness coach and educator, the deconstructing trauma guidebook author, coach, and trainer, a traditional indigenous healer, a mindfulness expert, an advanced yoga instructor, a master reiki practitioner, and a TRE provider.

Her company, Sacred Sol Healing Institute, is a peer-run organization that provides mental wellness and substance abuse recovery support resources through their deconstructing trauma program and indigenous clearing and trauma healing. Their healing-centered approach meets each person where they are at, offering hope, education, and life wellness support.

Based on the eight dimensions of wellness from SAMHSA, they offer support in habilitation (building foundational skills) and rehabilitation (regaining lost skills). Guiding their community in restructuring positive life styles, they advocate and educate mindfulness, appropriate daily life skills, healthy habits, and safe, balanced routines.

Their modalities are all holistic and deeply rooted in Native American teachings, producing positive, lifechanging results. They serve the public, including at-risk, underserved, and marginalized populations. At Sacred Sol Healing Institute®, their trauma-responsive holistic services and programs integrate equity, trauma-informed approaches, recovery, and a commitment to data and evidence. They facilitate wellbeing, mindfulness, daily resilience, stress reduction, harm reduction, substance abuse recovery, prevention, and trauma resolution.

They have developed the Deconstructing Trauma™ Program, which is integrated into all of their services and programs and is available to all through the Deconstructing Trauma guidebook and interactive workbooks. The Deconstructing Trauma program teaches a healing-centered life approach, allowing individuals to safely peel back the layers of trauma that have occurred throughout their lives.

Renee believes that by deconstructing our past trauma, we can learn to safely navigate our mental, physical, and spiritual well-being. Her curriculum is based on positive social development; through this process, behaviors, perspectives, and attitudes are learned, offering long-term positive changes in relationships and interactions involving oneself, peers, and family. She teaches that, as we learn to release negative and unhealthy behaviors that have manifested from our trauma, we are able to reprogram to positive mindsets and healthy behaviors. Her Deconstructing Trauma program includes insightful daily awareness tools, mindful behavior modification strategies, a revolutionary positive behavior resilience method, and energy healing therapy. The combination of these specific approaches has a significant impact on the release of trauma, chaos, pain, and negativity.

Renee explains that we have all been affected by trauma in some way. By creating health, wellness, resilience, and balance in all areas of our lives, we have the opportunity to reduce trauma, toxic stress, sadness, depressive states, low energy, anxiousness, panic, ACEs, substance abuse, addiction, mental health challenges, compassion fatigue, burnout, absenteeism, and more.

She started this journey to figure out why her life was so uncomfortable and why she couldn't be comfortable in her own skin. This journey was so profound, time-consuming, and frustrating that she decided to start keeping track of her findings and the tools that were making a difference in her life, just in case other people might want to utilize them. She knew for certain that if they could work for her, they would work for anyone who was open to change. And through this journey, the Deconstructing Trauma program emerged. Renee has invested countless hours in the information presented through this program, gathered through years of research, training, and self-development.

The Deconstructing Trauma Program offers unique information presented in a specific way to produce optimum results. Thousands have benefited from this format—a world of information gathered in one place with the specific intention of utilizing simple social development skills that will change our lives. As we release chaos, pain, and negativity, we begin to heal.

Through Sacred Sol Healing Institute, Renee provides trauma-healing holistic services and programs. She works with individual clients remotely as well as in person. She also offers many group programs, such as trauma-responsive staff resilience trainings, substance abuse recovery groups, restorative justice groups, grief and healing groups, suicide prevention training groups, deconstructing trauma groups, mindful movement groups, peer support-mental health and adult addiction groups, and motivational speaking seminar options for organizations. For more information, contact us through our website at www.sacredsolhealing.com.

In addition to Sacred Sol Healing Institute, Renee works and volunteers at many locations and in her community, including restorative justice groups, community corrections, addiction recovery treatment centers, suicide prevention events, substance abuse recovery events, community healing events, Native American ceremonies, tribal organizations, local associations, colleges, universities, schools, military bases, medical organizations, health and wellness healing fairs, and more.

She provides a healing-centered approach and holistic care, focusing on the whole person; in this way, you become your own best resource.

She says we all need healthy life-support skills. There is hope; we are not alone. She shares her mission, values, goals, and vision with the world. Her resources are not intended to diagnose, cure, or treat. To learn more, visit her at www.sacredsolhealing.com.

Mission: Resolve barriers to access by providing trauma-responsive resources worldwide

Values: SACRED: Sustain, Appreciate, Care, Respect, Encourage, Daily

Goal: Build self-efficacy, acceptance, and love through holistic healing and wellness

Vision: Heal Ourselves, Heal The World®

Renee is grateful to reside along the Klamath River. Her heart and soul will always be with the river; it is the umbilical cord of the people, their very life. She believes we all have a right to heal, no matter where we are, where we have been, or where we come from. This work can reach all people, in all places. Her goal is to make this information available to all who desire a positive change in their lives.

We can be whole. We are enough. We are not alone;
there is hope. RF

www.ingramcontent.com/pod-product-compliance
Lightning Source LLC
Chambersburg PA
CBHW060854120626
46553CB00001B/77